LEAVING THE SOUTH

LEAVING THE SOUTH

BORDER CROSSING NARRATIVES AND THE REMAKING OF SOUTHERN IDENTITY

MARY WEAKS-BAXTER

University Press of Mississippi / Jackson

The University Press of Mississippi is the scholarly publishing agency of
the Mississippi Institutions of Higher Learning: Alcorn State University,
Delta State University, Jackson State University, Mississippi State University,
Mississippi University for Women, Mississippi Valley State University,
University of Mississippi, and University of Southern Mississippi.

www.upress.state.ms.us

The University Press of Mississippi is a member of
the Association of University Presses.

First printing 2019
∞

Library of Congress Cataloging-in-Publication Data

Names: Weaks-Baxter, Mary, author.
Title: Leaving the South: border crossing narratives and the remaking of
Southern identity / Mary Weaks-Baxter.
Description: Jackson: University Press of Mississippi, [2019] | Includes
bibliographical references and index. |
Identifiers: LCCN 2018021899 (print) | LCCN 2018025249 (ebook) | ISBN
9781496819604 (epub single) | ISBN 9781496819611 (epub institutional) |
ISBN 9781496819628 (pdf single) | ISBN 9781496819635 (pdf institutional)
| ISBN 9781496819598 (cloth) | ISBN 9781496819765 (pbk.)
Subjects: LCSH: Rural-urban migration—United States—History—20th century.
| Migration, Internal, in literature—History and criticism. | African
Americans—Migrations—History—20th century. | Southern
States—Population—History—20th century. | Migration, Internal—United
States—History—20th century.
Classification: LCC HB1971.A3 (ebook) | LCC HB1971.A3 W43 2019 (print) | DDC
307.2/409730904--dc23

British Library Cataloging-in-Publication Data available

FOR BRENT AND ANDREW

CONTENTS

ACKNOWLEDGMENTS

This book, *Leaving the South: Border Crossing Narratives and the Remaking of Southern Identity*, tells a personal story I share with millions of other Southerners who left the South to settle in other parts of the country. Because much of what I discuss here is concerned with that journey, this book is, in many ways, one I've been working on all my life, and I have many people to thank for their help along the way.

Over the years my work has benefited greatly from the connections and friendships I have made through attendance and presentations at various conferences, including the Southern Women Writers conference at Berry College and meetings of the Society for the Study of Southern Literature and the Robert Penn Warren Circle. Early on in the writing process for this book, William Andrews and Fred Hobson were gracious in writing letters of support for a research grant for the project. My thoughts on much of what I discuss here has evolved through work on various research projects, including two anthologies that I coedited with Carolyn Perry. I'm ever grateful for her friendship.

Many people at Rockford University were a part of helping me get this book to press. The university was generous in providing support through the Faculty Development Committee and the Hazel Koch endowment, including funds in support of a sabbatical, expenses for conferences, and assistance with the research, manuscript preparation, and permissions fees. My colleagues and friends have also been quite encouraging and supportive. Faculty in the Gender Studies program, especially Stephanie Quinn, Tara Wood, Sharon Bartlett, and Belinda Wholeben, were instrumental in helping me think through the conceptual framework for my chapters on gender. Our discussions for various gender studies projects have helped me to grow as both a scholar and a teacher. John Burns introduced me to the work of Juan Felipe Herrera and helped me in thinking through my discussions of crossings along the Mexican-US border, and my department chair, Bill Gahan, read an early version of my introduction and made encouraging advice. I owe a special debt of gratitude to Catherine Forslund and Chris Bruun for the time and energy they each have taken to offer suggestions for research and to read and comment on my manuscript, and for our lunchtime discussions at Flatlanders on writing, work, and life in general.

As a professor at a small liberal arts university, over the years I have taught courses in such a wide range of areas that it is difficult to sum them up here. Although I'm especially grateful to my students enrolled in my Southern Literature course in spring 2017 who helped me wrestle with some of the issues of the final chapter of this study, my students in a broad range of classes from American Literature and Gender Studies to Rhetoric and Writing were part of classroom discussions that helped me formulate many of the ideas that came together to form this book. Two students, Meghan Peper and Kylee Bear, also worked for me as research assistants, tracking down sources and double-checking quotations.

Staff at Rockford University helped tremendously in my final preparations of the manuscript, including Jeannette Blum, who provided secretarial assistance. Pam Ward and Kelly James, director of Howard Colman Library, both took time to help me with scans of illustrations for this book, and Audrey Wilson was patient and helpful in locating interlibrary loan resources for me.

Family members, too, have been supportive and encouraging. The networks of the Baxters, the Lindsays, the Blacks, and the Suhrs on my husband's side and the Weakses, McMahans, Bayers, Reeds, Corgans, and Wrights on my side of the family have always been there for me, sending me articles on Southern Literature via the Internet and asking me how my writing was coming along. My parents, Tom and Elizabeth Weaks, have been steadfast in their support for me, and my sister Becky Brandvik and her husband, Neal, opened their home to me for visits where we talked about the South, Southern politics and history, and literature.

Most of all, I want to thank my husband, Brent, and our son, Andrew, who have been patient in giving me time and space to work, have made many a trip back down South with me, and have literally taken the journey of writing this book with me. I'm here in the Midwest and not back down South because of the life we have built here together in northern Illinois. My hope for Andy, who completed his college applications as I completed my final revisions on this book, is that during this next stage of his life, he will discover a career that brings him joy and meaning. For Brent and Andy and our family life together, I will always be grateful.

LEAVING
THE SOUTH

INTRODUCTION

Borders and Border Narratives

The drive into town isn't very far—no more than five miles. My family and I live on the outskirts of the village of Roscoe, hometown to NASCAR driver Danika Patrick and a bedroom community to the larger, more urban Rockford. The drive is one I make almost every day for drop off and pick up at my son's school, and for trips to the grocery store and the public library. Spring of 2017 a flag appeared at one of the houses along my route: one-half US flag on the hoist side and one-half Confederate flag on the fly end. The flag has been flying there for months now. This isn't the first time I've seen a Confederate flag in our community. It wasn't too long ago that another fellow living on my route would fly it, and kids in the "truck club" at my son's school sometimes fly it from the backs of their pickups. Perhaps what might—or might not—be surprising is that I live in northern Illinois, near the Wisconsin state line, not far from the suburbs in the outer reaches of Chicagoland. I've seen Confederate flags flown in the Midwest before, but they continue to startle me when I see them, and this new flag—this melded flag that sets the US flag alongside the Confederate—leaves me troubled. Can there really be such a thing? On the Internet, I find that I can easily purchase one of these flags as well as a license plate, a beach towel, and a rear window graphic emblazoned with its image.

For years now I've heard Southerners lamenting about whether or not there still is a South, but this new flag leaves me wondering more about what the United States as a whole is becoming. In many ways it seems not so surprising given recent events in the news: white supremacist marches, a revival of the KKK, and the continuing question of race in America. Is the Confederate

flag—this representation of a Southern past best left behind—becoming once
again a part of our American reality? Did it ever stop being part of that reality?
What does it mean, too, when the Confederate flag is flown hundreds of miles
away from the South, appropriated by Americans outside the region? Perhaps
this blended flag speaks some truths about where we are now as a country.
Many analysts hailed the election of an African American president as signaling
a postracial America, but this flag suggests otherwise. Despite the bloodshed
of the Civil War, despite the civil rights movement, despite the fact that our
nation twice elected an African American president, the deeply rooted issues
of race have never gone away.

Maybe I see myself in that flag, too—subdivided because of where I came
from, carrying with me a regional past that at once ties me to love for Southern
family and home, but also to feelings of shame and heartbreak because of the
South's tainted past of slavery and racism. Identifying as a white Southerner,
I've lived in northern Illinois for close to 30 years now, after living in various Southern and border states including Florida, Tennessee, West Virginia,
Georgia, and Missouri. The progression of my life has been increasingly northward, and when I began my professional career, I jumped the line into the
North. I was part of the largest mass migration of Americans in the twentieth
century: the mass migration OUT of the South. This book, *Leaving the South:
Border Crossing Narratives and the Remaking of Southern Identity*, is a collective narrative but also my own—my attempt to come to terms with my own
displacement and to make the passage as well, and to attempt to understand
what that mass migration of Southerners and Southernness from out of the
South has meant to the United States as a whole.

Leaving the South looks at narratives of and about those who left, how narratives about that displacement challenged concepts of Southern nationhood,
and how narratives about leaving remade and reconfigured how Southern
identity was and still is interpreted and represented. I am interested specifically
in how depictions of the South, particularly in the media and popular culture, prompted Southerners to leave the region; how Southerners who left the
region were portrayed by others; what happened to Southerners who crossed
over from South to NotSouth (to take a slant from William Faulkner); how
border crossings and being caught in the liminal spaces between South and
NotSouth defined (and continue to define) Southernness. Such an undertaking
has particular meaning because of the massive numbers of Southerners who
left the region—what Southern writer Shirley Abbott describes as the South's
"one perennially reliable export commodity" (190). Historian James Gregory
frames this exportation on an even grander scale, identifying twentieth-century
Southern out-migration trends as creating a Southern diaspora. As Gregory
shows in the chart included as Figure Intro.1, millions left the region to settle

elsewhere, with the number of departures for whites peaking in the 1950s and for African Americans in the 1970s. No other region of the country saw such large numbers of out-migration in the twentieth century. No other region of the country has struggled so much with its image and lost so many people to other parts of the United States.

The movements of Southerners—and people in general—are controlled not only by physical boundaries that can be marked on a map but also by the narratives that define that movement. Narrative is central in building and sustaining borders and in breaking them down. My aim here in this study is to examine the ways that what I call Southern border crossing narratives have been used to control the movements of people: how narrative defines and labels not only the movements of people but also moving people themselves, aligns groups of people and divides them, and builds literal walls and breaks them down. I look here especially at the intersections between territorial borders and narrative, and the ways that narrative can realign boundaries and redefine what physical borders mean. I look at the border between South and NotSouth not as just a physical line to cross, but as a space to navigate, and for that reason, I rely heavily on border theory to make my point. I am interested in not only the perceptions of those who left the South, but also the ways others attempted to shape representations of Southernness and assert control over both the actual lives and the stories of those who departed. My study examines the ways in which actual and imaginative borders that set apart the South from other regions of the country were negotiated, how border narratives figured in the construction of twentieth-century Southern identity, and how border narratives were used to create group affiliation and divisiveness. While the plantation mythology was the identifying representation of Southernness in the nineteenth century, for the twentieth century, Southernness was redefined by the experiences and representations of Southerners who were leaving the region. I examine here what makes "the South" "*the* South" and what it means to be a "Southerner" from the perspective of those who left. The representation of the departing Southerner figures prominently in literary texts and in popular culture, and the influence of that representation on the production of Southernness is key in understanding not only the way Southern culture has been interpreted both inside and outside the region, but also the impact of what has been called the "Southernization" of the United States. My hope, too, is that in focusing on Southern border crossing narratives, I can grapple with issues that have broader and even global implications and consequences.

Framing my study is a tension at the core of human nature: the tendency to wall off and set apart, and the urge (and oftentimes the necessity) to cross over boundaries and borders. Borders play a dual role, both as boundaries or limits and as places to cross. And it's clear that we humans are obsessed with them.

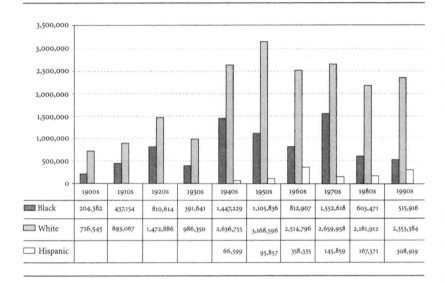

	1900s	1910s	1920s	1930s	1940s	1950s	1960s	1970s	1980s	1990s
Black	204,382	437,154	810,614	391,641	1,447,229	1,105,836	812,907	1,552,618	603,471	515,916
White	716,545	893,067	1,472,886	986,350	2,636,755	3,168,596	2,514,796	2,659,958	2,181,912	2,353,384
Hispanic					66,599	95,857	358,335	145,859	167,371	308,919

Figure Intro.1. Estimated Number of Southern-Born Leaving the South Each Decade. From *The Southern Diaspora: How Black Southerners and White Southerners Transformed Twentieth-Century America* by James N. Gregory. Copyright © 2005 by the University of North Carolina Press. Used by permission of the publisher. www.uncpress.org.

Borders are surveyed and walls are built, so we can maintain lines between "us" and "them." We pay expert surveyors and mapmakers to ensure these lines are the most accurate possible, and we fight wars because of them. Some argue that we create borders to maintain order, while others point to our deep-rooted desire to keep the "other" out. At the most southern reaches of the United States, along the San Diego highways that cross over into Mexico, bright yellow road signs like the one represented in Figure Intro.2 became an iconic image of illegal immigration in the 1990s. Headed with the word "Caution," the signs pictured the silhouettes of a running family of three—a man and a woman hunched over, pulling along a young girl behind them—warning drivers to watch for Mexican families fleeing the border guard, to watch out for border crossers who were "invading" US territory. Now only one remains—and it won't be replaced when it's gone. Illegal immigration along the California border is down, according to an article in the *LA Times*, "the result of California's diminished role as a crossing point for immigrants striving to make it to America" (Carcamo). Yet even as the number of illegal immigrants drops and as former US poet laureate Juan Felipe Herrera laments "187 Reasons Mexicanos Can't Cross the Border," President Donald Trump insists on building a wall between the United States and Mexico, and making Mexico pay for it. In many ways, the United States now seems controlled by a bunker mentality that has left Americans barricaded, afraid of what lies beyond the nation's borders and what might force its way in. Of course human beings want naturally to draw lines. We want to protect our spaces from intruders, want to be able to put a name to who we are, distinguish ourselves from others. But, of course, we also construct borders for divisive purposes, oftentimes paying little attention to the deep psychological impact on persons and communities fenced in by them and the debilitating effects of living as a refugee who has been forced across a border to escape persecution or poverty or war.

Although historically, boundaries that humans have chosen as demarcations have typically followed geographical and geological formations such as water-ways and mountains, borders have been built on artificial lines since far back in human history. For Emperor Hadrian, who ruled over the Roman Empire from CE 117–138, the wall that became known by his name was intended to separate off the Romans from the "barbarians." Spanning seventy-three miles through northern England close to the border with Scotland from the Irish Sea to the North Sea, Hadrian's Wall stood, in most places, 14 feet high and lined by a ditch that was 9 feet deep. On the opposite side of the world, but with similar goals in mind, the Celestial Empire of China began its own massive wall project not that many years before. The Empire's Great Wall built by various Chinese dynasties from the third century BC to the seventeenth century CE has a total length of over 12,000 miles and is so massive that it is the only human-made structure that can be seen from the moon. Like Hadrian's, the Great Wall of China was intended to protect "civilized" peoples from the "savage" forces beyond the Empire's boundaries. While borders are as old as early humans' territorial instincts, the modern concept of borders and the politicization of them is obviously much more recent. "It is borders and the threats to them from beyond (and before) which they conjure up that makes the nations and not vice versa," according to geographer John Agnew (416). In effect, nation building revolves around not only common social and political ideologies that bind people together, but also the tendencies of human societies to create enemies to struggle against, to marginalize, and to wall out. While that enemy might, of course, be based in very real circumstances of human abuse and outrage, we humans also conjure enemies by summoning them up within our own imaginations and from our own fears and insecurities. Thus nation building is as much about having common enemies as it is about common ideologies and cultural bonds among people. Though we tend to think of walls as built to stop invading armies, recent archaeological studies of Hadrian's Wall speculate that might not have been the case. A post at one of the Roman forts along the wall was not one of hardship. Some Roman soldiers even lived with their families in military settlements along the wall, and although there were deaths among

Figure Intro.2. Caltrans Caution Signs. Image by Cindy Carcamo. Copyright © 2017. Los Angeles Times. Used with Permission.

military personnel, no references have been found to fighting along the wall (Curry 114–15). Instead of holding back attacking armies, the wall was probably intended as a means to control the flow of people across the border (Curry 122). Likewise, in our day and age, and especially in our modern world of jet fighters and missiles, walls and barriers including the Iron Curtain, the Berlin Wall, Cuba's Cactus Curtain, the Bamboo Curtain, the DMZ, the Ice Curtain, and the growing barrier between the United States and Mexico that has been dubbed the "Great Wall of America" are not so much walls intended to hold back armies, but instead the movement of people.

Understanding who we are as individuals can mean knowing our attachment to specific nations and continents, but even more particularly the borders our ancestors crossed. Nowadays, we can even map out those migrations with the aid of modern science. The National Geographic Society claims to be able to help the common everyday person "unlock" their DNA and the migration patterns of their ancestors with a simple, mail-order kit. Pledging a pain-free collection of your DNA sample and offering a "remarkably comprehensive picture of your genetic ancestry going back hundreds, even thousands of years," the kit, according to the Society, can "go beyond historical records and the family photo album" so you can "discover your deep ancestry." For only $199.95, you can "find out what routes they took, and how they left their mark in your DNA" ("Geno" 65). The sales pitch is intriguing not only because of the promises it makes to purchasers, but also because a study of this sort recognizes the migrations of peoples across borders rather than the attachment to particular places. Digging down to the very heart of who we are means not just understanding the places our ancestors stayed, but, perhaps even more important, the crossings that they made and why they made them.

Because borders are not simple lines of demarcation between places, peoples, and nations, but instead complex spaces, I write here within the context of discussions about bordering and use the term borderlands to signify that borders are not fixed. They are unstable and fluid, and as human constructions, they can be erased and redrawn. Although humans may identify borders as lines that trace topographical formations, such choices also indicate particular human decisions. Humans choose, too, how deeply borders are drawn: who can cross over; who controls the border; what crossing a border signifies (freedom? abandonment? loss? the load of a burden? the necessity of code-switching?). Essentially, bordering is a process, a complexity of social constructions through which differences are articulated and enacted. I recognize here, too, the commonalities between geographical bordering and other types of borders, such as temporal borders (for example, between childhood and adulthood), gendering (including socially constructed binaries), and textual borders.

In studies of the relationship between crossing borders and cultural identity, migration is associated with not only estrangement, but also change and growth. At the beginning of the twentieth century, before Irish emigrants to the United States began their journey across the Atlantic, they were oftentimes given what was referred to as an "American wake." The wake was intended not only to represent the individual's impending physical displacement from Ireland, but also the community's feelings about migration and exile. Paul White uses this example in his essay "Geography, Literature and Migration" to explain migration as a metaphor for death in human lives and in literary texts (6). But migration has also been used, according to White, to suggest an "awakening or rebirth, relating to the migrant's transition to adulthood, to modernity, or to real self-discovery" (7). Although migrants might be described as "lost" to the communities that they have left, in actuality, they are oftentimes "lost" before they leave because they do not fit in (2). Migrating or making the passage from one place to another means not only creating a new identity, but also gaining an independence from the place that was left behind and acclimating to the societal framework of the place at the end of the journey. Yet even the most well-adjusted might still to some extent remain in the spaces in between, that is, the liminal space or the psychological borderlands. In effect, the migrant never actually reaches the "other side," always existing in not one place, but three. On the one hand, the borderlands can mean greater freedoms and a broader perspective for looking at the world, but existing in the liminal spaces can also potentially lead to a life consumed with feelings of displacement and alienation.

Border crossings can best be reflected upon within the context of theories of liminal space and liminality, especially in the work of French ethnographer and folklorist Arnold van Gennep, whose seminal book *Les Rites de Passage* (1909) focuses on the specific event of crossing the threshold from one human stage to another and the rites of passage that "accompany every change of place, state, social position and age" (94). Breaking this progression into the three phases of preliminal (separation), liminal (transition), and postliminal (incorporation), van Gennep frames initiation rites of childbirth, childhood, marriage, and death within the context of movement across physical borders, or what he identifies as "territorial passages." Reminding readers that a threshold is "only a part of the door," van Gennep explains that "most of these rites should be understood as direct and physical rites of entrance, or waiting, and of departure—that is, rites of passage" (25). Decades later, anthropologist Victor Turner carried these concepts a step further in his seminal book *The Forest of Symbols: Aspects of Ndembu Ritual* (1967) by focusing more specifically on the transitional stage, describing liminality as the "margin" (93), "the realm of primitive hypothesis, where there is a certain freedom to juggle with the factors of existence" (106). Locating liminality within ritual as van Gennep did, Turner describes the "transitional-being" (95) as "betwixt and between," "at once no longer classified and not yet classified . . . neither one thing nor another; or may be both; or neither here nor there; or may even be nowhere" (96–97). Turner places particular importance on liminal spaces because as he says, "phenomenon and processes of mid-transition . . . paradoxically expose the basic building blocks of culture" (110). On the one hand, we might assume that the margin does not represent the "real thing," that is, the markers of a particular society or culture, but in fact, it is the dividing line, what separates one human from another and one experience from another, where conflict resides and where meaning is found. If the culture of a society encompasses the distinguishing markers that set one people apart from another, then it is in the liminal spaces where those identifiers are made apparent. It is in the borderlands where those differences are actualized and navigated. Thus someone who crosses a border that is a dividing line between two cultures is necessarily unique in particular ways.

Turner also distinguishes between what he calls "marginals" and "liminars." Although both are "betwixt and between," he writes in *Dramas, Fields, and Metaphors*, liminars are "often moving symbolically to a higher status, and their being stripped of status temporarily is a 'ritual,' an 'as-if' or 'make-believe' stripping dictated by cultural requirements." Marginals, on the other hand, "have no cultural assurance of a final stable resolution of their ambiguity" (233). He describes them as people who are simultaneously members (by ascription, optation, self-definition, or achievement) of two or more groups whose social definitions and cultural norms are distinct from, and often even opposed to, one another. . . . [T]hey often look to their group of origin, the so-called inferior group, for communitas, and to the more prestigious group in which they mainly live and in which they aspire to higher status as their structural reference group. (233)

Because, as Turner explains, marginals "usually . . . are highly conscious and self-conscious people," within this group there also tend to be "a disproportionately high number of writers, artists, and philosophers" (233). Framed within the context of Turner's work, my book looks specifically at Southerners who have left the South as this sort of marginal and ultimately as a group that I argue redefines Southernness in the twentieth century.

More recently, within the fields of cultural studies and literary studies, and particularly in postcolonial theory, the concepts of bordering and liminality have been used to explain power structures, colonized spaces, an in-betweenness, and a hybridity experienced by peoples who find themselves on margins as refugees and displaced persons. While Turner's concern is more specifically with the transformative nature of ritual, Homi Bhabha claims this "in-betweenness" and hybridity in a context of borderlands created by colonialism and identifies this liminal space as a "third space" (6). Gloria Anzaldúa describes these "in-between spaces" as a "third country," where the "prohibited and forbidden" reside, "the squint-eyed, the perverse, the queer, the troublesome, the mongrel, the mulato, the half-breed, the half dead" (25). Situating the border crosser in a space set apart and displaced, she also views this opportunity as liberating, the site of the *new mestiza*: "Not only does she sustain contradictions, she turns the ambivalence into something else" (101). Within the context of my study here, in chapter 1, in particular, I examine ways that the South's borders were drawn historically through the colonization of particular groups of people (including African slaves and Native Americans), but my main focus in the chapters that follow is on the Southern diaspora and on the representation of leaving the South. I take as a given, that as the editors of *Gendering Border Studies* explain, borders should be studied as "discursive practices that create and negotiate meanings, norms and values and thereby shape lived experience" (Altink and Weedon 2).

More particularly, what defines liminal space in human cultures—here, Southern culture specifically—is the narrative associated with the passage. In effect, it is not the action of movement itself that creates meaning, but instead the narrative associated with that passage. In the United States and throughout US history, for example, crossing borders has meant fulfilling the nation's and the individual's supposedly God-given right to land and property (at least for those who were of the "right" color and ethnic heritage), and looking back instead of forward (usually westward to the frontier) was seen as unprogressive and un-American. President Andrew Jackson gave that movement particular meaning when he asked, "What good man would prefer a country covered with forests and ranged by a few thousand savages to our extensive republic, studded with cities, towns, and prosperous farms ... filled with all the blessings of liberty, civilization and religion?" Pushing back the border of the frontier meant that Americans were bringing "civilization" to the wilderness, ridding the continent of those "savage" forces that only stood in the way of what Jackson believed to be progress. By 1845, political writer John O'Sullivan claimed a God-given right to that westward push, a Manifest Destiny for the nation and the necessity of westward expansion to ensure that American Democracy survived. Just several years after the West was declared closed by the head of the US Census Bureau in 1890, historian Frederick Jackson Turner argued that this movement westward was the defining event of American history: "The existence of an area of free land, its continuous recession, and the advance of American settlement westward, explain American development" (1). Although, of course, Turner's Frontier Thesis as it came to be known looks at US history through blinders, with no regard for the impact of, say, slavery or the removal of indigenous populations who were the rightful owners of the land, Turner's thesis claimed a particular history for the nation that was ultimately cemented by many history books and within the American imagination. Generally a movement from east to west, with some side tracks in directions such as south into Florida, expansion into the frontier has always been defined by and equated with a narrative of freedom, prosperity, looking forward to the future, and the potential for beginning anew.

While the frontier border between "barbarian" and "civilized" was being pushed westward, a blockade of sorts—both literal and figurative—was creating "the South," and more and more so, that nation building was creating a Southern mythology that labeled the South as genteel and "civilized" and other Americans as those who needed walling out. Lines—particularly the Mason-Dixon—were being drawn and solidified. In large part because of the geographical differences that made the production of cash crops such as cotton, tobacco, and sugarcane possible, the entrenchment of slavery in Southern society, and the political debates on slavery that surrounded the formation of the country, by the time of the Revolutionary War, the boundary between North and South was generally recognized as the Mason-Dixon Line and the Ohio River. Even as early as 1800, Southerners saw their region as threatened by the "Other" beyond the South's borders, and what Charles Reagan Wilson has called a "siege mentality" was rapidly developing (586). The division between the South and the rest of the United States was spanning broader and broader. In the context of Southernness, crossing the border from South to North and vice versa carried with it a much more complex symbolism than westward crossings. By the 1830s, a distinct Southern culture had evolved—one based on a code of honor, values, customs, myths, and manners meant to cloud the racism and economic stratification at the heart of Southern society. In large part, establishment of Southern nationhood was achieved through the creation of a "blockade narrative." For Southern whites, the borders of the South became not only political tools to contain African American slaves, but also defining lines that solidified difference. For Southern blacks, crossing the Mason-Dixon Line or the Ohio River meant freedom, while for Southern whites generally, the move meant entering enemy territory. Even though the South ultimately lost the Civil War, even though attempts to separate to form a new nation were quashed with the loss of the war, it was the failure of the Southern Cause that solidified the South as what W. J. Cash called "not quite a nation within a nation, but the next thing to it" (viii). Nationhood for the Confederacy meant not only holding the borders of the South from Northern attack, but also claiming the line as a valid, physical marker of difference. If the nineteenth-century South laid claim to the name "Dixie" to set it apart from the rest of the United States, so, too, did the twentieth-century South solidify difference with monikers such as "the Solid South" and just plain "the" South. Even today, commentators speak of the political force of the South and in doing so, not only identify lingering distinctions between American regions, but also make a case that difference remains.

Despite the 150 years that have elapsed since the Civil War, the conflict continues over the South's borders and who is allowed to identify themselves as "Southern" and to call the region home—even those who are living within the South's borders. In a recent interview, former poet laureate of the United States Natasha Trethewey, for instance, described her poems as "not only about racism and the sense of psychological exile created by that, but . . . very much of an assertion of my entitlement to own the South, much as white Southerners own it—the deep knowledge that this is where they'll bury me" (Loftus 23). One particularly poignant example of Trethewey's struggles to claim both her psychological and physical connections with the South is her poem "Pastoral." With the skyline of Atlanta in the background, the persona of the poem dreams she is with the Fugitive poets, lining up with the "brotherhood" for a photo that recalls one taken of Allen Tate, Robert Penn Warren, John Crowe Ransom, Donald Davidson, and Merrill Moore in 1956 during a reunion of the group at Vanderbilt University. Accepting the offer of a bourbon as the sound of bulldozers fill the air, the persona deals with the complications of following in the literary footsteps of Southern white male writers who claimed to "flee nothing but the Brahmins of the Old South" but who were, for the most part, ingrained in the racism and chauvinism of the early twentieth-century South. The sound of his voice "just audible above the drone / Of bulldozers," Warren tells them all "where to stand" (of course an allusion to the poets' efforts to defend an agrarian way of life as opposed to an industrial way in their 1930 book *I'll Take My Stand*). As the photographer's backdrop pictures "a lush pasture, green, full of soft-eyed cows / lowing, a chant that sounds like *no, no*," the persona accepts the offer of a drink, going ahead to line up with the poets. She is in blackface, telling them, "*My father's white . . . and rural*," as the photographer's camera "freezes us." "*You don't hate the South?* they ask. *You don't hate it?*" (35). Set in urbanized and out-of-control growth Atlanta, where Trethewey as a child lived with her mother after her parents' divorce and where she taught as a professor at Emory University until relocating north to Chicago in 2017 to teach at Northwestern, the poem deals with the persona's conflicted attachment to a region that labels her as at once "Southerner" and "Other." Trethewey's persona takes her stand, refusing to let herself be crowded out of the picture, forced over the line outside the boundaries of the place that defines her and that she calls home.

Being pushed outside the South's borders is not only an actual physical struggle for Trethewey but also a conceptual, abstract one. For Trethewey, the question of who "owns" the South is in large part a question of who has the power to say what the South is—who defines it, who is entitled to claim "citizenship." Although the South can be defined by geographical lines on a map—most frequently as the states that joined the Confederacy during the Civil War along with border states including Kentucky, West Virginia, and Oklahoma—"the South" can be understood more fully, as scholars have been pointing out for years now, as a concept, an imagined construct rather than an actual physical place. "This South that we hold collectively in our minds is not—could not possibly be—a fixed or real place," writes Jennifer Rae Greeson in her book *Our South*, "It is a term of the imagination" (1). More generally, the framework for such an assertion can be found in Benedict Anderson's argument that a nation can be defined as an "imagined political community." It stands to reason that a nation must be "*imagined*," Anderson claims, "because the members of even the smallest nation will never know most of their fellow-members, meet them, or even hear of them, yet in the minds of each lives the image of their communion." Such a community is one that people will die for—even though they might not personally know the people for whom they fight (6–7). Foreshadowing Anderson's work years earlier back in 1901, E. A. Ross, a sociologist, identified what he named the concept of Social Control and examined what he referred to as the Social Influence "by which a social group is enabled to hold together" (viii). Pointing to the growing power of the press, the influence of the education system, and improvements in communications, Ross noted "the ease of comprehending distant persons and situations [that] enables fellowship to overleap the limits of personal contact" and concluded that "one of the most notable results is the rise of the nation" (435).

In many ways, it has been this sort of media as well as fiction and poetry, music and music recordings, consumer-goods packaging, radio and television programming and advertising, film, and the Internet that have been responsible for creating the region that is the focus of my study here in this book, the American South. And there hasn't been a shortage in recent years of publications about the representation of the region and the commodification of Southern culture. Back in the early 1970s, in his book *The Enduring South: Subcultural Persistence in Mass Society* (1972), John Shelton Reed looked at the impact of economic development in the South and the influence of American mass culture on what Reed calls "southern distinctiveness" by asking questions such as "What is 'Southern-ness'?" "Who is a Southerner?" and "Where is 'the South'?" In his revised edition published in 1986, he asked, "Will the South Prevail?" That same year, with a book cover featuring a picture of the Walton family of Walton's Mountain fame, Jack Temple Kirby's *Media-Made Dixie: The South in the American Imagination* was published, considering "History High and Low" by focusing on texts ranging from Erskine Caldwell's *God's Little Acre* to Shirley Temple's "Bojangles" Robinson musicals. More recent years have seen the publication of Leigh Anne Duck's *The Nation's Region: Southern Modernism, Segregation, and U.S. Nationalism* (2006), Allison Graham's *Framing the South: Hollywood, Television, and Race during the Civil Rights Struggle* (2001), and Karen Cox's *Dreaming of Dixie: How the South Was Created in American Popular Culture* (2011). The Appalachian South has had special attention in books like J. W. Williamson's *Hillbillyland: What the Movies Did to the Mountains and What the Mountains Did to the Movies* (1995). Scholars like Tara McPherson in her book *Reconstructing Dixie: Race, Gender, and Nostalgia in the Imagined South* (2003) have also directly tied the representation of the South to narrative, noting that "The South today is as much a fiction, a story we tell and are told, as it is a fixed geographic space below the Mason-Dixon line" (1). Likewise, Scott Romine asserts in *The Real South: Southern Narrative in the Age of Cultural Reproduction* (2008) that despite claims the South is "gone for good," through narrative "we are still reproducing and naturalizing the South *as place*" (9). The very recent *Creating and Consuming the American South* (2015), a collection of essays by noted scholars and edited by Martyn Bone, Brian Ward, and William A. Link, attempts to go one step further to "reorient our attention to the ways in which ideas and stories about 'the South' and 'southernness,'" according to Bone, "have social and material effects that register in various local, regional, national, and transnational scales" (1). Looking to other possible areas of scholarship, Bone proposes in his introduction that "we need to pay more heed to how discursive and marginal Souths interact with and impact social and material realities" (18). I hope my book can do just that.

My examination of Southern border narratives is built on the framework of border theory. I take here as a given that there is a close link between the physical borders of the South and the narratives written about passage across and through them, grounding my thinking in statements like Stephen Wolfe's in a recent special issue of *Nordlit* on border aesthetics and border works that "aesthetic activity participates in the processes by which people relate to real and conceptual geographies in which they live and through which they move" (2). Recognizing space as a social construction, Wolfe is part of the Border Poetics/Border Culture Research Group, which is currently working to develop a theoretical framework for what they call border poetics. I use border poetics here as a way to explain the relationship I see between border crossings and narratives about those crossings, and rely heavily on this definition of border poetics as framework for my argument:

> Border poetics focus on narratives and other symbolic forms, and on the important subjective dimension which cultural forms mediate in the public sphere. . . . Border poetics examines borders as forms of representation, the role of narratives of bordering, individual border crossings as well as grand narratives of border formation and erasure. It deals with passages as well as hindered passages in various ways (e.g. failed/prevented crossings or cases where crossings of the physical border does not imply crossings of symbolic borders as e.g. cultural or social borders). (Border Poetics Research Group)

"The kernel," the group says, of border poetics is "that borders on the level of presentation and on the level of the world presented are intimately connected." Identifying narrative as the centerpiece of border poetics, the research group breaks down border narratives into two types, border formation and border crossing:

> Border formation has traditionally been viewed as a top-down process in the hand of power elites. A more dynamic view of bordering allows for the possibility of bottom-up agency. Another way of saying this would be to say that as in Homi K. Bhabha conception of national identity, the border is a product of a tension between the pedagogic and the performative. By extension, the border comes about as a product of the grand narratives of border formation and the minor narratives of day-to-day border crossing. (Border Poetics Research Group)

The research group also emphasizes the importance of recognizing different types of border figures. Within the context of border poetics, for example, border crossers can be seen as passive or active, and border figures associated with these narratives range widely, from "migrants, refugees, [and] border guards" to "smugglers [and] borderland dwellers." Typical border figures identified by the research group include "walls, rivers, bridges, seams, windows, doors, skin, veils, masks, faces, fronts." My plan here is to explore this relationship between physical borders and cultural production through specific examples of Southern border narratives, and I follow the research group's lead by using their specific terminology in my book as a way to distinguish the various motivations behind and the impact of these two very different types of narratives. In chapter 1 of this book, I deal specifically with border formation narratives, but subsequent chapters focus on border crossing narratives. I have used the phrases border crossing narrative and border formation narrative to center my discussion on the border itself because despite a border crosser's best attempts, life will always be lived on this line.

Examining border crossing narratives places a lens on the complex layers of Southernness and the ways in which those texts construct Southern identity and Otherness, create codes of reference that include and exclude border crossers, and negotiate the borders and liminal spaces that border crossers pass through. Border narratives wield power over Southerners—both fictional and real-life ones. Southerners left their native region in droves, particularly in the first half of the twentieth century, motivated by stories of the riches of the West and the freedoms of the North. Others have found and shaped their own identities because they are readers of border texts and have become active participants in those narratives. The following pages explore these narratives—ones in texts ranging from novels and autobiography to photographs and paintings, newspaper stories, and blues and country music. My intent here is to be broad ranging to suggest the importance of looking at Southerners and patterns of crossing, and to speculate on why and how border crossings out of the South shaped Southerners' perceptions of themselves, molded and manipulated conceptions of gender, race, and class that have evolved as Southerners crossed over and imagined and reimagined themselves. I plan, as well, to examine the interconnections among these very different sorts of texts to focus on the commonalities among them as border narratives. Some do, in fact, like Toni Morrison's *Jazz* (1992), span the boundaries between genres—in this case fictional novel and the music of jazz—to show how thoroughly and deeply these narrative patterns are woven through representations of Southernness. Most importantly, I'm concerned with the differences in perceptions of the South between those who stayed and those who left.

My plan here is to examine border narratives of and about Southerners leaving the South to look for patterns and the ways those narrative patterns converge and diverge. In identifying the boundaries of "the South," I use the definition of the US Census Bureau: Alabama, Arkansas, Delaware, the District of Columbia, Florida, Georgia, Kentucky, Louisiana, Maryland, Mississippi, North Carolina, Oklahoma, South Carolina, Tennessee, Texas, Virginia, and West Virginia. Of course, though, this list does not give a cut-and-dry view of what the South is. Some of these states, after all, did not secede during the Civil War and one—West Virginia—chose new statehood by joining the Union. Others like Oklahoma are borders themselves, reflecting divided regional loyalties and diverse topographical landscapes. Such considerations emphasize the point that Southernness is conceptual, rather than solely the lines on a map. In considering the time period to discuss, I have attempted to be expansive, but because Southern out-migrations peaked in the 1950s, that decade is my centerpiece in this study, with much attention to the first half of the twentieth century to the increasing numbers of out-migrations in those decades. I'm interested as well in the latter half of the century as out-migrations continued, and I reflect upon this movement in the context of present-day concerns with border building and nationalism, as well as what has been called the Southernization of America. In effect, border narratives of and about Southerners leaving the South have become a cultural phenomenon, a cultural pattern and artifact. Southern border narratives are both personal and communal ones, but even in the personal, there are threads that link the individual to the community. In effect, this book is about the borderlands and the liminal spaces that migrating Southerners maneuver, but it is in even larger part about who controls those narratives, how those narratives are controlled, and how narrative can influence the actual movements of people. Who controls the story of the migrants' passage? Timothy Brennan asks, for example, in his essay included in *Nation and Narration*, what is the language used to define the person making the passage? Is the person defined as a "wanderer" or a "refugee" (61)? The words carry very different meanings and connotations. Some, like Thomas Wolfe, saw the label of "wanderer" as empowering. Robert Penn Warren referred to himself as a DP (Blotner 256). Who has control of the labeling? Who has control of the narrative?

Patterns of Southern migration narratives have been outlined before. Focusing specifically on African Americans in *Canaan Bound: The African-American Great Migration Novel* (1997), Lawrence R. Rodgers says that in his book he wants to address questions such as these: "As the migrating population has gone from the rural south to the urban north, how has this group reimagined its conception of identity in literature? How has a population that has been racially marginalized and economically disadvantaged also confronted geographic displacement from the foundational roots of its southern culture?" (4). Indicating that his goal is to survey chronologically, aiming to show the development of the African American Great Migration novel, he recognizes the broad spectrum of outcomes for the migrants represented in the novels: "finally rejecting the North and remigrating south, by rejecting his or her racial identity and recrossing the color line, by lashing out at forces beyond the migrant's control and falling victim to them, by submitting to the superior power of the environment, or, more rarely, by making a successful and triumphant transition from south to north" (29). Focusing on the departure of African American migrants as well as their adjustments in a new place in *"Who Set Your Flowin'?": The African-American Migration Narrative* (1995), Farah Jasmine Griffin explains that migration narratives by and about African Americans leaving the South generally represent four "pivotal moments": an incident that prompts the move northward; a first encounter with the city; navigation of the new landscape and the negative consequences of migration; a "vision" of the promise and the dangers of the new place (3). Griffin and Rodgers's books map out the stages of African American migration narratives—one looking at the development of novels and the other looking more generally at all types of narratives, including novels, poetry, music, and visual arts that share similar patterns from the representation of the departure to the arrival in the North. More recently, in *Ain't Got No Home: America's Great Migrations and the Making of an Interracial Left* (2014), Erin Battat takes a narrower historical view by focusing on Depression-era migration narratives, but looking across the boundaries of race. Examining internal as well as external migrations, Battat asserts that writers of the period used migration narratives as a "project of building an interracial, anticapitalist movement" (3).

In contrast to Griffin, Rodgers, and Battat's work, my study crosses boundaries of race to make a more far-ranging claim about Southern border narratives and their role in the twentieth century. Race, gender, and economic status can have profound effects on the nature of the migrant's journey, the adjustment of the migrant, and the ultimate decision of the migrant either to stay put or return home to the South, and for that reason, I look more broadly to reflect the multiplicity of Southern racial and cultural backgrounds and thus include African Americans, whites, Hispanics, and Native Americans. But because of the relative sizes of these populations in the South, my focus has been more specifically on black and white Southerners. I must emphasize, however, that my work here is not attempting to be exhaustive in surveying Southern border formation and border crossing narratives. Instead, my hope is that my representative examples can show how border narratives transformed definitions of "Southernness" and "the South." My terminology is also different from that used by Rodgers, Griffin, and Battat in that I use "border narrative" rather than "migration narrative" to add emphasis to the implications of navigating the border between North and South and finding the way through.

Five basic assumptions give a frame for my undertaking here. First of all, crossing the border from the South into the NotSouth is seen as transformative. The borders of the South represent a power struggle to retain a uniqueness to the South and to promote Southern exceptionalism. This border is different from others within the United States because it separates a region off that saw itself (perhaps still sees itself) as a separate nation. Movement across the border of the South outward thus also meant leaving an internal nation and crossing over into the larger nation—not crossing the US border from an external country. While passage across the Mason-Dixon Line into the North literally meant freedom from slavery for African Americans before the Civil War, crossing the border in the postbellum years and in the twentieth century meant claiming freedom from entrenched Southern racism and Jim Crow. "Water flows because of gravity. People flow because of symbols and hope" (viii), Richard Wright says in *12 Million Black Voices* (1941). "Black migrants became a river across the land because their slave forebears had dreamed that the North Star pointed the way to a mythic 'Freedom Land' where blacks were free and unpersecuted" (viii). The power of crossing the border for African Americans and white Southerners' distrust of anyone from outside the borders of the South ingrained a deep divide that still remains today, perhaps not as literally as the days when African Americans were legally required to move to segregated train cars when they crossed the Mason-Dixon, but just as psychically for some who hold on to continue fighting the war.

Second, Southerners are, in a sense, "marked" because they have passed over. Those markings may come in a variety of different forms, with accent, physical appearance, food choices, and hygiene being the most prominent. These markings, as James Gregory explains in *The Southern Diaspora*, have been highlighted in and promoted by the media to gain viewership and readership. Although narratives may tell individual stories, they still share commonalities. There is collectivity in the marking of passage and in the representations in narratives about that crossing. Southerners, according to Gregory, were marked by labels such as the "maladjusted migrant" and the "dangerous" migrant. Gregory says that both black and white Southern migrants were represented in this way, needing help through social services because of their inability to adjust. While the representation in the media of black Southerners, especially in the 1950s and 1960s during the civil rights movement, "became increasingly complicated," whites were often represented as "innocents lost in the city" (72).

Third, controlling a text—how it is dispersed and consumed—can have a powerful impact on personal and communal identity and on how a border is identified and interpreted. We humans are surrounded by texts that transport us, many that intentionally engage us in the experience of entering and becoming part of a narrative world. Studies of the role that narrative plays in human lives, such as Richard J. Gerrig's book *Experiencing Narrative Worlds: On the Psychological Activities of Reading*, show that although fictionalized texts such as novels and films are typically seen as transporting us into narrative worlds, so, too, do texts such as history books, newspaper articles, and visual art. The goal of a text is to influence us in some way—perhaps to amuse us, to persuade us, to motivate us. "It is a rare conversation among adults that does not depart from the here and now," according to Gerrig (7). We tell stories, we relate details about our weekends, something we saw, an experience we had. Narrative worlds and our experiences in them are universal and inescapable. Noting the influence of reader-response theory, Gerrig points out that the experience of entering into a narrative requires the reader to shed at least portions of the self. Reality for us as readers experiencing narrative becomes the reality of the text itself. Although being "transported" by a text also suggests a passivity, reading a narrative is still like taking a journey, for the traveler always returns to himself or herself in some way changed (13, 16). Yet, if as Douglas Reichert Powell explains in *Critical Regionalism*, "telling the story is the practice that sustains the identity of the place it comes out of" (12), then who has control of the telling also has control of the representation of a place, and by extension, of a people. Recent scholarship on outbreak narratives, for example, points to the ways that narrative has been used for divisive purposes to bind groups of people together in opposition to an "other." Outsiders or marginalized peoples, such as migrants, strangers, and travelers, are often represented as a "social contagion," at once "an agent of dangerous and productive change" (Wald 26). The first chapter of my book looks especially at the power plays throughout Southern history that created a South that identified outsiders as a "contagion" as a means to assert control over the system of slavery and the culture of the South.

Fourth, texts can provide readers with what K. Anthony Appiah in his study of social reproduction in multicultural societies identifies as a "script," that is, a narrative "people can use in shaping their life plans and in telling their stories" (160). Musical texts, for example, can be powerful "scripts" that help listeners face life—its changes, its emotions, its traumas—and show them that others share similar experiences, hardships, and heartaches. In "Sing Me Back Home: Nostalgia, Bakersfield, and Modern Country Music," music historian Rachel Rubin describes the white migrants from the South as experiencing a "split consciousness" similar to the "doubleness" that W. E. B. Du Bois identified as the experience of African Americans who struggled with the conflict between their citizenship and the lack of full empowerment in American society. An "iconic South" that appears in the music helped Southern migrants deal with the implications of making the passage from South to NotSouth. With little hope or intent to return to the South, these migrants experienced displacement from their Southern homes and marginalization in the places they landed. Rubin describes the country music singer as "a mediator in a cultural clash" and refers to Buck Owens as an example, pointing to the opening lines of his 1972 song "Streets of Bakersfield": "You don't know me, but you don't like me" (101–2). Other singers and songwriters served as mediators as well. While the lyrics of music may themselves relate stories of departure, separation, and coping, the music itself became a binding mechanism as people shared types of musical expression and a common story.

Lastly, I assert that the narratives I examine here are ones without resolution. Even if a Southerner leaving the South hopes to fully acclimate to the new place where he or she has landed, that transition will never be complete. The past will always be there. Rodger Bromley calls these narratives "'borderline' narratives," "texts of 'incomplete signification' and hybridity, constituted by in-between spaces in which indistinct and indefinite diasporic identities are negotiated" (67). Although Bromley uses terms different from ones I use here to identify patterns in diasporic cultural fictions, he reaffirms that crossing a border entails a complex situation that will never be resolved. My work here, too, is strongly influenced by Gloria Anzaldúa. Writing of the border between Mexico and the United States and more broadly about lines of nationalism in general, Anzaldúa describes the borderlands as "physically present wherever two or more cultures edge each other, where people of different races occupy the same territory, where under, lower, middle and upper classes touch, where the space between two individuals shrinks with intimacy" (19). Even though this "struggle of identities continues," she says, and "the struggle of borders is our reality still," ultimately, "one day the inner struggle will cease and a true integration take place" (85). Conversely, others argue for the importance of recognizing the borderland as a site that can be manipulated for divisive purposes. Scott Michaelsen and David E. Johnson in their introduction to *Border Theory: The Limits of Cultural Politics* (1997), for example, label Anzaldúa's interpretation of the "so-called borderlands" as "the site of a new cultural production, a new *mestizaje*" as instead a "dream" (28–29). Although on the one hand, I find that Anzaldúa's interpretation of the borderlands is one that can help me to come to my own very personal conclusions and resolutions about being a border crosser, on the other hand, I recognize in my discussion here the highly charged power struggles over Southern borders and over the narratives about crossing them.

For that reason, I begin my book with a chapter entitled "Southern Border Formation Narratives: Controlling the Flow of People," aiming to give context for the rest of my book by looking into Southern history to examine ways border formation narratives have been used to manipulate the historical and cultural significance of crossings into and out of the South as a way to gain control of the boundaries of the South and to define the South as a nation unto itself. This chapter examines the construction of hegemonic devices used to disrupt cultural continuity for Africans enslaved and brought to the South and to sever the psychical umbilical cord connecting them with Africa; to wall out cultures, especially Native American, deemed "uncivilized"; to extend slave territory into contested spaces and thus beyond the South's borders; to shore up borders and boundaries that helped formulate Southern exceptionalism. Most importantly, this chapter gives a historical base for understanding the complications and implications of border crossings in the twentieth century and for giving a context for examining the ways border crossing narratives from this period have grappled with, reacted against, and responded to entrenched patterns and power struggles.

The chapters that follow examine the spaces where territorial borders and textual frames intersect and how control of textual frames can shape territorial borders. I open this section of my study with a chapter entitled "The Border Crossing Narrative and the Disruption of Southern Borders" and turn in this chapter to the transformations that take place as borders are crossed. In the liminal spaces, "South" and "Southernness" were reinterpreted as an identifier carried by those who left the region as new communities were formed by the crossing and as those new communities found themselves somewhere in between: Southern yet Not-Southern. In effect, this new "nation" is one that is outside the confines of the physical space of the region that is historically referred to as the "South." It was a region of the imagination that displaced Southerners carried with them. This chapter examines the power of border crossing narratives to break down and reconstruct definitions of Southernness and the South. Looking broadly at different types of texts, including personal accounts, advertising, creative literature, newspaper articles, and visual art, this chapter reflects on the ways that the physical movement outward across Southern borders bound migrants in new communities as they experienced the departure, disconnection from family and friends in the South, the road itself, and the acclimation to a new environment. Border crossing narratives not only created and were created by these new communities, but they also redefined communal identity, thereby disrupting definitions of Southernness and reinterpreting what Southernness means. Most importantly, this chapter gives a framework for understanding the communal narratives that I examine in later chapters.

Chapters 3 and 4 focus on ways that gender and race shape perceptions of border crossings and how gender and race become gatekeepers for those who attempt to pass. Chapter 3, "Securing the Border as a Creative Site: Southern Masculinities and the Urge to Tell," looks at the traditional American male success story of making the way in the world as a self-made man and how that image was reinterpreted in the context of Southern masculinity in the first half of the twentieth century. Focusing on novels written by Thomas Wolfe, Ralph Ellison, William Styron, Truman Capote, and Robert Penn Warren, the chapter builds on earlier scholarship that identifies a turning point in the early part of the twentieth century from the idealized images of planter and slave to new models of masculinity for blacks and whites: "the Christian gentleman, the masculine martial, and the self-made man" (Friend xvi). My claim here is that new narrative patterns were embraced and popularized—particularly by the generation who came of age in the 1920s through the 1940s—that set male characters on journeys outside the South to encounter that world and to find success. In fact, a mania of sorts evolved around this narrative as portrayed by Thomas Wolfe, who represented wandering as opportunity for introspection, movement as cleansing and a means to remake one's self, and liminal space as a site of creativity for the neophyte writer and, most notably, a masculine zone. I end this section by reflecting on how this journey is altered when the male encounters racial oppression or sexual prejudice. This chapter on Southern masculinity is paired alongside chapter 4, "Southern Womanhood and 'The High Cost of Living and Dying in Dixie,'" to reflect on the ways gender impacts border narratives. If, as Julia Kristeva says of Woman, "the biological fate that causes us to be the *site* of the species chains us to *space*: home, native soil, motherland" (33–34), then the South has laid claim not only to women's bodies but also to their containment in space. Women's bodies are literally the embodiment of the line, reflecting gendered patterns of border building that identify Woman as symbolic border guard of nations and communities, as who it is that needs "saving" when outsiders threaten. Working within this context, the chapter focuses on autobiographical writings by Shirley Abbott, Zora Neale Hurston, and Eudora Welty, and highly autobiographical novels by Evelyn Scott and Harriette Arnow and examines ways Southern women look to the horizon to claim it, struggle with firmly ingrained models of Southern womanhood, and attempt to break free from these patterns.

While I examine texts as performative in the sense that they shape and create experience, I look specifically in chapter 5, "Rescripting What It Means to Be Southern: Musical Performance as Border Narrative," at communal spaces and the role of music and performance in border crossings. Migrants leaving the South found that border narratives set within music could help them break from the places they had come from, navigate the transitional spaces, and identify with others who had made a similar passage. Music as diverse as the blues, jazz, gospel, and country carried narratives of displacement. Music helped departing Southerners to validate their experiences, see the value of who they were as people, and help formulate new communal spaces. Cultural symbols and values shared by migrants through their music came to redefine Southernness as Southerners departed the South and set forth on journeys that would forever change their perspectives on who they were and where they came from. This chapter looks specifically at the ways that border narratives in music disrupted definitions of "Southern" and the "South," claimed new frameworks for defining "Southernness" and new cultural heroes to create a Southern culture that was/is of the South, but not *the* South, and how performance bound communities together and even became a means of freedom for groups of Southerners, specifically African American women. Perhaps most important, I look at how the road of the migrants transformed music labeled as "Southern" into music that was more consumable and ultimately more "American."

Ending my study of the twentieth-century South, chapter 6, "And Then They Drown?: Faulkner's Quentin Compson Lost in the Borderlands," focuses on one specific border crosser as a means of looking closely at the ways border narratives are formulated and the consequences of such narratives as they are passed through multiple perspectives for varying purposes and aims. Quentin Compson in *The Sound and the Fury* and *Absalom, Absalom!* is a victim of the Lost Cause, a failed border crosser. Surrounded by characters who like him are border crossers—the Canadian Shreve, the little immigrant girl, and Thomas Sutpen—Quentin isn't one of those survivor-narrators at the end; he doesn't make it through the passage and across the border and instead, drowns in his past, unable to leave the liminal space to pass on to the other side. He forever remains in the borderland, and rather than drawing strength from his in-betweenness, is swept into a vortex of hopelessness and despair. Through Quentin, Faulkner makes clear the pressures and dangers of the divisions between black and white, between North and South, and the inability of Southerners like Quentin to successfully navigate the borderlands. Faulkner's Quentin also seems the most indelibly inked reminder of what the consequences may be of the border narrative gone awry and the warnings to a culture of the harm of building walls and not bridges.

While chapters 2 through 6 reflect on ways that Southern border crossing narratives have shaped the representation of the South in the twentieth century, my concluding chapter, entitled "Anywhere South of the Canadian Border," turns my discussion back again to border formation narratives to examine them within the context of larger US and global twenty-first-century concerns. On the one hand, markers of Southernness are fading: the physical markers along the Mason-Dixon are disappearing, stereotypically Southern cultural phenomena such as NASCAR and country music appeal to Southerners and non-Southerners alike, and claims of uniquely Southern identifiers such as high church attendance and military enlistment really aren't so exclusive to the

South. On the other hand, strategies of Southern border building are rearing their heads in American society: Confederate flags, the Southern Strategy in politics, women as border guards, as who needs "saving" when Mexicans cross the border into the United States. I close with a discussion of Southern border formation narratives that have been rewritten and consumed by and for different groups of people beyond the South and how those narratives have blurred the line between South and NotSouth. I wrestle with questions about twenty-first-century wall building and what happens when the border itself moves.

Essentially, my book focuses on the South's story as a sort of paradigm. In a time of calls for building a physical wall between the United States and Mexico, and growing nationalistic movements and isolationist tendencies around the globe, I reflect on that friction between the human urge to build walls and the desire to move freely, to cross borders. What I conclude here is that Southern border crossing narratives not only collapse boundaries established by Southern exceptionalism and nationalism, but they also reframe Southernness within a broader American context and in doing so, reconstruct American national identity and American perceptions of borders, bordering, and the liminal spaces in between. The movement of Southerners has had important consequences for the United States more generally, and the impact of this mass migration has in many ways rewoven the fabric of American society on political, sociological, and economic levels. Of course the South has been Americanized as well by the movements of people into the South, by the standardization of mass media, by the ease of transportation between regions, by the evolution of the "Sun Belt," but as historian James Gregory has explained, the Southerners who left the South have forever altered the character of the United States as a nation. While Gregory focuses in his study on the effects of movement and on migration stories, especially in mass media, as "factors in history" (44), I focus on the border itself, examining Southern border crossing narratives and how those texts have remade what "South" and "Southern" mean. Reflecting on issues of nationhood, boundaries, and walls that are so intently being considered in our current national and international landscapes, I propose, too, that this diaspora South can, in effect, be viewed as a "South" carried by those who migrated, a South informed by memory of a place rather than a physical presence, a South not of specific physical geographical location but of the imagination.

CHAPTER 1

Southern Border Formation Narratives: Controlling the Flow of People

If songs can create borders—draw lines between people and regions—then the song "Dixie," originally entitled "I Wish I Was in Dixie's Land," certainly has. Supposedly written by Daniel Emmett, who worked in vaudeville in the 1840s and 1850s, and who composed two American folk classics, "Old Dan Tucker" and "Turkey in the Straw," "Dixie" was originally performed as a comical piece to be sung in blackface for the vaudeville stage. The story goes that during the cold, chilly New York winter of 1859, Ohio-born Emmett, who spent most of his life in the North, found himself daydreaming of Southern landscapes and warmer weather. Vaudeville troupes typically toured Northern states during the summer months and went south for the winter. According to the legend, out of daydreaming for "the land of cotton, / Cinnamon seed and sandy bottom" came the words and the music for a song that was a smash hit for Emmett. The song "Dixie" quickly caught on and was popular among Southerners and Northerners alike. Two years after the song debuted on the New York stage, the *New York Clipper,* a trade paper of the theater industry of the time, described the song as "one of the most popular compositions ever produced. . . . [It] had been sung, whistled and played in every quarter of the globe" (Sacks 3). By 1862, the name "Dixie" was identified with the cause of the South and symbolized the ties to a Southern homeland for Confederate soldiers on the front. Representing the perspective of a persona who looks nostalgically back to "Dixie Land, where I was born"—perhaps from a spacial distance or a temporal one—the song represented not a reality, but an ideal, and one that held power. Abraham Lincoln was said to be an admirer, and on the day that the Confederacy surrendered, he asked that the song be played for a crowd gathered outside the White House. "I have always thought that 'Dixie' was one of the best tunes I ever heard," Lincoln was quoted as saying the next day on April 10, 1865. "I had heard our adversaries had attempted to appropriate it. I insisted yesterday that we had fairly captured it" (Hall 10). In the same way that Lincoln believed having "fairly captured" the song meant a symbolic as well as an actual victory for the Northern armies, so, too, did subsuming the song for the cause of white supremacy become of paramount concern for those hoping to perpetuate a Southern society based on prejudice and subjugation. By the middle of the twentieth century, while the leaders of the civil rights movement gathered forces around "We Shall Overcome," those who rallied against them countered with "Dixie."

This first chapter of my book begins with a short history of the song "Dixie" to help me achieve several purposes. This account of the song's composition and the rise of the song's popularity show how an imaginative work about displacement and about crossing back over into the South's borders "to live and die" there played a significant role in the construction of Southern nationhood. Abraham Lincoln understood so much the power of the lyrics and tune of "Dixie" in inciting wartime fervor on the battlefield and on the Southern homefront that he claimed it as a spoil of Northern victory, thereby showing that texts can be controlled and claimed like other instruments of war. But what complicates the history of this song with lyrics told from the perspective of a Southerner who is far from home are the multiple layers of claims that have been made to the song itself. According to historians Howard L. Sacks and Judith Rose Sacks in their book *Way Up North in Dixie: A Black Family's Claim to the Confederate Anthem*, Dan Emmett actually learned the song from Ben and Lew Snowden, two African American musicians who were part of the Snowden Family Band. Making their living by farming in Knox County, Ohio, the same county where Emmett was born and raised, the Snowdens were well-known musicians in the area who performed for both black and white audiences. Performing their music and dance routines in communities as far as 75 miles from their home, the Snowdens were popular entertainers at family, church, and community gatherings. Although Emmett's 1904 tombstone in Mount Vernon identifies him as the man "whose song 'Dixie Land' inspired the courage and devotion of the Southern people and now thrills the hearts of a united nation," three miles north a cemetery marker for the Snowden brothers identifies them as the ones who "taught 'Dixie'" to Dan Emmett (Sacks 1–3).

Ellen Cooper Snowden, mother to the two Snowden brothers, was born in 1817 on a plantation in Charles County, Maryland, a region at that time where strong-knit black communities were rooted in a distinctly African American culture. Ellen Cooper and her future husband, Thomas Snowden, moved west to Ohio with white families (Ellen was 10 and Thomas 23), and both found free-dom from slavery in Ohio. Among the first African Americans in the county where they settled, the Snowdens fought back against injustices they faced, including a lawsuit that Ellen Snowden brought against some whites who were described in court papers as having "denied her the opportunity to plant crops." Although Ellen and Thomas Snowden were freed from the plantation system of Maryland, their move to the Ohio territory also brought with it the isolation and varied conditions for African Americans living in antebellum Ohio (Sacks 14–15).

The Snowdens' music both celebrated and perpetuated their African American folk heritage. The instruments they used were similar to those in Southern antebellum black string bands, and according to the Sackses, the Snowdens "connected to—perhaps conjured—lost family members, black kin and friends in Maryland, and more broadly, the shared culture of black Americans." They also faced the "peculiar sensation" of a divided self not unlike what W. E. B. Du Bois experienced, at once recognizing and resisting the expec-tations of whites while also attempting to honor and perpetuate their African American heritage (13–14). At the heart of the Snowdens' story and their music is a narrative of geography and displacement: the separation of their family—especially for Ellen—from family, friends, and the African American commu-nity in Maryland. If African American music expressed anger and resentment about the racism of the time, typically those attitudes would have been veiled, "'safe' from the ears of uncomprehending whites." The Sackses argue that "We listen to 'Dixie,' then, for its black voice, its expression of themes of diaspora in the North—generations before the Great Migration made its promises and its disappointments known to the nation" (16). Nevertheless, even though we might listen for the "black voice" of the song, a voice of self-determination and individual expression, and even though "Dixie" may be rooted in a story of African American movement and migration, the song still remains one that was, in effect, stolen for divisive purposes. What is important for a study of Southern border crossing narratives is not only the way in which the song "Dixie" was appropriated from African American folk culture, but also the ways in which a story of African American migration was claimed by whites and became an argument for Southern white patriotism and ultimately white supremacy.

This first chapter in my book deals specifically with how border formation narratives have been used to create the physical and imaginative boundaries that contain the South and thus framed it as "almost a nation within a nation." As "a story we tell and are told" (McPherson 1), the South was created and continues to be created by those who have been able to wrest control of the region's "story." The song "Dixie," for example, has a complex history of being captured, retaken, freed, and captured again. If the original song was written by the Snowdens, laid claim to by the Northerner Emmett, and then smuggled away and maintained as a communal narrative of the Confederate South, then "Dixie" was ultimately freed by Lincoln, brought back as property of the Union before it was reclaimed as a symbol of entrenched and stubborn Southern determination that the "South should rise again." Essentially, this chapter in my book is concerned with how the borders of the South have been constructed and maintained through the control of border formation narratives, by means of top-down hegemonic discourse.

The trans-Atlantic slave trade, for example, laid claim to the collective narrative of the at least 12 million Africans who were captured and forced to suffer the atrocities and horrors of the Middle Passage and slavery in the New World. Enduring the Middle Passage meant facing perhaps the most horrendous and cruel conditions ever imposed upon one people by another and the largest imposed mass migration and displacement of a people ever in the recorded history of humankind. African slaves who reached the New World were beaten into submission, categorized as subhuman, forced into harsh labor conditions, and stripped of their identities by slaveholders who valued personal monetary gain and power over the sacredness of human dignity and worth. The journey itself across that Middle Passage often became the tie that bound slaves together in the New World. "Far from wiping out all traces of their cultural, social, and personal past," according to Howard Dodson and Sylviane A. Diouf, "the Middle Passage experience provided Africans with opportunities to draw on their collective heritage to make themselves a new people." Cut off from the familial and cultural bonds of Africa, slaves formed new bonds with other slaves on the ships, relationships that were viewed as being as close as kin. In Jamaica, slaves referred to those who had suffered the Middle Passage with them as "shipmates." In areas where Creole was spoken, the word *bâtiments* was used, and in Suriname, *sippi* (Dodson and Diouf 23). But as generations passed and those who had made the passage died, those relationships forged in a collective narrative of the nightmare of the Middle Passage also faded. While psychological repression of the experience of the crossing is certainly understandable, loss of the narrative itself—the story of the tortuous Middle Passage from Africa to slavery in the Americas—also severed the tie of Africans to their homeland.

The accounts that do survive point to the hegemonic forces working against the authors as they struggled to control their own life narratives. Yet while Olaudah Equiano's *Interesting Narrative of the Life of Olaudah Equiano* (1789) records the tortures of the Middle Passage, the "galling of the chains . . . the shrieks of the women, and the groans of the dying . . . a scene of horror almost inconceivable" (48), poet Phillis Wheatley represents the journey to the New World as a blessing and a godsend in her poems "On Being Brought From

Africa to America" (1773) and "To the University at Cambridge" (1767). Born in West Africa in 1753 and held as a slave in New York State and ultimately freed, Wheatley writes in her poems of "being brought from Africa to America" and describes her "native shore" as "the land of errors, and Egyptian gloom." It was the "gracious hand" of God, she says, that "[b]rought me in safety from those dark abodes." Her poems do not portray the atrocities of the Middle Passage, but instead claim "'Twas mercy" that set the journey going, and the "gracious hand" of God, the "Father of mercy," that brought her to a life in Christ in the New World. Her story of coming to Christ revolves around God's grace that "brought" her out of the darkness of Africa. Wheatley takes control of her story of the Middle Passage by claiming God as the one who "brought" her rather than the slave traders who piloted the ship named "Phillis." But in doing so, she frames her story in the context of the traditions of those who colonized her. Although I do not dare assume to be able to read Wheatley's religious convictions from the poem, I believe it is important to remember that she identifies herself as a devout believer not only to gain power over the society that enslaved her, but also to proselytize for Christianity.

Not until the time of the civil rights movement in the 1960s and 1970s, however, did the attempt to retrace the journey across the Middle Passage become a possibility for large numbers of African Americans and an established cultural phenomenon. Alex Haley's 1976 book *Roots* traced Haley's own family lineage back to Kunta Kinte, his Gambian ancestor who was captured and bound into slavery. The book won numerous awards and was made into a television miniseries that was reportedly viewed by 130 million people ("Alex Haley"). Alice Walker examined the conflict between reclaimed African roots and the Southern past in her highly anthologized "Everyday Use" (1973), the story of a mother and her two daughters, Maggie and Dee, who represent the rural folk past of Southern blacks and the more forward-thinking educated blacks who have fled to the cities. Although readers typically see Dee—the sister who wants nothing to do with the homemade quilts and simple living of her mother and her sister Maggie—as lacking in substance and connection to family, Dee represents the strong desire of many African Americans during the 1970s to reconnect with their African roots. She takes the name "Wangero" not only because she wants to reclaim her African past, but also because she does not want to claim ownership of a narrative of a people who have been enslaved and renamed with Anglicized names. Instead, she wants to lay claim to the homeland of her people, the departure place for this narrative of slavery—not to her African American past. In fact, though, the trouble with Dee is that she wants to wipe out the story of the Middle Passage. She does not want to see herself as connected to a people who have struggled through the bonds of slavery and fought for the freedoms of their brothers and sisters.

Narratives of the Middle Passage have been at once surrounded by deep emotion and even controversy. The conventions and prejudices of the times led Wheatley's master, John, to attest to the authenticity of the poems and his fellow Boston gentlemen to sign their names to a letter confirming that they knew Phillis to be a slave who had been taken from Africa and a woman capable of writing the poems attributed to her. The validity of Equiano's narrative was questioned by his contemporaries and more recently by modern-day scholars, some pointing to his baptismal record in Westminster, England, as indicating he was born in "Carolina" rather than in Nigeria. Thus, these claims point out, Equiano could never have experienced the Middle Passage as a slave. Alex Haley was sued three times in connection with *Roots* (including once by writer Margaret Walker, who charged he had plagiarized from her novel *Jubilee*), while other critics argued that his book was not based on historical fact as Haley claimed, but instead on a fictionalized narrative of his ancestral story. Noted historian Henry Louis Gates was quoted as saying, "Most of us feel it's highly unlikely that Alex actually found the village whence his ancestors sprang. *Roots* is a work of the imagination rather than strict historical scholarship" (Beam D1). Even though the factual details of Haley's book might have been questioned, *Roots* still had an incredibly powerful impact on the general population. The book and television miniseries that was produced from it reclaimed for many African Americans a communal story that had been all but wiped out by the institution of slavery and became a cultural phenomenon that both validated the African past and *reclaimed* a racial and cultural narrative for many African Americans.

Other narratives of the Middle Passage have gained similar power. Award-winning illustrator Tom Feelings believed that in reclaiming the Middle Passage, "this part of our [African American] history could be told in such a way that those chains of the past, those shackles that physically bound us together against our wills could, in the telling, become spiritual links that willingly bind us together now and into the future." Brooklyn-born Feelings responded with his book *The Middle Passage: White Ships / Black Cargo*, probably his best-known work and winner of the 1996 Coretta Scott King Award, which collects 64 narrative paintings that illustrate the suffering and the atrocities of the Middle Passage—the beatings, brandings, savage torture, and rape of his people. Feelings says that he "began to see how important the telling of this particular story could be for Africans all over this world, many who consciously or unconsciously share this *race memory*, this painful experience of the Middle Passage." The image included here from Feelings's book (Figure 1.1) shows the chained figure of an African male whose body—the trunk and the upper portion of his legs—encapsulates a diagram of the interior of a slave ship, with human beings lined row upon row like livestock. Feelings suggests here that within the chained African is this historical fact of the Middle Passage—this race memory that lies deep at the core of all those who were stolen from Africa into slavery and their descendants. This narrative is one that defines his people, yet one that is difficult to face for so many reasons. But according to Feelings, in the retelling of the story, "that painful Middle Passage could become, ironically, a positive connecting line to all of us whether living inside or outside the continent of Africa."

Writing of the importance of Equiano's slave narrative for African studies, Professor Catherine Ancholou of the Awuku College of Education in Nigeria reclaims this narrative of passage as well. Calling the narrative the "anchor," a text studied "in every discipline," she asserts that as an African, Equiano

> makes it impossible . . . to forget the issue of slavery and the fact that we have millions and millions of our brothers and sisters who are now no longer part of us, but who have now gone through this experience of slavery, who have now become part of another culture, but who are equally part of us, and who are yearning to connect. Equiano's story, more than any other story, carries that authenticity, that impetus and that imperative to connect, to not forget, to remember, and to take responsibility for the actions of our forefathers.

Both Feelings and Ancholou assert the power of reclaiming the narrative of crossing. Indeed, according to Feelings and Ancholou, it is not only through retracing the steps of the ancestors, but also through understanding the significance of the threshold separating African peoples that wounds of the past can be healed. The Middle Passage is at once a dividing line and a boundary that binds together two peoples—Africans in Africa and Africans in the diaspora—who share a common history.

Laying claim to Equiano's narrative also foregrounds an even larger scale struggle for control of the historical narrative of American slavery: the why and how and to what end Africans were enslaved, moved, and displaced and the consequences of that displacement. Paul Gilroy, one of the leading voices in deconstructing and revising that narrative, published his groundbreaking book *The Black Atlantic: Modernity and Double-Consciousness* in 1993, aiming to rescue African "roots" and "routes" through the Middle Passage from the hegemonic control of the Western narrative that identifies the modern world as a "white" invention. In his monumental study, Gilroy claims a significance for the Atlantic and "questions of 'race' and representation" that he says have been "so regularly banished from orthodox histories of western aesthetic judgement, taste, and cultural value" (9). Focusing on the Atlantic Ocean as what he identifies as "one single, complex unit of analysis," Gilroy encouraged cultural historians to look at the Atlantic in the context of modernity and to examine

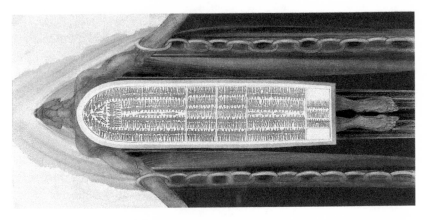

Figure 1.1. Untitled image of human body packing diagram inside of black body as vessel. From the collections of Yale University. Used by permission of The Tom Feelings Collection, LLC.

it within a transnational context (15). Suggesting that historical studies tend to be segregated along racial lines, Gilroy argues for looking at what he calls "another, more difficult option: the theorisation of creolisation, métissage, mestizaje, and hybridity" (2). Looking to J. M. W. Turner's 1840 painting "Slavers Throwing Overboard the Dead and Dying—Typhon Coming On" (Figure 1.2), Gilroy identifies the slave ship—in movement across the Atlantic, across the waters between Africa, the United States, the Caribbean, and Europe—as "a central organising symbol":

> The image of the ship—a living, micro-cultural, micro-political system in motion—is especially important for historical and theoretical reasons.... Ships immediately focus attention on the middle passage, on the various projects for redemptive return to an African homeland, on the circulation of ideas and activists as well as the movement of key cultural and political artefacts. (4)

Reconsidering modernity within the context of the Black Atlantic and the African diaspora, Gilroy's book established Africans' central role in the development of modern society by reclaiming the liminal space of the Atlantic Ocean. In effect, Gilroy reclaimed the borderland and revised the border narrative that colonized Africans who were enslaved and set far from their homeland to other parts of the world, showing how this space became the site of a "double consciousness" for W. E. B. Du Bois and a "double vision" for Richard Wright and claiming a nationalism for blacks in the liminal space of the Atlantic.

In the same way that establishment of the Atlantic slave trade was possible only through European narratological control of the Middle Passage, settling the New World meant colonizing Native Americans by creating

Figure 1.2. J. M. W. Turner, *Slavers Throwing Overboard the Dead and Dying—Typhoon Coming On.* Museum of Fine Arts, Boston.

and perpetuating the image of the "savage" Indian world and the "civilized" European, and reframing the border between wilderness and "civilization" as one that was necessary for and endorsed by God. Similar to the "cure" narrative as a means to build nationalism, a version of the "cure" narrative was employed by Europeans who believed that they were the ones who could bring religious salvation and civilization to native peoples in the Americas by conquering them, claiming the land for European kings and queens, and establishing European-styled communities and plantations. The New World and its people was a place that needed "saving," and its moral and social contagion needed to be contained and cured. One of the first of those European texts about the early exploration and settlement of the American South was written by Cabeza de Vaca. Serving as provost marshal and treasurer of a royal expedition to North America that departed from Spain in 1527, Cabeza de Vaca was responsible for keeping the books, overseeing the enforcement of Spanish law, and seeing that the investments of Emperor Carlos V of Spain were protected. He was determined to explain his own actions in his account of the expedition and encourage others to finance future expeditions to the New World. After the expedition leader Pánfilo de Narváez decided to split his men into land and sea forces, the expedition met again and again with disaster. Cabeza de Vaca and the members of the land party first went ashore in the Tampa Bay area, but after they took captive a Native American chief in what is now north Florida, they were forced to leave Florida and sail for the island that would be known as Cuba in a boat they had built. They landed instead on the western coast of the Gulf of Mexico, where they were at first welcomed, until, as Cabeza de Vaca explains, "half the natives died from a disease of the bowels and blamed us." In effect, the Europeans carried the contagion—not the cure. Leaving the coast with only a small group of survivors remaining, they began their wandering that took them into what are now the northern regions of Mexico. Not only does Cabeza de Vaca write in his narrative about the challenges of making the physical passage across the border of the ocean between Spain and the wilderness of what would become the southern United States, but he also creates a psychological boundary around himself as he defines himself as a Spaniard (a Christian) against the Other—the Native Americans or the Not-Spaniards (the "barbarians"). Like Hadrian and the Celestial Empire in China before him, he believed that the "savages" needed walling out.

Formulating his narrative as at once a captivity narrative and a conversion narrative, Cabeza de Vaca sets himself apart from the Native Americans as a conquistador who compares his ordeal to Jesus's 40 days and 40 nights in the wilderness. Like Jesus, he also performs "miracles." He often overlooks the similarities between his European ways and those of the Native Americans, seeing them as "barbarous people" who are "ignorant of time," even though they live lives more closely connected to the natural world. Cabeza de Vaca is, in effect, captured by the text of the Bible, which gives him strength to struggle through his ordeal and sets him apart as the carrier of "the Word" to a people that he and his fellow Europeans see as dispossessed heathens. Of course, though, he saw himself as a sojourner, eventually returning to Europe and to "civilization."

As Cabeza de Vaca becomes what Alan J. Silva identifies as an ethnographer, a sort of anthropologist of the sixteenth century, he also becomes a participant in the Native American communities that he and his party visit. He observes their rituals, but he also takes part in some of them. He writes of shedding his clothing just as the Native Americans do and losing the outer façade of the conquistador, including the horse. Increasingly, he is observed by the Native Americans, especially the men, as he becomes an object to colonize in their eyes. He eats raw meat, including horses. The loss of Cabeza de Vaca's horse and clothing, according to Silva, represents "the destruction of the discoverer as mythic hero and the substitution of a man simply trying to survive." Essentially, the "old, imperial self is at war with the new, refashioned one." This divided self that resides in the liminal spaces also forces Cabeza de Vaca into the role of "Other," forces him to cross the line between European and Native American cultures. By taking the role of ethnographer, his original goal as colonizer and conqueror becomes more complex. In his narrative, Cabeza de Vaca at once expresses the needs and wishes of the native population from the perspective of the outsider, but in doing so, he also rejects the objectives and motivations of the colonizers. He reframes the story of his border crossing so that it is more acceptable to readers who might be troubled by the aims of colonization. Silva points out that Cabeza de Vaca is identified as heroic because he has been spiritually and physically tested and has passed through those ordeals. "Enslavement" is now referred to as "conversion." The "conquistador" is now a "missionary" whose chief goal is the kingdom of God—not the riches of earth.

While Cabeza de Vaca has been credited with returning to Spain with a more enlightened view of Native Americans that was more compassionate and progressive, he also intentionally reframed the story of his sojourn in the New World as one that would bring salvation to what he believed was a heathen people. He reconstructs his role in the liminal space—no longer "Other" encountering the "savage" and crossing the line into "uncivilized" territory. He passes into the borderland as the "missionary" with a new mission not to conquer, but to save. From those earliest years, the history of European conquest of the Americas revolved around borders and who had control of them. Narratives like Cabeza de Vaca's also gave Europeans, in general, a mission for seeing that the wilderness was conquered for God with the additional benefits that along the way Native Americans would be controlled and "civilized," and land would open up for European settlement and potential moneymaking enterprises. The spaces in between were both the place of contact and of conflict, a boundary that was continually moving westward. Crossing into that "in-between" world signified for Europeans the progress of civilization; the entire movement west was essentially an attempt to control liminal space, which was, in effect, a constantly moving borderland.

In the more northern region of what would become the South, at the Jamestown settlement of the Virginia colony in the early seventeenth century, the English pursued tactics similar to Cabeza de Vaca's, attempting to sway the opinions of the Crown and the English people that the settlement—and the liminal space between civilization and wilderness that it represented—was a worthy and profitable enterprise. Forced to the center of these efforts was Indian Princess Pocahontas, who, as legend tells it, singlehandedly turned the wrath of her father Powhatan from Captain John Smith and saved his life. The real story, however, is much more complex and reflects John Smith's misunderstandings of the event. The story of Captain Smith's "saving" by his supposed love interest does not appear in Smith's first account, but it does appear in his 1624 version, which was written seven years after Pocahontas died in England. More recent scholarship asserts that if, indeed, the event actually took place, the interpretation of the episode was marred by Smith's inability to understand Indian cultural practices and his own foggy recollections. Smith even gets her name wrong. He identifies her by her childhood nickname, "Pocahontas," rather than by her real name, Matoaka. Contrary to Smith's recollection of the "saving" incident, Matoaka was only 11 or 12 years old at the time. And there was no romance (Weaver 144–46).

While on an expedition outside the Jamestown settlement in 1607, Smith and his men came upon an Indian party led by the brother of Wahunsenacawh, who was the leader of the Powhatan nation and became known to the whites as Powhatan. Smith and his party were taken to Powhatan, who asked why the white men were settling on native lands. Smith explained that they were seeking security from attacks by the Spaniards and their ships were in need of repairs because of damages they had sustained. Powhatan responded by offering them protection and food. The ceremony that Smith described was actually an adoption or initiation ceremony intended to claim Smith as an "Anglo-Powhatan," to symbolically kill and then rebirth him as someone who navigated the line between cultures; instead of threatening his life, the ceremony was actually meant to signify an agreement between Powhatan and Smith. According to Jace Weaver, the ceremony sealed a "sacred covenant by which the English agreed to a subordinate position in the Powhatan Confederacy in exchange for protection and succor. . . . John Smith became a Powhatan. There was no longer a 'John Smith' to them. He was now Nantaquod" (146). Within a year following Smith's captivity, the colonists had become distracted by the search for gold, even forsaking practical considerations like the farming of food and hunting, and within two years, Smith had sailed for England, never to return to the Virginia colony. Matoaka was told that he had died. Tensions grew between the colonists and the Indians as whites raided Indian communities for food and Indians fought back as the colonists attempted to claim more land as their own (Weaver 147).

With the increasing unrest, one of the leaders of the Virginia colony, Captain Samuel Argall, concluded that a way to bring peace was to capture Matoaka. She was, and a ransom was set, but Powhatan didn't respond for three months. Jace Weaver points to this as evidence that perhaps she wasn't his biological daughter, but instead a "daughter" of his tribe (148). While she was held, she was instructed in English ways and in Christianity, and fell in love with John Rolfe. She married him and gave birth to their son. The general consensus was that with the wedding came peace between the Indians and the colonists, but what peace meant was also tainted by the motivations of the English to take Native American lands. In a 1616 letter to Queen Anne, John Smith proclaimed that by marrying John Rolfe, "an English gentleman," Pocahontas—"the first Christian ever of that Nation, the first Virginian ever spake English, or had a childe in marriage by an Englishman"—had "at last reject[ed] her barbarous condition" (Qtd. in Price 173). Even though she was probably not an actual princess within the Powhatan tribe, Pocahontas was represented that way by the

Virginia Company and by Smith, who proposed to Queen Anne that the English might through Pocahontas "rightly have a Kingdom by her means" (Smith).

When in 1616, the Virginia colony became in critical need of additional funding from the Crown, Sir Thomas Dale concluded that the best means of ensuring the success of the colony and its expansion was to organize a delegation to England that would bear products of the New World and Pocahontas herself. As Jace Weaver tells the story, the ship *Treasurer* set sail to England with a load of "exceeding good tobacco" and "other such lyke commodyties," including sassafras and sturgeon caviar (148). On board, as well, were Matoaka, who was by then known as Lady Rebecca Rolfe, along with her husband, her son, and her brother-in-law, who had been sent by Powhatan on an "espionage mission" to find John Smith and to survey the numbers of the British enemy and to take stock of their resources. On what was a carefully orchestrated trip that was intended to gain public support for the Virginia venture, Lady Rebecca met with Sir Walter Raleigh and other dignitaries, was introduced to Ben Jonson and John Donne, and had an audience with Queen Anne and King James, who was said to have been concerned that Rolfe held a potential claim to the Virginia colony because he had married a "princess" (Weaver 149). Rebecca also met with John Smith, but it was not a meeting of "unrequited love." According to Smith in recounting what happened, Maotaka sternly said to Smith, "You did promise Powhatan what was yours should bee his, and he the like to you called him father being in his land a stranger, and by the same reason so must I doe you." Pointing to the fact that the colonists had told Maotaka and her people that Smith was dead, Maotaka lashed out at him, explaining that "your Countriemen will lie much" and accusing Nantaquod of breaking his agreement with Powhatan, abandoning her people, and thus wrecking the alliance between the Indians and colonists (Weaver 150). Alden Vaughan wrote of the meeting, "The pity is that Powhatan's most successful representative to the Court of St. James did not live to share with her father what she had seen and heard, for she seems to have envisioned a Virginia that expanded, rather than displaced, her natal society" (55). She died in Gravesend, most probably from influenza, before she could set sail for home and was buried there.

The space between "civilized" society and "savage" Native Americans that Europeans tried to control is figuratively represented in this portrait of Pocahontas (Figure 1.3), who is dressed in the full regalia of an English noblewoman of the seventeenth century, renamed as the Anglicized "Rebecca," and baptized as a Christian. Originally a 1616 sketch by Simon Van de Passe that was used to create an engraving that commemorated Pocahontas's journey to England, the image shows not only a Native American woman bound tightly in the clothing of the Europeans, but also encircled—essentially controlled and contained—by a framework that holds her tightly in check. For Europeans, the issue of settlement revolved around securing the boundaries—keeping "civilization" within the borders—and control of the liminal space, seeing that the borderland between Europeans and Native Americans was secured, reimagined, and controlled. If the New World was framed as a place that needed civilizing and containing, then Maotaka's story was reworked to make it more consumable and more acceptable for Europeans and a rationalization for continuing to assert their control over the New World and its people. Indeed, it is a narrative that remains in popular culture today, in part because of Disney's claim to Pocahontas.

Because the early settlement of the Americas essentially revolved around the European notion of labels and lines on a map, including the Virgin Queen's name given to the Virginia colony and lines of settlement drawn on a piece of paper, the complications of borders and borderlands were at the forefront. In the 1760s, after the Seven Years' War with the French, colonists were dismayed that the British king would hold them back from moving westward to settle land that they believed had opened up to them by the end of the war. With the Proclamation of 1763, the Crown had made an agreement with Native Americans west of the ridge of the Appalachian Mountains that white settlers would not invade their territory. Although the Proclamation was intended to encourage peace between the Native Americans and the settlers, the colonists saw movement westward to claim land west of the ridge as an act of defiance against British tyranny and a way to assert their independence from the British Crown. Ignoring treaties with Native Americans, settlers moved westward anyway. According to Natalie Inman, "freedom from British tyranny across the mountains was as much or more about the 'liberty' of unfettered territorial expansion than it was about the concerns illuminating patriot activity further east" (258). As settlers pushed beyond boundaries set in treaties between Native Americans and the Crown, hostilities intensified as colonists settled illegally on Indian lands. By the early 1770s, as the British lost control of frontier territories, the Proclamation line was wiped out and land-hungry white settlers poured across the Appalachians, further increasing tensions with Native tribes.

Europeans differed ideologically from Native Americans in their conceptions of space, property ownership, and boundary setting, but even when European forms of treaty-making bound whites and Indians over property, whites were often quite willing to break those agreements. Whereas Native Americans viewed land as something that could be purchased as a place to settle, they also typically believed that land could be shared for hunting. Increasingly, though, Indian tribes recognized that whites were easily swayed to break treaties for profit and political gain. Oftentimes, too, whites misunderstood whether or not anyone in particular held rights to Indian property and who specifically had authority within any given tribe to sign treaties or

Figure 1.3. Simon Van de Passe, *Matoaka als Rebecka daughter to the mighty Prince Powhatan.* Library of Congress, Prints & Photographs Division, Miscellaneous Items, LC-USZ62–8104.

speak for an entire Indian population. And while a particular chief in one tribe might hold such authority, in another tribe the person or people with similar power might be vastly different—or even include women. As a result, according to historian Peter Nabokov, "Native Americans lost far more of their land and independence by the bloodless process of signing treaties than they ever did on the battlefield. Indeed, most of the violence between Indians and whites flared up because Native Americans were being deprived of the very land promised them in earlier treaties" (Nabokov 117).

One of the largest tracts of land that Southern Native Americans lost through treaty included what is now the northern section of Middle Tennessee and the entire state of Kentucky. When in 1774 North Carolina land speculator Richard Henderson began negotiating the Treaty of Sycamore Shoals with the Cherokee for the Watauga settlements in present-day east Tennessee, he expanded the negotiations to include Cherokee hunting grounds south of the Ohio River and north of the Cumberland River. Although the colonial government deemed the treaty illegal, following the American Revolution, newly formed state governments were more in favor of the acquisition of the land. The treaty also created sharp divisions among the Cherokee. While Little Carpenter continued to work for peace through treaty-making, his cousin Dragging Canoe, Cherokee chief Oconostota's great-nephew, declared war against the settlers and warned, "You have bought a fair land, but you will find its settlement dark and bloody" (Inman 263). Chief Oconostota lamented that "Whole nations had melted away in [the] presence [of white settlers] like balls of snow before the sun, and had scarcely left their names behind, except as imperfectly recorded by their enemies and destroyers" (Qtd. in Inman 263).

Early presidents of the new United States believed that Native Americans should be removed from the South. Both Thomas Jefferson and James Monroe made the case that Native Americans should exchange their lands in the Southeast for territory west of the Mississippi River, but no action was taken during their administrations. As a major general leading the military campaign against the Creek Indians in the Battle of Horse Shoe Bend, Andrew Jackson led efforts by the US government to force the Creek to surrender 20 million acres of land. Becoming a driving force in efforts to remove Native Americans from their property, over the next decade, Jackson was involved in 9 of the 11 major treaties that resulted in Indian removal. Hoping to hold on to at least some of their lands, the Creek and other Southeast Indian tribes including the Cherokee and Chickasaw continued negotiating treaties with the whites despite the fact that the treaties typically collapsed as more white settlers poured into territory reserved for the Indians in those very same treaties. Many Native Americans negotiated in good faith, accepting themselves "to be under the protection of the United States of America, and of no other sovereign whatsoever." Yet when Andrew Jackson became president, he used this assumption as evidence that the federal government had the right to remove Native Americans from their lands and to resettle them in territory west of the Mississippi River. The means to do so was the Removal Act of 1830, which offered incentives for Indians to move westward, but also opened up opportunities for Jackson and his administration to coerce tribes into signing treaties and to force them off their lands. Signing nearly 70 removal treaties that removed close to 50,000 Indians from their lands, Jackson went so far in his plan for removal that he refused to recognize a Supreme Court decision ruling that the Cherokee Nation was sovereign and not subject to the laws of the state of Georgia. Negotiating the Treaty of New Echota with a chief from an unauthorized faction of the Cherokee Nation rather than with Principal Chief John Ross, Jackson set in motion the Trail of Tears, calling out federal troops and state militia to forcibly remove the Cherokee from their lands given by earlier treaties with the US government. Estimates are that up to 4,000 of the 15,000 to 16,000 Native Americans pushed west on the Trail of Tears died en route (Office of the Historian).

After the Indian Removal Act of 1830, only remnants of Native American tribes remained in the Southeast, and only the Cherokees had government status in the eyes of Washington. Yet while the act had been highly debated and the consequences well known across the country, there continued a subtler removal of Native Americans from the Southern states east of the Mississippi. Those who remained faced increasing isolation and violence against them because they had stayed. According to Theda Perdue, the South and the US federal government operated together to continue to remove Native Americans from the region so as "to solidify a biracial South and reinforce white power long after the Trail of Tears ended" (4). The presence of Indians made more difficult Southern attempts to bolster a racial system based on polarities of black and white, particularly by the early twentieth century, when Jim Crow laws became problematic because the South was actually a multiracial society. "As states segregated not only schools but also transportation and public accommodations," writes Perdue, "these people presented legislators with a conundrum: How could they fit a third race into a biracial legal system?" Typically, Southern states responded by identifying Indians as "colored," barely mentioning Indians in Jim Crow statutes, labeling marriage between Indians and blacks as having "tainted native people's Indian blood," barring Indians from spaces identified as "whites only," and not recognizing Indians as an option on government documents (Perdue 9). Whereas in the border state of Oklahoma where Native Americans had been resettled in large numbers in the Jacksonian era, Indians were legally identified as white, they were not given full US citizenship rights until 1924.

Perhaps the project of framing out the South gained even tighter controls of mapping out borders between the South and the Other with the Mason-Dixon Line. Certainly, it has been this border that has had the most power in formulating the boundaries of the place that became known as *the* South. The history of the line reaches back to the colonial period to a border dispute between the Calvert family of Maryland and the Penns of Pennsylvania. Although Maryland and Pennsylvania were in the earliest years formed by groups in pursuit of religious freedoms, the economy in Maryland became focused on single cash crops. While the Pennsylvania citizenry was composed substantially of yeoman farmers, tradesmen, and merchants, Maryland's plantation economy revolved around tobacco production, which depended upon slave labor. The line was hotly contested by both colonies in large part because the land was still under settlement, and violence often broke out. Although Calvert and Penn attempted to negotiate the dividing line between the two colonies, the decision was ultimately left to the Lords Board of Trade back in London. The border between Pennsylvania and Maryland would be at 40 degrees north in a line that stretched westward into Indian territory. Despite the decision from London, neither Calvert nor Penn agreed, so the dispute continued, even long after the two men had died.

Increasingly concerned about the unrest along the border and strongly influenced by the mentality of the time that was grounded in reason and enlightenment, the British believed that to bring order to the colonies and to unite the people, a dividing line was necessary. Taking little notice of the differing character of the cultures they divided in their mapmaking and caring most about the economic implications of the disruptions along the border, the royal administrators made the decision to send Charles Mason and Jeremiah Dixon to the colonies to draw the imperial line that was intended to settle the dispute. The British government, according to historian John C. Davenport, "did not understand exactly what it was drawing a line between" (36–37). Davenport creates a striking image of a British power caught up in drawing lines on white paper, defining places by the lines that they themselves created. Control of the colonies, they maintained, came from the ability to place lines on a page. The lines "looked so tidy on paper." Like their British counterparts, Mason and Dixon believed that disagreements between colonists "never had . . . amounted to anything a well-drawn line could not remedy" (41). As part of the British Empire and of their age, Mason and Dixon were skilled, well-known mathematicians and astronomers before they arrived in the colonies. Mason had worked at the Royal Observatory in Greenwich, and they had been sent as a team to Cape Town, South Africa, by the Royal Society of London to observe the first transit of Venus in a hundred years. Both saw their jobs as scientific endeavors intended to bring British order to a less civilized outreach of the Crown. Mason was particularly adept at recordkeeping and brilliant at visualizing a line imposed upon nature where no topographical boundary existed. Mason and Dixon arrived in Philadelphia on November 15, 1763, to begin their work, which finally culminated with a marker at mile 233 on October 9, 1767, not far beyond their crossing at the Great Warrior Path.

The line gained greater significance as the conflict between pro- and anti-slavery movements intensified, and Southern exceptionalism became more deeply entrenched. When Pennsylvania abolished slavery in 1780, the division between Maryland and Pennsylvania grew deeper. By 1789, the Northwest Ordinance had extended the line even further west via the Ohio River, and by 1800, according to Davenport, "quarreling Americans . . . began to develop an obsession with lines, lines of separation and compromise" (53). In 1820, the Missouri Compromise was passed, extending the Mason-Dixon Line along the Ohio River and then all the way to the Pacific Ocean and further grounding slavery into American policy and culture. In effect, a new state in the Union could also be transformed by the Mason-Dixon if the state fell above or below the line. The Missouri Compromise granted statehood to Missouri and Maine, allowed Missouri to enter the Union as a slave state and Maine as a free state, and extended the Mason-Dixon Line from the point where the Ohio River enters the Mississippi River all the way to the Pacific Ocean. In 1845, Texas, which would ultimately join the Confederacy in the Civil War, entered the Union as a slave state under this "compromise," further solidifying the hold of the institution of slavery in the United States. Even though the Missouri Compromise was ultimately ruled unconstitutional in the Dred Scott case, it had already solidified the Mason-Dixon Line as a boundary around which American political and social life revolved.

During the Civil War, the necessity of crossing the Mason-Dixon Line became of paramount importance to Robert E. Lee and the Confederate army. With Missouri, Kentucky, and Maryland all remaining with the Union during the war despite their Southern leanings, the Virginia border became the physical border for the Confederacy. But the true border of the Confederacy remained the Mason-Dixon Line. Although a Confederate Maryland offered a strategic foothold for the South, pushing across the Mason-Dixon Line into Pennsylvania offered even greater rewards and a symbolic victory: the North would be pushed into a defensive role, Northern morale damaged, and Northern security questioned, and Southerners would be motivated by their army's success. Abraham Lincoln recognized the power of the line as he ordered his generals to wipe out the Confederate army if it came too near Pennsylvania. In fact, for not only Lee, but also for the armies of both sides, the Mason-Dixon Line became an obsession. If the Southern army succeeded in moving the line of demarcation into the North, not only would the South have gained a stronghold in war, but also the psychological upper hand.

Yet while Lee might have been obsessed with crossing the line in order to retain it during the Civil War, the postbellum South engraved that demarcation into the cultural and political landscape. "As soon as the Confederates laid down their arms, some picked up their pens and began to distort what they had done and why," writes James Loewen. "The Confederates won with the pen (and the noose) what they could not win on the battlefield." Jim Crow laws and the postwar South's creation of an elaborate mythology of "moonlight and magnolias" made the Mason-Dixon Line the mark that signaled even in trains that crossed it that the laws were different as African Americans were forced to move out of "Whites Only" cars as they entered "Dixie." The Spaniards and the British in the earliest days of settlement, the Confederate and Yankee generals during the Civil War, and finally segregationists in the postwar South understood the powerful tool of mapmaking, the power of cartography and using the page itself as a means of control. As Amy Propen notes in her article "Visual Communication and the Map," scholars who study the rhetorical strategies of mapping "understand the map as an ideologically charged, cultural artifact" (236). Maps "convey meaning," according to Propen. They "not only *reflect* renderings of the world, but they also *create* these renderings" (237). In clinging to the line, the South gained power, power that came from the narrative claiming that the North had not succeeded—the division between the South and the rest of the United States had not been erased. Borders were ideologically charged, continuing to convey meaning and reflecting a view of the world that still claimed Southern difference.

Much of the power attributed to mapmaking actually comes from border narratives themselves. Because the liminal margins of cultures and nation-states are used to imagine and create ways of envisioning nationality, they were also employed as hegemonic devices to reinforce and expand the borders of slave states and reigns of terror. Borders can be used to build a nation, as a way, according to Russ Castronovo, "to imagine the limits beyond which it might expand, to scout horizons for future settlement, to prepare the first line of attack." In effect, liminal space becomes the proving grounds for imperial expansion. Castronova points to the example of John Latrobe's 1855 book *The History of Mason and Dixon's Line*, beginning with a passage written by Latrobe that identifies the Mason-Dixon Line not as divisive but as binding and creating purpose: "There is, perhaps, no line, real or imaginary, on the surface of the earth—not excepting even the equator and the equinoctial—whose name has been oftener in men's mouths during the last fifty years." Claiming a significance for the 233-mile Mason-Dixon Line that is second only to the 25,000-mile line that encircles the globe, Latrobe, a white Southerner from Maryland, points out to his readers that the Mason-Dixon Line did not always suggest a divided nation. In elevating the Mason-Dixon Line, Latrobe intended to bind together his readers as Americans with the ethnocentric notion that the Mason-Dixon was more important than the equator and that sectional discord in the United States was more significant than any other political situation in the world (195–97). "Latrobe's comments are right on the mark," Castronovo explains, "instead of fragmenting regions and identities, boundaries may encourage consolidation and consensus" (202). The same year that Latrobe published his book, he traveled to Pennsylvania where he lectured on national disunity and argued that the line itself was not the location of instability. He instead envisioned a time when "the Mason and Dixon's line of politics will gradually change its position until, as cloud-shadows pass, leaving earth in sunlight, we shall be seen, of all, to be a united and homogeneous people" (Qtd. in Castronova 202). In effect, Latrobe aimed to revise the meaning of the border and rewrite the way the line was interpreted. With the Compromise of 1850, that unity and homogeneity was made real as Northerners agreed—in support of a system that they regarded as cruel and immoral—to hunt down escaped slaves who had entered Northern territory. In effect, borders were blurred as the injustices of slavery became Northern law.

This blurring becomes especially apparent in narratives such as Harriet Jacobs's 1861 *Incidents in the Life of a Slave Girl*. Even though Jacobs fled across the Mason-Dixon Line from slavery in the South to freedom in the North, she remained trapped in this liminal space, always fearful that she would be discovered and sent back South again into slavery. At the end of *Incidents* when she shields her identity by taking the name Linda Brent, Jacobs says that she must remain "closely veiled," hiding her face so that she will not be discovered. She has made the physical journey into freedom, but the passageway remains controlled by the institution of slavery. Even after a white friend named Mrs. Bruce buys Linda's freedom, and Linda no longer fears to show her face, the narrative emphasizes that Linda has not fully gained her freedom. Jacobs uses this liminal space strategically to urge support of the Northern cause during the Civil War, arguing that the passage to freedom has not yet been fully won. Her story ends, as she says, "not in the usual way, with marriage." Instead, because of slavery, she laments, "The dream of my life is not yet realized. I do not sit with my children in a home of my own" (302). Jacobs urges her readers to act, claim, and win the passage to freedom for all.

The literal border controlled other narrative patterns as well. Frederick Douglass's border narrative, for instance, points not only to the power of a border to control groups of people, but also the power that texts have to shape ideological movements and nation building. In Douglass's 1845 *Narrative*, passing over the Mason-Dixon Line is what transforms the slave into a human being. Douglass figuratively crosses that boundary as he fights back against the physical abuses of Mr. Covey and ends with the well-known phrase, "You have seen how a man was made a slave; you shall see how a slave was made a man" (52). Yet despite his powerful critique of the Southern slave system, Douglass's criticism "stopped at the Mason-Dixon Line," according to Michael Bennett. Bennett argues that because Douglass was writing under the influence of Garrisonian abolitionism and William Lloyd Garrison himself, and because he depended upon Northern audiences to make his living, in fact, "Douglass's experience of slavery, mode of narration, and position in an unjust economic system are mutually transformed when he crosses the Mason-Dixon Line" (95). Using the allegory of the North as heaven also became problematic. Noting the influence of *Pilgrim's Progress* during the time period and on Douglass's *Narrative*, Bennett points out that *Narrative* "follows it closely—from the narrow gate, over the slough of despond, through the valley of humiliation, and onward to the celestial city." In effect, in order for *Narrative* to find success, it "had to fit through the narrow gate of the nineteenth-century black spiritual autobiography's generic codes and the expectations of that genre's readers" (96).

The transforming powers of the line were also a centerpiece for popular Southern novels of the nineteenth century that were intended to sway Northerners into believing that Southern slavery was a benign and even beneficial practice. Representing the Southern plantation system as benevolent and honorable, plantation novels rode on the popularity of local color and travel writing of the time period, but also attempted to capture Northern audiences in texts that pulled them across the line into Southern territory so that readers could be manipulated into seeing the "true" nature of the Southern slave system. In reading these books, Northern audiences were captured by texts that forced readers to cross the line into the South to see truths that supposedly were not apparent and were clouded by perspectives in the North. Such a pattern of Northerners crossing the border into the South was especially popular in novels by nineteenth-century Southern women writers, including Maria McIntosh, Mary Virginia Terhune, and Caroline Lee Hentz, who very intentionally used border crossings made because of marriage.

Perhaps one of the best examples of this sort of border crossing narrative is Hentz's *The Planter's Northern Bride* (1854). A transplanted Northerner herself, Hentz is probably best known for this novel, a defense of the Southern plantation system, which Hentz wrote as a response to Harriet Beecher Stowe's *Uncle Tom's Cabin* (1852). Born in Massachusetts, Hentz moved to Cincinnati in 1832 and lived in the South during her adult life. *The Planter's Northern Bride* tells the story of Northerner Eulalia Hastings, who finally sees the flaws in her abolitionist father's views on slavery and marries Russell Moreland, a wealthy Southern planter. The novel is full of kind and generous slave masters, miserable runaway slaves, and controlling abolitionists—a thorough and blatant support of Hentz's adopted Southern homeland. Moreland first meets

Eulalia in her small village in the North. "The Flower of the village," Eulalia is "highly educated and accomplished," and "universally beloved and admired" (39). Love-interest Moreland carries two blemishes that make him unsuitable for marriage: he is a divorced man and a Southern planter. Yet Hentz tries to strike a chord of sympathy for Moreland, who says he chose to leave the South to become a "wanderer" not because of business profits, but because he wished to "escape from sad and bitter recollections" of his marriage (97).

Hentz tries a number of tactics to sway Northern readers. Portraying the South as an Edenic garden, Hentz depicts the Hastings children who listen intently to Moreland's account as too sheltered and too controlled by their father to recognize what sort of world truly resides below the Mason-Dixon Line. Even Moreland's great love for Eulalia will not help him win over her father, but perhaps it went a long way in helping to sway Hentz's contemporary audience of readers. Moreland remains in her village week upon week, as if enchanted by a spell. Recalling Hastings's proclamation that he would see his daughter to a New England grave before she married a Southern slave master, Moreland ultimately resolves he will fight for her hand to the bitter end. Yet even Moreland's profession of deep love for Eulalia and his promise that in the South she will be "surrounded by affluence and comfort, the mistress of faithful, affectionate beings" do not sway her father (106). As Moreland dramatically places his hand on the door latch to leave, sure that Hastings will never allow their marriage, Hastings conveniently adds that if Moreland were "an humble missionary to some heathen land, I would give her to you in the name of the living God." That is indeed the case in the view of the planter. "I look upon myself as a missionary," he claims. "I look upon every master and mistress in our Southern land, as missionaries appointed to civilize and christianize the sons and daughters of Africa." The South, according to Moreland, has brought more than ten times the numbers of converts to Christianity through slavery than he estimates possible if all American missionaries were sent to Africa (108–9). It is only with this unlikely comparison that Hastings finally consents.

As the newly married couple journey South, Eulalia crosses from maidenhood into marriage, from Northern girlhood to Southern plantation mistress. Never having seen a train much less traveled on one, she is at first "started as if a fiend from the infernal regions was approaching her" (178), and on the steamboat she suffers through a night of motion sickness and sleeplessness as a storm passes through. "A young traveller" (179), with the "elastic feelings of a child" (190), Eulalia becomes a woman in the liminal space as "the world enlarged upon her vision!" (191). She gains a new perspective on slavery as she journeys southward, "cradled" (198) on her husband's arm, "bathed in that calm, celestial light" (199). Passing over the border becomes a birthing experience for her. At first unsure that she will be able to fulfill her duties as plantation mistress, she tells her husband that she will be looking to him for guidance, yet his "guidance" quickly has her convinced she is the one who is prejudiced. She has, after all, only had contact with free African Americans, whom Moreland describes as "generally far more degraded, more low in the scale of being, than the slave" (202). Describing Northern philanthropists as ready to "stand back with a *holier than thou* written on their brows" (202), Moreland assures her that in the South, she will "see the negro, not as he is at the North, an isolated, degraded being, without caste or respectability . . . but surrounded with the socialities of life . . . free from the cares and anxieties that rest so heavily on us" (204). Then, he tells her, she will be able to make up her own mind about slavery. Symbolically transformed from her "otherness," Eulalia scorns at an uncouth Northerner on the boat who confronts her husband about his slave interests.

As Eulalia settles in at the plantation, she gains confidence as she is "initiated in the mysteries of plantation life." First riding a "gentle little pony" to accompany her husband as he makes his rounds, she soon forges a new courage and worldliness, riding out on even "the most spirited and high-mettled" horse (340). All she sees is orderly, neat, and tidy, and all is under the "watchful guardian providence" of her husband (341). At the sound of a bugle blast, the slaves begin their "grand march" from the fields, carrying baskets of cotton on their heads, with the small children carrying their baskets and beaming with "an air of self-importance and pride" (331). Eulalia is full of pride, too, for it is her husband whom the slaves gather round as a father—not as a conquering king. She recognizes, too, that "she must share that responsibility" (332), for she has been transformed from a child to the "presiding Queen of his princely home" (231). Hentz deftly parallels Eulalia's initiation into the maturity and responsibilities of womanhood and marriage with her recognition of the "truths" of the Southern plantation system. In effect, Hentz represents Eulalia's border crossing from North to South as one that empowers her as a woman and gives her a life of purpose as a maternal figure and as a Christian bringing others to Christ.

While antebellum Southerners like Hentz remained in the South and promoted a Southern story of a beneficent slaveholding system, other white Southerners left the region for good, during the Civil War and Reconstruction, hoping to form enclaves, "purified" communities intended to preserve Confederate values. The best known of these groups settled near Santa Bárbara, Brazil, in the 1860s and 1870s, where the climate was similar to that in the southern United States. White Southerners who had fought for and supported the Confederacy and who remained in the South tried a similar isolationist tactic, shoring up the borders, perpetuating the myth of the Lost Cause, solidifying a line that had been a military prize, and turning the essential worship of the line into a fetish. The Civil War might have ended with Southern defeat, but the line became the South's means to continue the fight for Southern nationalism.

If the line remained, then so, too, did the South remain as a separate "nation," as a place set off from a North that was represented as industrialized, commercialized, and money hungry. The South didn't become "Dixie" until the Civil War, and the song "Dixie" didn't become popular until the war. Likewise, the borderland between North and South remained an area of contention—a space that in itself held power for those who crossed the threshold and into the liminal space and for those who endeavored to control that space.

The South attempted to bolster other borders as well—not just the Mason-Dixon Line. To the south, the border between the Southern states and Mexico was and continues to remain a more porous boundary, in part because of the US desire—and the Southern US desire—to expand territory. While the United States laid claim to more territory with the annexation of Texas in 1845, the South also laid claim to another slave state. Even though the Treaty of Guadalupe Hidalgo, which ended the Mexican-American War, seemed to lay a clear boundary for Texas on the Rio Grande, the border between Texas and Mexico even into the twenty-first century continues to be a contested site. As the adage goes, "I didn't cross the border; the border crossed me"; with the signing of the treaty, many Mexicans found themselves living in US territory but not holding the same rights as Anglo-Americans who poured into Texas to settle and took possession of land that had in some cases been passed down through generations of Mexican families but was taken from their control because of racist laws that governed the new state. In effect, the land border that frames the southernmost part of the South created a liminal space within the South itself. This "newly deemed 'opened' space," according to Bernadine Hernandez, was, in effect, "reconstructed" by the treaty, by a legal document that favored Anglo-Americans and left Mexican Americans displaced (2).

This liminal space is the focus of the first novel written in English by a Mexican American woman, *Who Would Have Thought It?* Written by María Amparo Ruiz de Burton and first published in 1872, the novel draws comparisons between the US government's annexation of Texas and Northern aggression against and defeat of the South in the American Civil War. A critique of northeastern Yankee society, the novel is set during the Civil War and Reconstruction, features Civil War battles, and comments on what Ruiz de Burton saw as the racism, corruption, and hypocrisy of Northern society. The story focuses on Lola Medina, who is saved from a tribe of Native Americans in California by medical doctor James Norval and brought back east to live in his New England home. While the novel deals with the racism that Lola experiences in the North because her skin was dyed black by the Native Americans to conceal her light skin, it also reflects Ruiz de Burton's own classism, elevating Mexicans such as Lola, who is actually descended from an aristocratic Mexican family. According to Hernandez, Lola is "an outlet to portray dispossession and loss." In fact, Hernandez says, Lola stands for "everything the Confederacy stood for" (7). As evidence, Hernandez points to the conclusions of Rosaura Sanchez and Beatrice Pita, who edited Ruiz de Burton's letters and reasoned that she "sympathized with the defeated Confederacy, seeing in the South's defeat a mirror of the defeat of Mexico in 1848, and in Reconstruction, a clear imposition of Yankee hegemony in the Southern states" (Qtd. in Hernandez 6–7). The wife of a federal military officer, Ruiz de Burton chose the language of the colonizer—not the colonized—to tell her story, reflecting the border circumstances of her own life.

The difficulties of laying claim to both a personal identity that honored a person's culture and rights as a US citizen while living in the border region were a constant concern of the Hispanic immigrant press. Nicolás Kanellos explains that since its inception in the nineteenth century and until present day, the Hispanic immigrant press has resisted assimilation. Kanellos points, for example, to what was a characteristic urging by the *Corpus Christi El Horizonte* (The Horizon, 1879–80). Addressing its Mexican readers in 1880, the editors advised them not to become US citizens because of the discriminations they faced in American society. "We shall always be foreigners in the United States and they will always consider us as such," the editors claimed (Qtd. in Kanellos 321). Perhaps having a common language of Spanish allowed Hispanics to better preserve their cultures, no matter the country from which they originated. Notably the first Spanish-language newspapers published in the United States were based in Southern cities: *El Misisipi*, which was founded in 1808 in New Orleans, and *La Gaceta de Texas* (Texas Gazette) in 1813 in Nacogdoches, Texas. Although these two papers had claims to being the first, they were followed by hundreds more, which published news and creative work, as was typical of the day, but endeavored to reprint the literary and intellectual writings of well-known Hispanics (Kanellos 314). In effect, if a newspaper can create nationhood, then this was the goal and the result. This effort intensified after northern Mexico and Louisiana became part of the United States and the Hispanic population was rapidly outnumbered by Anglo settlers. According to Kanellos, newspapers became a means not only to preserve culture, but also a way of "protecting and preserving" Catholicism as Hispanic communities became increasingly populated by Protestants (314). Hispanic cultures were preserved by other means as well. By 1900, about 150 cigar factories had opened in West Tampa and Ybor City in Florida that employed large numbers of Cuban immigrants. Because the job of rolling cigars was a repetitive, arduous task, lectors were often hired by the workers and paid by them. Figure 1.4 shows a lector in a cigar factory in Tampa in 1929. Actually a tradition carried from Cuba and Puerto Rico, the lector provided an education to workers through Hispanic print culture, giving them an opportunity that typically was only available to more privileged classes of people (Kanellos 326).

Figure 1.4. Interior view of the Cuesta-Rey Cigar Company—Tampa, Florida. 1929. *Interior view of the Cuesta-Rey Cigar Company—Tampa, Florida.* 1929. Black & white photoprint. State Archives of Florida, Florida Memory. Accessed 26 Sept. 2017. https://www.floridamemory.com /items/show/27163.

Those who navigated this southern border of the American South were often celebrated in popular culture and the line itself became a site associated with rebellion. Corridos fronterizos, or border ballads, were written about border heroes such as Cheno Cortina, Gregorio Cortez, and Catarino Garza. Cortina, who was known as the Red Robber of the Rio Grande, came from a Mexican family that owned property on both sides of the Rio Grande, and he saw the consequences of the property disputes along the river that were the result of the defeat of Mexico in the Mexican-American War that ended in 1848. Leading a Mexican militia in raids against the Anglo-Americans who settled in the region, Cortina ultimately saw his forces fail as the Texas Rangers took control. Passed down through generations of Chicanos who navigated the border, the "everpresent *corridos*," writes Gloria Anzaldúa, "narrated one hundred years of border history. . . . These folk musicians and folk songs are our chief cultural mythmakers, and they made our hard lives seem bearable" (83). Woven deep within the culture of the border, the stories and the music claim a strength and a courage for those who continue to navigate through life in the borderlands.

The South's borders have thus been slippery ones. "One emphatically says 'the South,' with a capital 'S,'" according to Édouard Glissant, "as though it represents an absolute, as though we other people of the south, to the south of the capitalized South, never existed" (30). As numerous scholars have argued since Glissant wrote these words, the southern United States has failed to see, too, its complicit relationship with other slaveholding nations, pushing aside and labeling others as barbaric and uncivilized. John Lowe questions the border in his "'Calypso Magnolia': The Caribbean Side of the South," mapping the South as "in many ways the northern rim of the Caribbean—especially the coastal states of Texas, Louisiana, and Florida." In effect, the region that encircles the islands—the American South, Mexico, and northern parts of Central and South America—"embraces" the Caribbean. Because of traditional conceptualizations of nationhood, this view of the South and its relationship to the Caribbean constitutes a "counter-narrative," one that he believes might not be readily accepted in the "more mundane world of 'Southern-Lit-Nation'" (Lowe 54). I address these differences of opinion here to point to the malleability of the South's boundaries and to frame my main focus here in this book: the ways in which narratives about passage through those already porous and tentative borders have been used to reconfigure notions of the South and Southernness in the twentieth century.

In effect, the Southern myth of a stable boundary—one that the South could control—is exactly that: a myth. While this first chapter in my book attempts to identify the border formation narratives that shaped the region that became known as The South, the chapters that follow look at the ways those borders and thus the long-held belief of Southern exceptionalism have been disrupted and reconfigured by the movement of southerners out of the South. My focus here is specifically on those out-migrations and journeys beyond the South primarily (but not exclusively) in the first half of the twentieth century because it was in that period that the largest number of Southerners departed from the region. I look not only at the action of movement itself, but also more specifically the ways in which narrative has shaped those movements, given meaning to that passage from South to NotSouth, and the ways in which conceptions of Southern and US nationhood have been shaped by those border crossing narratives. On a broader political and humanistic level, I'm concerned as well with the hegemonic devices used to control the passage of people across borders and the necessity of recognizing the importance of deconstructing the narratives that we create and that are fed to us, narratives that control our lives and that shape who we are.

CHAPTER 2

The Border Crossing Narrative and the Disruption of Southern Borders

As the Great Migration got underway in the early twentieth century, the words "Bound for the Promised Land" were written in chalk on the sides of trains headed to Chicago from the Mississippi Delta. As it did in the antebellum South for slaves escaping slavery, crossing the border to regions beyond the South literally took on biblical proportions. Upon their arrival at the Ohio River, a group of 147 African American migrants reportedly "knelt and prayed, stopped their watches, and sang old spirituals, one bearing the words 'I done come out of the Land of Egypt with the good news.'" When an older African American man at a railroad station was asked where he was going, he replied, "I'm gwine to the promised land" (Kling 222). In the Far West, in the 1930s and 1940s, migrant poets and songwriters represented "old sunny Cal" as a place where "money grew on trees." Supposedly a veritable Land of Plenty, the California landscape promised ideal weather conditions, rich earth, golden citrus fruit, and an extended growing season. Back east, Muncie, Indiana, might not have been "old sunny Cal," but for Tennesseans, the city offered better economic opportunity than did the South, and the distance was not as far from home. In Fentress County, Tennessee, a map on the Forbus General Store noted the mileage choices for a migrant: "Muncie, 325.1 miles; Dayton, 300 miles; Indianapolis, 275" (Berry 23). Up in the West Virginia hills, mountaineers were also leaving. In part because of the foresight and business savvy of a migrant West Virginian turned realtor, increasingly large numbers of mountaineers relocated to the flatlands of eastern Ohio around the turn of the century, and from the 1940s through the 1960s, Cleveland Electric Company advertised northeast Ohio as "the best location in the nation" (Sisson). Clear lines were drawn between South and NotSouth, and NotSouth represented freedom, prosperity, and the American Dream.

Many Southerners were motivated to leave the South because of a push and pull. African Americans tended to leave the South for Northern cities such as New York, Chicago, and Philadelphia not only because of racism and poor economic conditions in the South but because of the deeply rooted image in African American history of the North as a promised land. And city life also had its draw. "When they fall in love with a city, it is for forever, and it is like forever. As though there never was a time when they didn't love it. The minute they arrive at the train station or get off the ferry and glimpse the wide streets and the wasteful lamps lighting them," Toni Morrison writes in *Jazz*. The "country people" from the South "know they are born for it. There, in a city, they are not so much new as themselves: their stronger, riskier selves" (33). White Southerners from Appalachia also headed north, but more particularly to Detroit and Chicago. Although white Southerners who left the Dust Bowl of Oklahoma for California were often depicted as poverty-stricken by writers and photographers such as John Steinbeck in *The Grapes of Wrath* and Dorothea Lange in *An American Exodus*, recent analysis of the Dust Bowlers indicates that their migration westward was actually more of "a tragedy in the rather privileged white American sense of the term." They were "neither destitute nor the dirt farmers of popular paradigms," but instead twentieth-century migrants pulled by the lure of American westward migration—not refugees (Gregory 10). Although African Americans typically migrated northward in the first several decades of the twentieth century, by World War II, they began to migrate westward in larger numbers. Other racial groups of Southerners were also moving. Native Americans living in Oklahoma during the Dust Bowl years left in increasing numbers during World War II for industry jobs in California. By 1970, twenty percent of all Native American adults living in the region had left (36). Migratory patterns for Hispanic populations moving out of the South increased more substantially in the 1970s, when Latinos born in the South outnumbered foreign-born Latinos in Michigan, Indiana, and Ohio (Gregory 35).

Crossing the border that marked off the South was transformative. Essentially, that doorway or threshold between South and NotSouth remade and redefined the Southerner who passed through it. Historians characterize the migrants who left the South as creating new communities that bound people together because of their movement. In effect, they came to identify themselves not by the physical places in which they lived, but instead by commonalities that they shared with others because they had left. They identified themselves through constructs of the imagination rather than by physical location on a map. James Gregory, for example, in defining the pejorative term "Okie" in the context of the Depression years and several decades that followed, notes that "Regionalism is not the issue here." The label refers not to a group of people identified with a specific place, but it has more to do with "character, values, and experience" (248). Lawrence Rodgers points to what he calls the "dynamic connection between northern residents and their southern roots." Oftentimes, African Americans returned to the South for extended visits, but whether or not they actually made the trip South, the region, according to Rodgers, "remained central to their collective urban consciousness" (17). Chad Berry explains in his study of the migration of Appalachian Southerners to Midwestern cities that despite the diversity of white Southern migrants, in large part as a response to the discrimination and ill-treatment they faced, many of them began to view themselves as a people who shared both ancestors and a history. As a result, seemingly disparate groups of migrants developed similar thought and behavior patterns because of the migration experience (136).

If in the nineteenth century, the Confederacy followed by the postwar Reconstruction South fought to hold back the forces of Northern aggression, in the twentieth century began what was a full-fledged assault on the border by Southerners themselves. In effect, whether intentional or not, whether departing Southerners rejoiced in their leaving or grieved over their displacement from "back home," the result was a more porous border around the region. If pre-twentieth-century Southerners attempted to shore up the borders, massive numbers of twentieth-century Southerners were breaking them down. If border formation narratives or top-down/hegemonic discourse had shored up those borders, then the physical act of border crossings and border crossing narratives are counterdiscourses or performative acts that renegotiate the border, reframe it, and even attempt to erase it. In effect, departing Southerners shared common texts of journeying, texts that ranged as broadly as family letters, columns in a newspaper, and music to creative literature, including fiction and poetry. Southern migrants became part of new communities that shared stories of displacement.

For Southern migrants, collective narratives became a way to reidentify and redefine themselves. Although the collective narrative for African Americans in the nineteenth century was the exodus narrative—the story of freedom from slavery by a flight to the North—that narrative was not as prominent in the first several decades of the twentieth century. The narrative was revitalized by the *Chicago Defender* and once again gained prominence and remained an influence into the civil rights movement. Southerners migrating westward in the twentieth century followed the paths of nineteenth-century Americans in their drive to settle the continent from coast to coast. Whites did not experience an exodus in the sense of leaving enslavement (although large groups of African Americans did migrate west to escape Southern racism, and John Steinbeck almost suggested as much for Dust Bowlers), but they did see themselves as journeying to regions that were said to offer greater financial security and prosperity, oftentimes a "land of milk and honey," such as the supposed agricultural gold mine of beautiful and bountiful California. For white migrants heading north into Illinois, Michigan, and Ohio, the collective narrative was frequently labeled as an odyssey with a return home to the South as the ultimate goal. Although Langston Hughes wrote of the African American's "one way ticket" out of the South to "Any place that is / North and East...West— / And not South" ("One Way Ticket"), whites who headed north out of Tennessee, Kentucky, and West Virginia oftentimes clung to this promise of a return home. One popular joke of the time told the story of a dying man going to heaven and finding himself before St. Peter, who offered a tour. After pointing out the various sections of the valley in heaven set aside for the different denominations, St. Peter pointed to a hillside set apart by a fence that surrounded it. When the newly arrived man asked who resided there, St. Peter replied, "Oh, these are all our West Virginia people.... They still think they have to go home every weekend" (Feather 3–4). Many Appalachian Southerners leaving for Midwestern cities such as Chicago and Detroit only intended to "sojourn," to stay in the city long enough to make a substantial amount of money and then return South. For many Southerners, migration became not a journey with a final destination, but an odyssey that eventually carried them home to the South—imaginatively and literally.

In each case, the collective narrative of that passage through the liminal space shaped the ways Southerners viewed themselves and the ways other people saw them. Yet whether the migrant stayed or just sojourned in the new place, making that passage out of the South disrupted both internal and external definitions of Southernness as Southerners and non-Southerners in other parts of the United States came into contact with Southerners who had made the crossing. Movement took on religious connotations as migrants experienced transformation described in a religious context, but also transformation into promises of a new life in the Promised Land of American prosperity and freedom. Yet in making this move, Southerners leaving the South were also "othered," as they become not *of* one place but of multiple regions—South, NotSouth, and the spaces in between. While residing in the liminal spaces between South and NotSouth could be freeing in many senses, it also left many migrating Southerners in the margins, feeling as if they had no homeland at all.

These collective narratives found their way not only into the literary texts of the twentieth century, but also into the popular imagination and popular culture, and shared similarities in pattern and perspective. These border crossing narratives, in general, tend to be patterned after two classic stories: the exodus and the sojourn/odyssey. Typically, the narrative is either one of escape from prior circumstances and dealing with attachment to a new place, or a move outside the South with the ultimate goal of a return, oftentimes after enough money has been accumulated. In both instances, the border crosser is captured by the narrative of escape that promises personal freedoms and prosperity— essentially the American success story. In no way do I see migrants of all races sharing the same stories of exodus or odyssey because of the racial injustices that threatened not only the individual lives but also the economic and social conditions of many Southerners. These narratives, however, clearly intertwine Southerners of all races and show something about the communities that were created and sustained as Southerners left the South. Claiming "ownership" to the very personal story of movement and migration, however, was impacted and influenced by other cultural, economic, and societal factors as well.

In Chicago, for example, the *Defender* newspaper played a dramatic role not only in reporting on the Great Migration of African Americans, but also in motivating African Americans to leave the South in great numbers. The newspaper, headed up by publisher Robert Abbott, hired train conductors to carry copies of the newspaper to the South and virtually hand deliver them to potential migrant readers. The newspaper even identified the start date of when the Great Migration would begin: May 15, 1917. That same year, California farmers began competing for the services of Oklahomans and Texans. San Joaquin Valley planters paid train costs for families willing to relocate and met the families at the station. Southerners heading west before the Depression years, in the teens and twenties, were in many cases influenced by ads that proclaimed "In California . . . you live life, elsewhere you merely spend it" (Gregory 8–9).

Like nineteenth-century migration stories of westward migration or exodus from slavery in the South, the narratives that prompted and portrayed twentieth-century Southern border crossings represented the threshold as one that was communally experienced. Whether organized by clergymen, community members, *Defender* agents, or industry agents or empowered by the words of a sermon, a letter, a newspaper ad, or just word of mouth, migrants' connections to a larger movement of Southerners crossing the boundary to life outside the region in many ways made their departures possible. In some cases, migration clubs helped ease the transition. Members of clubs were typically organized through family and friendship networks, a leader was chosen who was usually a prominent member of the community, train tickets were purchased at a group discount rate, and a date for departure was selected. In Jackson, Mississippi, migrant clubs generally included 40 to 75 members. Oftentimes, migrants made the decision to leave because of what James Grossman describes as a "feeling that it must be [the] best thing since everybody was doing it" (Grossman, *Land* 96–97). A return visit made an impact as well. One white migrant was noted as saying that "It leaves a good impression on the home folks that they are doin' well" if "they left in an old wreck and come back in a good car" (Gregory 27). In effect, the visiting migrant became the American success story in the flesh for those back at home—the literal picture of the hopes and desires of many who were still living in the South. For many who were Southern-born, material wealth and success were possible only if the border out of the South was passed. In a similar fashion, just plain gossip and stories circulated through Southern communities helped to fuel the desire to leave. The strength in knowing that family or friends were already settled in the new place made the leaving a little easier. Migration chains oftentimes linked Southerners considering the move to those who had already crossed and pulled migrants from home, and kept them in the new location. Being at once part of home back in the South and part of the community in the new place gave migrants the ability to linger in the liminal spaces, making the adjustments in some ways easier because others were making the same journey, experiencing the same disconnections and transitions.

When letters reached the South from migrant destinations in the North or West or when migrants returned home, the differences were clear. A "script" of what life could be like on "the other side," letters told family and friends back in the South about trips to major league baseball games in Chicago, a church revival where 500 people were saved, integrated schools, and voting privileges. Letters home were passed around, shared, and read, although many letters were couched with words intended to portray the difficulties as well as the advantages of migration, oftentimes the benefits were weightier, perhaps in part because of the writer's attempt to control their image and to look good as someone who had left home. Nevertheless, letters were powerful motivators; one letter, for example, was said to have "enticed away over 200 persons" (Grossman, *Land* 89–91). Essentially, the border could be crossed by the gaze through the words on a page before they were experienced by a physical move. Visual artist Jacob Lawrence captured those moments when a reader was lost in the words of one of those letters home in Panel #33 of his Migration series (Figure 2.1). Entitled "Letters from Relatives in the North told of the better life there," the image shows what appears to be a woman lying on her back on a bed, with a smaller figure, perhaps a child, sitting beside her. With legs drawn up in front, the child seems to be listening intently to the words of a letter. Lingering in the spaces in between—anticipating what that new life would be like in the North, but still in the South—the two figures on the bed seem to be caught up in the possibilities of what they might find on the other side of the border but perhaps too in the fears of what it will take to get them there. Lawrence's series on migration shows what led African Americans to leave the South, their journeys northward, and the lives they lived in the North where they arrived. "The choices made were hard ones," Lawrence wrote about the series, "so I wanted to make sure to show what made people get in those northbound trains. I also wanted to show just what it cost to ride them. Uprooting yourself from one way of life to make your way in another involves conflict and struggle" (*The Great Migration* n.p.). The struggle of crossing is a transformative experience, one that brings, according to Lawrence, "a kind of power, and even beauty" (n.p.) to the lives of those who may experience the passage.

While border crossing narratives told of hardships, they also pulled readers in to see themselves as a changed people. The words of a spiritual proclaiming "let my people go" or of letters from relatives in the North that told of prosperity and an equality in civic life enclosed readers in a new narrative—one that elevated the reader's position in society and gave them a means to change their lives. Although the impetus of a text may have been for the profit of a company or farm that wanted new employees who would accept low wages, migrating Southerners were also held captive by narratives that gave them hope for a better life outside the borders of the South. Thus the border crossing narrative also became a way for the narrator and the reader to gain agency over their own lives and to rewrite the script. For African Americans, the story of migration was a subversive act not only in pre–Civil War days as slaves saw the passage north as an escape to the Promised Land, but also in the twentieth century as railroad conductors smuggled in copies of the *Defender*. Having control over the text itself and becoming part of the story also meant taking action—moving, escaping, crossing the boundaries of the South into the North or the West or helping others to make the passage. Narratives of escape and freedom and potential elsewhere became ways for migrants to elevate their actions and reimagine themselves. Communities were forged in the crossing, and cultural heroes were made who became guides for those making the passage.

Essentially, then, the border was conceptually remade *because* migrants crossed it both physically and within the imagination—the two can't be separated. The Exodus story was for African Americans a story that had long represented their relationship with the South. Antebellum accounts of black out-migration, or slave narratives, framed accounts of subversion and revolt. If Harriet Tubman was called the "Moses of her people," then for African Americans hoping to escape northward out of "Pharaoh's Land of Egypt" and slavery, the North was the Promised Land, and the slaves were the chosen who would be delivered by God from slavery. A former slave from Missouri related the story of a Baptist minister who shackled his slave with a log chain that cut into the slave's shoulder bone. Ultimately, the minister's neighbors realized what was happening to the slave and insisted that the

Figure 2.1. Jacob Lawrence, *The Migration Series, Panel no. 33: Letters from relatives in the North told of the better life there*, between 1940 and 1941, Casein tempera on hardboard 12 × 18 in.; 30.48 × 45.72 cm. The Phillips Collection, Washington, DC, Acquired 1942. Jacob Lawrence's "Letter from Relatives" from The Migration Series. © 2017 The Jacob and Gwendolyn Knight Lawrence Foundation, Seattle / Artists Rights Society [ARS], New York.

minister free the slave from the chains. The ex-slave who related the story believed that God saw to it that the slave masters received their due: "No wonder God sent war on this nation! It was the old story of the captivity in Egypt repeated. The slaveholders were warned time and again to let the black man go, but they hardened their hearts and would not, until finally the wrath of God was poured out upon them and the sword of the great North fell upon the first-born'" (Kling 218). The narrative became real and wove together a story of an oppressed people breaking the bonds that held them. The story was a frequent one in church services and songs; as one ex-slave explained, "All us had was church meetin's in arbors out in de woods. De preachers would exhort us dat us was de chillen o' Israel in de wilderness an' de Lord done sent us to take dis land o' milk and honey" (Hopkins 10). Writer James Weldon Johnson described the unique power of the Exodus story: "there is not a nobler theme in the whole musical literature of the world" (Kling 211). Frederick Douglass wondered why anyone overhearing the words that African Americans sang at church would not understand the subversive implications: "A keen observer might have detected in our repeated singing of 'O Canaan, sweet Canaan, / I am bound for the land of Canaan,' something more than a hope of reaching heaven. We meant to reach the *North*, and the North was our Canaan" (Douglass 196–7). Song formed communal bonds and empowered some slaves to escape to the North. Others who remained in slavery oftentimes read these narratives with the only sign of hope as the time when they would make the passage into heaven.

Although Christianity was forced upon slaves by their white masters, according to Lawrence Levine, slaves engaged in "communal re-creation" by shaping a religion that blended Christianity with folk beliefs (29). Songs such as "Go Down Moses," which was also known as "Let My People Go," drew a vivid parallel between the plight of the Israelites in Egypt and those bound in slavery in the American South. With a call to "let my people go!" the song described the Israelites held in Egypt as "Oppressed so hard they could not stand." This narrative of captivity and freedom not only tied slaves to the Old Testament story of Moses, but also to the New Testament story of transformation through Christ. Eugene Genovese describes this "pervasive theme of deliverance" as a blending of likenesses of Moses, "the this-worldly leader of his people out of bondage," with Jesus, "the other-worldly Redeemer" (252). In the spiritual "Go Down, Moses," for example, Christ is identified as having "died for me" and "set me free" "Way down in Egyptland." Some scholars have also suggested that Moses even ranked alongside Christ (Kling 213).

The story of migration—the border crossing narrative—thus became a potent motivator and weapon against racism and racial inequality. The story of crossing—here more specifically the exodus story—literally overlaid the migration experiences of African Americans. Holding a central place in the African American community and traditions, this border crossing narrative equated movement with deliverance and transformation, flight from the Southern "Egyptland" with civil, social, and economic freedoms. The parallels that were drawn between the migrants' experience and the biblical story were concrete and clearly delineated. One such example was the Kansas Fever Exodus of the 1870s. Prompted in part by advertisements circulated by an ex-slave named Benjamin "Pap" Singleton and concern among blacks that they might be forced back into slavery with the end of Reconstruction, this exodus to Kansas prompted 20,000 blacks to leave Kentucky, Louisiana, Mississippi, Tennessee, and Texas. Believing he was in direct communion with God, Singleton viewed himself not as a messiah, but as "Father of the Exodus" or "Moses of the Colored Exodus." One elderly man who was part of the exodus to Kansas told a reporter for the *St. Louis Globe-Democrat* that "we's like de chilun ob Israel when dey was led from out o' bondage by Moses." He equated St. Louis with the Red Sea, "the place of deliverance between their former residences in the South and the Promised Land of Kansas" (Kling 220). Boll weevil infestations and floods were read as punishments on Southern whites by God. A Chicago pastor named

Harold Kingsley noted in 1930 that African American migrants "saw a parallel between [their] coming out of the South and the Hebrew children coming up out of the land of Egypt, out of the house of bondage" (Kling 222). Kansas became figuratively and literally a modern-day Canaan for African Americans in flight, and the journey itself—the passage through the Red Sea, the crossing from South into NotSouth—became the transforming power. Just as Africans who were carried to the New World felt a kinship with those who were bound with them on the slave ships, so too did those who migrated out of the South share a common bond, one that made their experience of bondage in the South and their deliverance from it into what Milton Sernett calls "a religious event— another chapter in the ongoing salvation history of African Americans, rich in symbolic and metaphorical content" (58). The African American narrative of flight from the South as the biblical Jews had fled Egypt became part of a collective memory, but also empowered the individual, giving a strength that encouraged more and more African Americans to make the journey. By the time of the Great Migration in the twentieth century, one migrant from New Orleans stated that "Every black man is his own Moses now," suggesting that for this migrant, the narrative had been internalized, taken as his own (Kling 220).

While the passage, the route of the journey, the liminal space in between can, of course, be the site of struggle and discord for the placeless and marginalized, it also can be a space of healing and the source of a communal voice that creates a new community out of brokenness and loss. If liminal space creates a situation where the migrant is at once "look[ing] in from the outside while looking out from the inside" (Bromley 5), this perspective can also be the origin of a new and united voice—a common narrative that gives a new people formed by shared experience and movement a sense of belonging and connection. Victor Turner sees "this betwixt and between period" as a time when a people and their leaders are more closely bound through a "mystical solidarity": "In this fruitful darkness, king and people are closely identified" (*Forest of Symbols* 110). Heroic voices and actions become shared ones, and the liminal space reaches mystical importance as the grounds for a more united people and vision. The heroic figure most frequently associated with the liminal space of the African American border crossing narrative is Moses. I am not, of course, the first to point to the role of Moses in narratives about African American migration out of the South, but I want to point out here the ways in which this figure disrupts notions of Southernness for departing African Americans.

As a figure of nation building—the new nation of the Israelites—Moses became a centerpiece for narratives that claim a new communal identity for African Americans. Moses made frequent appearances in literary texts by African Americans in the late nineteenth century, including Paul Laurence Dunbar's poem "An Ante-Bellum Sermon" (1896) from the collection *Lyrics of Lowly Life*, and written and oral texts by Frances E. W. Harper. Harper was captivated by the figure of Moses and wrote about him not only in her poetry and fiction, but also in her speeches. In her 1859 essay, "Our Greatest Want," Harper argued to other African Americans that "Our greatest need is not gold or silver, talent or genius, but true men and true women. We have millions of our race in the prison house of slavery, but have we yet a single Moses in freedom and if we had who among us would be led by him?" (*Brighter Coming Day*, 103). In 1869, Harper published *Moses: A Story of the Nile*, a retelling of the Moses story, and a novel entitled *Minnie's Sacrifice*, a version of the Moses story set during Reconstruction. Harper's 1885 article "A Factor in Human Progress" offered a self-sacrificial Moses as a model for African Americans who might be tempted away from their pursuit of racial freedom by alcohol and other distractions. "Had Moses preferred the luxury of an Egyptian palace to the endurance of hardships with his people, would the Jews have been the race to whom we owe the most, not perhaps for science and art, but for the grandest of all sciences, the science of a true life of joy and trust in God, of God-like forgiveness and divine self-surrender?" she asked (*Brighter Coming Day*, 279). Looking not only to Moses as a model for African American leadership, Harper saw, too, the qualities of a Moses as necessary to the individual. If Moses had not thought beyond his own individual desires, the Jewish people would not have had the true relationship with God that Harper purports that they had. She sees the highest spiritual level as only possible through following the lead of a Moses, sacrificing for community as Moses did, and healing a fractured world.

Moses remained a strong force in twentieth-century literary texts, particularly during the Harlem Renaissance. James Weldon Johnson's "Let My People Go" (1927), from his *God's Trombones: Seven Negro Sermons in Verse*, tells the biblical story of Moses in poetic form, but closes with a question intended for all "sons of Pharaoh" who enslave others, including those in the United States in the 1920s: "Who do you think can hold God's people / When the Lord God himself has said, / Let my people go?" (52). Focusing on Pharaoh's unwillingness to free the Israelites, the plagues God sent against the Egyptians, and the parting of the Red Sea, the preacher's sermon in Johnson's poem revolves around the Israelites' doubt of their god as the Egyptian chariots, or the border guards, close in, enforcing their control over the border and who is able to pass through. The illustration by Aaron Douglas included just before "Let My People Go" in the *Trombones* collection (Figure 2.2) shows this pivotal moment in the Israelites' crossing when the "children of Israel all lost hope; / Deep Red Sea in front of them / And Pharaoh's host behind" (51). It is in this liminal space—in the darkness of the journey itself—that the Israelites question Moses, wondering if perhaps "Slavery in Egypt was better than to come / To die here in this wilderness" (51). Here in the borderlands a "mystical solidarity" (to use

Victor Turner's phrase) forms between Moses and his people, and it is through that solidarity that the Hebrews are able to make the passage: "the Children of Israel all crossed over / On to the other side," united by Moses and their god, who "led the Hebrew Children on / Till they reached the promised land" (52).

Journalistic narratives had perhaps even more widespread consequences and impact. The *Chicago Defender*, for example, secured this image of the out-migration of African Americans as a journey of biblical proportions with stories that referred to the "exodus" and called for a Moses-figure who would be a race leader. Starting with a run of 300 copies, Robert S. Abbott quickly built readership to 16,000 by 1915. In part because of the paper's encouragement and the industry jobs opening up after the United States entered World War I, the African American population of Chicago increased by 148% from 1910 to 1920 (Sernett 155). Frequently reminding readers about the dangers faced by African Americans living in the South by quoting statistics on the number of lynchings in the region, the *Defender* printed schedules for trains headed north, advertised jobs in Northern cities, organized migrants into traveling clubs, and printed news from families back in the South in a feature called "News From Your Home Town." For readers outside of Chicago, the railroad was the mode of delivery that made the newspaper the first black paper to be circulated nationwide. Because Southern landowners attempted to block circulation of the newspaper, which was helping to drain their workforce, porters threw bundles of the newspaper from trains before they reached stations. The newspaper was circulated in black communities and oftentimes read aloud in homes, local businesses, and churches. In Laurel, Mississippi, an African American man reported that "people would come from miles running over themselves to get a *Defender*" (Grossman, *Land* 88).

Creating a common narrative for its readership, the impact of the newspaper was monumental. Particularly in the years from 1915 to 1919, the *Defender* appealed to Southern blacks to head out of the region to the more promising opportunities of Chicago. With the marvels of the Columbia Exposition of 1893 still a lingering memory, headlines, stories, and advertisements in the *Defender* portrayed Chicago as a place to achieve the American dream of prosperity and attain the manufactured goods that came along with that success. "I bought a Chicago Defender and after reading it and seeing the golden opportunity I have decided to leave this place at once," said a railroad worker in Tennessee in 1917 (Grossman, "Southern Distribution"). The magnitude of the Northern migration was suggested in headlines such as "Southerners Plan to Stop Exodus" and in a photo of the crowded Savannah train station with the headline "The Exodus." Carl Sandburg claimed in the *Chicago Daily News* that "*The Defender* more than any other one agency was the big cause of the 'Northern fever' and the big exodus from the South" (Qtd. in Henri 63). Historians have described

Figure 2.2. Aaron Douglas, from *God's Trombones: Seven Negro Sermons in Verse.* "Illustrations" by Aaron Douglas, copyright © 1927 by Penguin Random House LLC, copyright renewed © 1955 by Grace Nail Johnson; from GOD'S TROMBONES by James Weldon Johnson. Used by permission of Viking Books, an imprint of Penguin Publishing Group, a division of Penguin Random House LLC. All rights reserved.

the magnitude of the publication's impact, with William Barlow describing it as "a beacon for the African American migration to Chicago" (288) and Mark Anthony Neal making the case that "the American North, as constructed by the *Chicago Defender* and the narratives of the 'New Negro,' represented the possibilities of full citizenship for those who accepted the challenge" (12). Crossing meant transformation from dispossessed to citizen.

Perhaps the most extended retelling of the Moses story in twentieth-century African American fiction is Zora Neale Hurston's *Moses, Man of the Mountain,* which blends the biblical story with African American folklore and dialect. In her author's introduction, Hurston describes the Moses of Christianity as an "old man with a beard," "a great law-giver," who "had some trouble with Pharaoh about some plagues and led the Children of Israel out of Egypt and on to the Promised Land." Dying at Mount Nebo, he was buried there by angels. The book, according to Robert Hemenway, "kidnap[s] Moses from Judeo-Christian tradition, claiming that his true birthright is African and his true constituency Afro-American" (257). Pointing out that legends are fashioned by "people seeking to satisfy deeply felt personal needs," he notes that "we all believe in legends because we need to, because they satisfy our innermost compulsions, because we want to find epic qualities in the most unlikely place—the affairs of the earth." Hurston suggests in her book that even though Moses was an exceptional human being, he was also influenced and shaped by the legendary qualities that others assigned to him, even the flaws that came not so much from Moses's actual person but from those who wished to remake him (264). The exodus narrative has obviously seen many different iterations, depending upon the peoples who have retold it from their own perspective and experience.

Hurston grounds her story of Moses as a story of border crossings, a crossing with transfigurative powers. Note, for example, her repetition of the negative "no," "not," "none"—what Moses is no longer—and the phrase "crossed over" throughout the following passage (italics is mine):

Moses had *crossed over.* He was not in Egypt. He had *crossed over* and now he was not an Egyptian. He had *crossed over.* The short sword at his thigh had a jeweled hilt but he had *crossed over* and so it was no longer the sign of high birth and power. He had *crossed over,* so he sat down on a rock near the seashore to rest himself. He had *crossed over* so he was not of the house of Pharaoh. He did not own a palace because he had *crossed over.* He did not have an Ethiopian Princess for a wife. He had *crossed over.* He did not have friends to sustain him. He had *crossed over.* He did not have enemies to strain against his strength and power. He had *crossed over.* He was subject to no law except the laws of tooth and talon. He had *crossed over.* The sun who was his friend and ancestor in Egypt was arrogant and bitter in Asia. He had *crossed over.* He felt as empty as a post hole for he was none of the things he once had been. He was a man sitting on a rock. He had *crossed over*. (278–79)

The passage points to the ways Moses is changed *because* he passes over the border from Egypt into the wilderness that he and his people wander through. It is the movement itself that reworks and revises him in the liminal space so while the jeweled sword still remains strapped to his thigh, it is "no longer the sign of high birth and power." He is no longer any of what he had once been. According to Hemenway, Hurston points here to the "difficult process of constructing a new identity from the ground up" and how "Moses' life will be *transformed* into something entirely new when he comes to identify with the oppressed" (270). Using the language of borders, Hurston repeats the phrase "cross over" thirteen times to add emphasis to the journey that Moses experiences, the decision he made to leave, and the crossing that he makes with his people. The emphasis here is on the crossing itself and the resulting transformation. The borderlands become a place of contemplation, a place of a growing bond between a leader and his people, the Magico bond that Turner refers to. In stripping bare of the facts of his life—what made him the oppressor of his people—he no longer carries the symbols of Egyptian royalty. He no longer has friends who can "sustain him" but instead he becomes the sustainer, the deliverer of the Hebrew people.

Images of the Israelites and their leader Moses occur again and again in African American narratives specifically tied to crossing out of the South. Moses appears in Robert Hayden's "Runagate Runagate" (1962) in a name given to Harriet Tubman, "alias Moses," "Stealer of Slaves," and James Baldwin in his 1955 *Notes of a Native Son* states that "the Negro identifies himself almost wholly with the Jew" (67). Moses appears in the title of visual artist Jacob Lawrence's *Genesis Creation Sermon* and is channeled through the preacher who is portrayed in the series. Also referred to as *The First Book of Moses, Called Genesis*, the collection of eight multicolored silkscreen prints portrays an African American preacher and his congregation. First published as a collection in 1989, the edition—limited to 400 copies—shows the powerful and engaging speaking of an African American pastor, with the inside of the church coming to life with the story of creation as portions of the narrative are vividly represented outside the arched windows—the portals or figuratively the doorways—in the church. The third print of the series, "The Creation was Done and All was Well," is included here in Figure 2.3. Although Moses does not physically appear as Moses in the prints, he does through the title of the book—*The First Book of Moses*—and through the words of the story itself, for they are attributed to him. The story is his. The preacher, who is said to have been based on the Reverend Adam Clayton Powell Sr., pastor of the Abyssinian Baptist

Church in Harlem from 1908 to 1936, calls to life the story that Moses told in the Bible, and Moses's words are in the mouth of the preacher. Lawrence's choice of Powell as his model is highly significant. From western Virginia, Powell was particularly attuned to the large number of Southern migrants who were moving into Harlem and their religious needs. He was instrumental in moving Abyssinian Baptist from Manhattan to Harlem to help acclimate the large numbers of African Americans migrating to Harlem from the South.

Moses and the Exodus also significantly influenced the impact and the power of the civil rights movement. Martin Luther King Jr., in his "I've Been to the Mountaintop" speech (1968), most famously represented himself as a Moses figure whom God "allowed . . . to go up to the mountain" where he "looked over" to see the "Promised Land." Like the Hebrews who were enslaved by a Pharaoh who controlled them in part by keeping them fighting among themselves, African Americans will reach the Promised Land, King said, and they will make the passage to reach the other side to a land of freedom from the "Pharaoh." Equating the civil rights movement with the literal journey to freedom of those who fled from South to North out of the bonds of slavery in the nineteenth century, King very intentionally framed the civil rights struggle as a metaphorical journey to a new land. But similar to Harriet Jacobs, who ended her *Incidents in the Life of a Slave Girl* by saying that she had not yet fully gained her freedom to raise her own children in her own home, King signaled that the liminal space between and the journey from the racism of the South to the freedom of the North had not yet been secured. Still relegated to the liminal space between inequality and freedom, King saw himself and other African Americans with freedom in sight, but not yet attained. In effect, the liminal space is at once a place of division and a strategic location that gives a concreteness to the struggle for civil rights and points to the powerlessness that those struggling for racial equality continued to experience.

While the story of exodus is woven through African American narratives about migrations out of the South, it also became a framework for other racial groups of Southerners, who felt trapped in an economic system that lagged behind the rest of the United States through much of the twentieth century. Southern migrants were still drawn by the narrative of westward migration into a place of new beginnings and of the Californian cornucopia, and the story of exodus, an escape from those harsh conditions, renewed a westering spirit and reconnected Southerners with their American roots. With Manifest Destiny leading the way in the nineteenth century for migrants from all corners of the settled portions of the eastern United States, settlers flocked westward in search of new opportunities generally connected with the acquisition of land, of property. Although the out-migrations of Southerners into the West in the nineteenth century in no way reached the same proportions as those who moved westward in the twentieth century, the concept of the West as a place

Figure 2.3. Jacob Lawrence, *Genesis Creation Sermon III*. © 2017 The Jacob and Gwendolyn Knight Lawrence Foundation, Seattle / Artists Rights Society [ARS], New York.)

to start anew and as a place that represented a better life was as thoroughly rooted in Southern culture as it was in the North. Many Southerners, like the fictional Huck Finn at the conclusion of Twain's most famous novel, "headed to the Territory ahead of the rest" looking for adventure and freedom. Horace Greeley's "Go West, young man" proclaimed an essential myth for any American.

White Southerners left the South in the greatest numbers in the 1930s, and the destination for many of them was the West and California. In a March 1940 article entitled "Arizona Cotton-Growing Scheme Abets Migration to California" published in the *New York Times*, Byron Darnton identified several reasons for the drive:

> One is historical—west is the direction migrations have taken from the beginning of the country. Another can be laid at the door of Californians themselves. They have been shouting from the housetops for years about their climate, about their prodigious advances in business and farming, about the beauties of their State, about how pleasant life here can be. (20)

Popular media played a significant role, too. In Hollywood, although films such as *What Price Hollywood?* (1932) warned of the dangers of quick success, others like W. C. Fields's 1934 *It's a Gift* portrayed a West rich with promise. When Harold, played by Fields, moves to California to run a grove on property he has bought, the land is at first deemed worthless for planting. Ultimately, though, the property is bought by a fellow who wants to start a race track. The film ends with Fields squeezing orange juice into a glass (along with the contents of a flask), while his family takes a ride in their new car. The film industry also began its 40-year love affair with the western, which looked back nostalgically at the Western frontier and captured viewers in a text that most often portrayed white characters as taming "savage" Indian Territory. The western craze that started in the 1930s and produced the legendary John Wayne focused on the glory days of expansion. With films like *Covered Wagon Days* (1940) and Tex Ritter's *Roll Wagons Roll* (1940), the craze prompted the production of travel trailers called Covered Wagons. The story of the wealth and bounty of California reached into the grocery stores and homes of those with some money to purchase items from stores. In a 1941 book entitled *A Mirror for Californians*, Oliver Carlson notes in a chapter entitled "Some Call It Eden," "More potent and inclusive than even its high-powered publicity is the advertising work done by the products of fields, gardens and orchards, for no matter where you live in this broad land, California products come to you" (64). The grocery shelves themselves made the case to leave for distant California.

Home for white Southerners was portrayed in the national media as a place to escape, and whites, like blacks, experienced a push and pull. The media, for example, helped to exaggerate and extend typically Southern qualities into abnormalities and extremes, and to redefine white Southerners as "hicks" and "red necks." Articles similar to one entitled "He War Good to We Uns" that ran in the *New York Post* in 1941 were not uncommon. The *Post* reporter told of a visit in North Carolina with the "child bride of Knob Mountain," 11-year-old

Estelle Pruitt Downs, who had recently married 61-year-old Joe Downs, a grandfather of five. The article is filled with pictures of the couple together in their unpainted cabin eating corn bread and grease from pork and Estelle working on house chores. As the title proclaims, Estelle says, "he war good to we uns," meaning her and her siblings. Complete with chewing tobacco, spit, iron kettles, red clay, possum hunting, and a picture of Joe's first wife hanging on the wall of the cabin with her face covered by a burlap sack, the image created in the article is one that would have led readers to looks of indignation and pity (Kerkhoff 1,3). Others tried to reshape the images in the popular media. The governor of Oklahoma, Leon Phillips, was said to have been so irritated with the poverty-stricken image of his state in the media that when he was questioned by a congressional investigating committee about the conditions of the migrant populations headed west, Phillips made it very clear that not all of the migrants were poor and unemployed. Phillips noted that even a wealthy friend of his who worked formerly as a stenographer and banker had made the decision to head west because of the idyllic images of California that he had seen advertised (Gregory 17).

The migration westward in the twentieth century was framed as a story of pioneering akin to the migration of settlers in the nineteenth century, as a thoroughly American story. Although at times the traditional framework of western migration and settlement was derided and critiqued in the media, it still was what bound migrants together. They were referred to as "modern pioneers" who drove their covered wagons westward. Often their intent in moving west was laid squarely on the supposition that they were looking for adventure. Some of the newspapers published for migrants in the migrant camps bore names that pointed directly to this parallel, with names such as the *Covered Wagon News* (Shafter, CA) and *The Indio Covered Wagon* (Indio, CA). The sidebar to Paul Taylor's article for *Survey Graphic* magazine that accompanied a series of photographs by Dorothea Lange noted that "To many families put 'in a movie mood' by depression and drought California looks like a haven" (348).

The "record of human erosion" represented in Lange's photographs tells the story of this American Exodus. Paul Taylor, Lange's second husband and the author of the text included in the book *American Exodus*, states in his introduction to the 1969 edition that the photograph on the original dust jacket of the book was an image of the back of a truck headed west with the caption "Covered Wagon—1939 Style." Taylor verifies the connection that he and Lange saw in the western migration of Southerners during the Depression years and the nineteenth-century migration westward. He adds that the book is bookended and enclosed by this image of the 1939 migration with the "pioneer tradition" with a concluding section of photographs entitled "Last West" (11). Both Lange and Taylor in their joint introduction to the book describe the migration as a "giant tide," a "contemporary exodus" that "attains its most dramatic form on the deltas, the prairies, and the plains of the South, and in the tide of people which moves to the Pacific Coast" (14).

Lange's images also place in juxtaposition the consumer goods that had come to represent the American dream and the poverty and hopelessness of the individuals who were in pursuit of that dream and became a frequent theme in her work. The photos included here (Figures 2.4 and 2.5) juxtapose a person or persons alongside ads for products or services they cannot afford. Much as Thoreau who writes in *Walden* of the railroad that runs overtop the immigrant workers who build the railroads, Lange portrays people walking roads, resting, and congregating in tent camps alongside highways in photographs that show a market system that mocks the goals and aspirations of a people who are rooted in a history of movement and westering. The ads are larger than life and seem to be of greater importance than the real-life people who are represented as being in difficult, trying conditions. Such images also point to an evolving way of thinking in the United States. For so long the American Dream revolved around the acquisition of land. The dream involved ownership, but Lange's photographs point to the fact that the American dream was realigning so that it was increasingly concerned with the acquisition of consumer goods and leaving behind the Southern attachment to place and home. Certainly the actual conditions in the West proved the migrants wrong in their belief that the West always held promise and renewal. In a 1939 article in the *New York Times Magazine* entitled "The 'Okies' Search for a Lost Frontier," author Charles Todd speculated that the average Dust Bowl migrant would probably have this to say about California after they arrived: "They told me this was the land o' milk an' honey, but Ah guess the cow's gone dry, and the tumblebugs has got in the beehive." In the first five months of 1939, new arrivals numbered 20,000. "The 'covered wagons' are still rumbling across the border," Todd explained (Carlson 80–81).

The pull of Northern and Midwestern cities was likewise in large part the direct result of the rapid expansion of the consumer goods industry. Harriette Arnow, for example, shows in her novel *The Dollmaker* how Gertie Nevel and her family leave Appalachia for a Northern destination where acquiring the latest appliances such as a refrigerator becomes more important than owning property and settling down to run a farm. Because of strict immigration laws that were imposed after World War I, the number of European immigrants entering the United States dramatically decreased, and with it a large potential pool of factory workers. Southern workers were attracted to jobs in industries such as the Champion Paper Company in Hamilton, Ohio, and tire factories in Akron. So many workers relocated to Akron that the "Rubber City" became known as "the Capital of West Virginia." Mass exoduses from Appalachia between the

Figure 2.4. Dorothea Lange, Billboard along U.S. 99 behind which three destitute families of migrants are camped. Kern County, California. Library of Congress, Prints & Photographs Division, FSA/OWI Collection, LC-DIG-fsa-8b32706.

years 1940 and 1960 drained the region of 7 million people (Obermiller xii). The population shifted so much that one saying popular in Indiana was "Haven't you heard there are only 45 states in the Union? Kentucky and Tennessee have gone to Indiana, and Indiana has gone to hell" (Obermiller 10).

Migrants from Appalachia to Northern locations in Michigan, Illinois, and Ohio—because of their proximity to the South—often found only temporary homes. Migrants from these regions typically described themselves as sojourning for a time while they made money enough to move back home or as shuttle migrants who worked in the Northern or Midwestern factories during the seasons when there was work and then returned back home for the rest of the year. In many ways, then, Southern whites seem to have been struggling against the transformations of the border. When war production ramped up during World War II, Southerners were also attracted to distant factories by the prospect of a salary and duty to country. The intent of the migrant was to move to a new location to make money, but the ultimate goal was oftentimes to return home. This is certainly the intent of Gertie Nevel, who goes to Detroit in support of her husband, but whose final goal is always to return to Kentucky to purchase land and to farm. Migration becomes key to making the money

Figure 2.5. Dorothea Lange, Toward Los Angeles, California. Library of Congress, Prints & Photographs Division, FSA/OWI Collection, LC-USZ6–1470.

necessary to buy goods in exile, while the ultimate goal is to use the money to buy the land back at home. Chad Berry notes in *Southern Migrants, Northern Exiles* that "The story of the great white migration thus entails both a divided heart—emotional ambivalence about leaving—and economic success—solving the economic problems that were the main reasons for migrating" (8). Many saw themselves and intentionally defined themselves as border walkers, purposely remaining in the liminal space, in the psychological space between places. Migrants often first bought a car before other purchases because a car was the means to get back home (Feather 3).

Others, however, like Native American chief Wilma Mankiller, saw themselves as retracing the bitter routes of their ancestors. "I experienced my own Trail of Tears when I was a young girl. No one pointed a gun at me or at members of my family," Mankiller writes in her 1993 autobiography, *Mankiller: A Chief and Her People*. "No show of force was used. It was not necessary. Nevertheless, the United States government, through the Bureau of Indian

Affairs, was again trying to settle the 'Indian problem' by removal. . . . I cried for days, not unlike the children who had stumbled down the Trail of Tears so many years before. I wept tears that came from deep within the Cherokee part of me. They were tears from my history, from my tribe's past. They were Cherokee tears" (62). Trying to "memorize the shapes of the trees, the calls of animals and birds from the forest" as she took her last sight of Oklahoma before her family moved west to California in the 1950s, she hoped for "some kind of miracle" that would keep them from moving, even considering running away to avoid the move (70). Telling her story about her own "Trail of Tears" along-side the story of the Cherokee Nation, which she led as first female principal chief, Mankiller says that her family was not forced to move westward as her ancestors had been forced to follow the Trail of Tears in the nineteenth century, but instead the US government, wanting to "get out of the Indian business" (69), produced promotional brochures that promised a life out of poverty for Native Americans. Government workers knocked on doors, encouraging Native Americans to leave their homes with the lure of fewer financial hardships if they moved off the reservation. Similar to the propaganda mentioned earlier in this chapter, these brochures that Mankiller writes about—ones "showing staged photographs of smiling Indians in 'happy homes' in big cities" (69)—promoted a move outside the region to California and to cities like Chicago as the way to a "better life." Instead, Mankiller says, displaced Native Americans generally only found "life in a tough, urban ghetto" (73). She describes all ten of her family piling into the train going westward as "look[ing] like a darker version of the Joad family from John Steinbeck's novel, *The Grapes of Wrath*" (71). Mankiller writes about reaching California and trying to acclimate—or at least fit in—reading aloud with her sister in the evening, trying to lose her Oklahoma accent (103), and of her family eating beef sandwiches with gravy for breakfast because when they scanned the menu at the restaurant where they ate their first breakfast in California, they could not find the biscuits and gravy they were accustomed to back at home in Oklahoma (71). Mankiller writes, too, of her experiences confronting prejudices against her and her family because of their race, and her feelings of isolation and her attempt to reconnect with her Native American heritage, especially after the death of her father. Ultimately, as a mother of two children, Mankiller was able to return home to Oklahoma to live; as she says, "the circle had to be completed" (205).

The goal for many was, in fact, to remain in the liminal spaces where they could find security and safety—at once holding on to their home in the South, but always preparing and considering ways to make their return. The title of Obermiller, Tucker, and Wagner's edited collection of essays, *Appalachian Odyssey: Historical Perspectives on the Great Migration*, points to a signifi-cant narrative that Arnow's *Dollmaker* represents. Although the narrative was certainly not one as common as the exodus story or the story of Westward migration, the odyssey sums up the journey of many Southern migrants who did not move as far from home and always intended to return. Although the editors of *Appalachian Odyssey* begin with the statement that their book "does not offer a single narrative, trope, or account that purports to explain the whole event" of the Great Migration of peoples from Appalachia, their title does, in fact, point to a narrative that is summative for many: a narrative that defined their future as one of return to the South (Obermiller xi). Many Southerners defined their sojourning as steps along the way in an ultimate plan to return "home" and even viewed that liminal space as a space that would help them retain their Southernness and hold on to their regional identity. Despite, however, these goals of returning, this crossing back and forth resulted not in a "true" Southern identity (whatever that means!), but a hybrid one and created a border between South and NotSouth that was porous and permeable.

The narratives that drew the migrants to places outside the South were, however, frequently replaced by ones written or rewritten by those they confronted on the other side. The narrative that held them captive in making the journey was oftentimes replaced by a new narrative when the migrant reached the destination. If a hybrid nature—part place of departure and part place of arrival—is said to give power to the migrant who remains in the borderlands, then the new communities that Southerners found oftentimes tried to push them out of the borderlands and back into the South. African American church leaders voiced their concern that the story of their people was being rewritten when the AME Council of Bishops appealed to congregations to offer help to migrants who were, according to the council, experiencing a "new form of bondage." In 1917, the pastor of the Union Baptist Church in Philadelphia told new migrants that they had not reached Canaan: "For there are those here in charge of the land and the government who are of another race" (Kling 222). The failed promises of hope for a new and better life in the North are clearly portrayed in books like Arnow's *The Dollmaker* and William Attaway's 1941 novel *Blood on the Forge*, which tells the story of three African American brothers who leave sharecropping in Kentucky for work in a steelmill town in Pennsylvania. Comparing Attaway's novel with Arnow's story of white Appalachian migrants, Stacy I. Morgan parallels the journey northward on the train in startling ways: Arnow's migrants sleep "the smelly, moaning, coughing, muttering, sleep of cattle penned too closely in a strange barn" (136), while Attaway's are "bunched up like hogs headed for market, riding in the dark for what might have been a year" in what Morgan describes as in "the manner of Middle Passage experience" (724), rather than in the "optimistic spirit" (723) generally equated with the Great Migration and the train ride into freedom. When Attaway's migrants reach the North, they work on machines called "mules," suggesting "America's unfulfilled promises of enfranchisement ('forty acres and a mule')" (716). "Attaway and his protagonists," according to Morgan, "soon seem to join Richard Wright in perceiving little difference between southern 'Lords of the Land' and northern 'Bosses of the Buildings'" (723).

The meaning of the passageway out of the South was thus layered with complexities. Even though media representations of the North and the West drew Southerners to places they thought would be the living embodiment of the scriptural Promised Land, the media also did its share to help create and solidify images of Southerners as dangerous to the communities they migrated to in a struggle between that top-down hegemonic discourse and the everyday experience of crossing the border. "The Hillbillies Invade Chicago" headlined a story published in *Harper's* in 1958. Starting the article with the statement that Chicago's "toughest integration problem" has "nothing to do with Negroes," the author of the article describes white migrants to the city as living as close as possible to the way they supposedly lived back home. They remove window screens so they can sit in windows half-clothed, "dispose of their garbage in the quickest way" (suggesting that it is pitched rather than disposed of properly), fail to supervise their children and to teach them that incest is morally wrong, and are "usually proud, poor, primitive, and fast with a knife." In Detroit, according to Louis Adamic in his 1935 article entitled "The Hill-Billies Come to Detroit" for the *Nation*, a man was best able to get a job if he put on a Southern accent; "another good way . . . is to look and act stupid" (Gregory 65). Essentially, then, migrating Southerners felt the push on the other end as well, as they crossed the border to find themselves isolated by characterizations that othered them.

Although in the first several decades of the twentieth century, Southern white migrants were treated as most any other migrating Americans, during the second period of migration from roughly 1935 until 1970, according to James Gregory, the media represented both black and white Southern migrants as "people who would play out a tense drama of maladjustment in the big cities" (78). Gregory identifies the "maladjusted" and the "dangerous migrant" as two stereotypes of migrants that Western and Northern whites seemed to fear. He notes, too, that while white migrants were generally labeled as hillbillies, marked by the outcome of the Scopes trial in Tennessee and the media representations of poor whites from *Tobacco Road* (1932) to *The Beverly Hillbillies*, the portrayal of blacks in *Amos and Andy* radio and television shows and Richard Wright's character Bigger Thomas in the best-selling novel *Native Son* (1940) had a powerful impact on the ways that migrating blacks were viewed. Black and white migrants were increasingly analyzed by sociologists and labeled by theories that became popular with the publication of Robert Park's 1928 essay "Human Migration and the Marginal Man" (Gregory 67).

If Southern blacks looked to the North as a promised land, the double labeling of being Southern and black produced ever harsher living conditions for African Americans. When a black swimmer was killed at a southside Chicago beach by whites in July 1919, four days of violence erupted and 38 people were killed, with the majority being black. "A week of lurid front-page articles dominated newspapers across the country," according to James Gregory, with headlines such as "Flying Squadrons of Blacks in Automobiles Fire into Crowds of Whites" and "Negroes Storm Armory in Effort to Obtain Arms and Ammunition." The Associated Press, on the third day of the rioting, reported the number of people involved in the fighting as "a hundred thousand negroes and an equal number of whites." The inflated number of African Americans, according to Gregory, "effectively counted among the rioters nearly every black Chicagoan who could walk" (48–49). Carter Woodson wrote in his 1918 essay entitled "The Exodus During the World War" that black Southern migrants "are not wanted by the whites and are treated with contempt by the native blacks of the northern cities, who consider their brethren from the South too criminal and too vicious to be tolerated" (186–87). The image of the migrating Southerner was literally high-jacked.

The language used to describe the new white arrival also had profound effects as migrants were recaptured by pejorative names that rewrote their stories of flight, escape, or resettlement. John Hartigan Jr. states in *Racial Situations: Class Predicaments of Whiteness in Detroit* that the name "hillbilly" during the 1940s and 1950s was used as "a strict act of boundary maintenance, shoring up an imperiled sense of white identity.... Like any cultural matter that threatens an established symbolic order, the dirtiness of 'hillbillies' caused great anxiety among native white Detroiters" (88). Although during those years the term was used more specifically to denote a geographical identity, those who were "out of place" living in the city, as years have passed, the term has become more generally used—according to Hartigan "misapplied"—to describe people without any Southern connections but who in some way have "transgressed the mores associated with, or evidencing a desire for, the upward mobility that is so integral to ideological constructions of whites" (88). In a similar fashion, the name "Okie" came to define people not just from Oklahoma, but all migrants from Southern regions who had made the journey westward into California, even though the term supposedly originated from a journalist in California named Ben Reddick who saw a number of cars in migrant camps with Oklahoma license plates that read "OK." He wrote "Okies" on the back of a photo of a camp and the automobiles, and the name was used in a caption in the newspaper.

In many ways, the dark, naturalistic quality of Paul Laurence Dunbar's *The Sport of the Gods* (1902), the earliest novel about the Great Migration of African

Americans from the South, could also be a quality that holds true of many border crossing narratives. The consequences of movement are shaped by the race, economic conditions, gender, and cultural background of those who move and settle in a new place. Pushed out of their comfortable life in the South by not only the prejudices of whites, but also the resentment of other African Americans, Dunbar's Hamilton family moves to New York City, a place they believed would be one where no one "would look down upon them" (78), that "seemed to them the centre of all the glory, all the wealth, and all the freedom of the world" (77–78). Finding instead that they must "battle with the terrible force of a strange and unusual environment" (212), ultimately, Berry and Fannie Hamilton return to the South, only to find that they cannot reconstruct the life that they had left behind there. The novel ends with a sobering statement: "they knew they were powerless against some Will infinitely stronger than their own" (255). In effect, a Southern background and accent left many a migrant with the mark of their journeying, a mark that became a label of Otherness and of a life in the spaces in between. For Southern border crossers, narratives that told of their leaving the South not only shaped the journeys that they made, but also the very lives they lived in the places where they landed.

CHAPTER 3

Securing the Border as a Creative Site: Southern Masculinities and the Urge to Tell

During the Civil War, the Confederate obsession with holding the line and fighting to retain the physical boundaries of the South as a distinct nation also framed a struggle to hold back the intrusions and influence of a model of white manhood distinctly different from the Southern version. On the Northern side of the Mason-Dixon Line stood the Self-Made Man, a figure ingrained in American nationalism and myth, while on the Southern side stood the gentleman, who according to legend, "moved soft-spokenly against a background of rose gardens and dueling grounds, through always gallant deeds" (Qtd. in Kimmel 51). Although the Civil War has for many years now been examined as what historian LeeAnn Whites first called a "crisis in gender," sociologist Michael Kimmel has looked more specifically at the war in terms of masculinity and at the ways in which the war represented a clash between two distinct models of American manhood. "Northern and southern men questioned each other's manhood, both on the battlefield and in rhetorical skirmishes," according to Kimmel, and "The Civil War pitted Confederate chivalry against Self-Made Yankees and signaled the triumph of the urban industrial entrepreneur over the genteel southern patrician" (50). While the Southern gentleman supposedly represented honor, chivalry, morality, and a strong commitment and attachment to place, the Self-Made Man, according to an 1838 description, was "made for action, and the bustling scenes of moving life, and not the poetry or romance of existence." The Self-Made Man was, says Kimmel, "a man on the go. . . . Mobile, competitive, aggressive in business, . . .

temperamentally restless, chronically insecure, and desperate to achieve a solid grounding for a masculine identity" (Kimmel 13). Solidified in the American mind in the late nineteenth century in books by writers such as Horatio Alger, the Self-Made Man typically had his start as a displaced, homeless boy in pursuit of wealth and success. Oftentimes he was in search of a father figure, having been orphaned or left to support a struggling mother (Kimmel 96).

Narratives of young men passing across borders—from rags to riches, from country to town, from east to west—were prominent as both cultural and literary phenomenon in the late eighteenth and nineteenth centuries in the North as well as in the South. The image of the young Ben Franklin departing from Boston and entering Philadelphia with penny loaves under his arms and few personal items on his back became not only a model for Franklin's son but a cultural icon for generations of Americans who dreamed of a rise in the world like the one he experienced. In the nineteenth century, American politicians clung to the story of making good from nothing, Southerner Andrew Jackson pulled himself up by his bootstraps to become president, and Alger saw huge success with his "rags to riches" books including *Ragged Dick* (1868) and *Luck and Pluck* (1869). American nation building depended upon the transforming power of the literal passage from one place to another—from Old World to New World, from Eastern settlement to Western frontier, or, as in the instance of Franklin, from Boston to Philadelphia—and evolved into a figurative journey from humble beginnings to monetary and professional independence and success. The Self-Made Man was, of course, a representation that held sway in the antebellum South, but the slave system of the South laid greater claim to models and representations of manhood, and the defining images of Southern masculinity in the period evolved into models of master and mastered that shaped and gave power to the slaveholder.

Standing out as the Confederate hero who fought to preserve the physical marker of the South's boundaries and the image of the iconic Southern gentleman, Robert E. Lee, in the postwar South became the model for a new sort of Southern manhood. According to Craig Thompson Friend in his introduction to *Southern Masculinity: Perspectives on Manhood in the South since Reconstruction*, actually three new models evolved in the Reconstruction years and the years leading up to World War I: "the Christian gentleman, the masculine martial, and the self-made man—[who all] coexisted uneasily in the South and across racial boundaries" (xvi). Even though Jefferson Davis had eluded capture by dressing as a woman, "'chivalree' was not dead." And chivalry found its physical manifestation in General Robert E. Lee, seemingly the model of the Christian gentleman in the flesh, who was characterized by his "self-esteem, self-control, and a respect for the dictums of war" and his willingness in the postwar South to preserve "the intractability of southern civilization even with the defeat of the Confederacy." Lee, and by association, the Christian gentleman, was "honorable, master of his household, humble, self-restrained, and above all pious and faithful" (Friend xi). If in the antebellum period models of Southern manhood were clearly delineated along the lines of race as master and mastered, according to Friend, in the postwar years, African American men were "empowered . . . to publicly challenge white attempts to emasculate them." The Christian gentleman was also a model for African American manhood, offering a "'race-neutral language' for masculinity" (x–xi). The second masculine model was the masculine martial, which "filtered those ideals [of the Christian gentleman] through the war experience" and evolved into public representations of white power, including lynchings, to show control over African Americans. The third model was that of the Self-Made Man, whom Friend identifies as specifically related to the late nineteenth-century ideals of the New South and Henry Grady, and the promotion of industry, capitalism, and agricultural diversification as means to bring the South out of poverty. Friend explains that the New South tried to construct the Self-Made Man as what he calls "the hegemonic form of masculinity in the South, as it had become in the North" (xv).

What I propose here is another model of masculinity that became prominent in the first half of the twentieth century among both black and white writers of the period—a Self-Made Man of sorts. This new model of Southern masculinity takes possession of the liminal space as an intellectual space and a creative site, and is not one who was of Henry Grady's New South, but one who sought education and financial success outside the South and who was haunted by the Southern past. My focus here in this chapter is on the representation of this new model of Southern masculinity in literary works by writers Thomas Wolfe, William Styron, Robert Penn Warren, Truman Capote, and Ralph Ellison. The characters I focus on, including Wolfe's Eugene Gant, Styron's Stingo, Ellison's Invisible Man, Warren's Jed Tewksbury, and Capote's unnamed narrator, are all characters who are neophytes like those Victor Turner describes, who are "not yet classified" (96), who are crossing over Southern borders, looking for the potential of new lives on the other side. "Since neophytes," according to Turner, "are not only structurally 'invisible' (though physically visible) and ritually polluting, they are very commonly secluded, partially or completely, from the realm of culturally defined and ordered states and statuses" (98). They are stripped bare—sometimes literally—with "no status, property . . . rank, kinship position" (98). Although Wolfe labeled this journeying as "wandering," I would argue that even Wolfe's Eugene Gant knew where he was headed—across Southern borders and out of the region. Always the movement is outward from home, and that means leaving the South, but that movement is not always part of a young man's intent. In some cases, that journeying also reflects social constraints and prejudices that create a push and pull for the young man who is crossing. He also encounters border figures that block passage (walls, veils, skins, faces), provide passage across (bridges, windows, doors, rivers, railroad tracks), or hold the line (border keepers, border guards).

Crossing out of the South represents not only a coming of age for these young men, but also the loss of home attachments and the connections to a past and familial ties. For black and white Southern males coming of age in the first several decades of the century, the narrative of crossing the liminal divide between South and NotSouth revolved specifically around passage *from* a world marked by the tragedy of slavery, entrenched racism, an evolving white guilt and shame over a history mired in loss, and consistent and ever-present labeling of the South as a cultural backwoods of the United States. Leaving the South meant leaving home, but also a region that Baltimore essayist and editor H. L. Mencken described in 1917 as the Sahara of the Bozart, "almost as sterile, artistically, intellectually, culturally, as the Sahara Desert" (*Prejudices* 136). When in 1925 the Scopes "Monkey" Trial on evolution in Dayton, Tennessee, drew national attention, Mencken described this cultural wasteland as the site of "hill-billies" and "peasants" (188) who were being brainwashed by the "degraded nonsense . . . being rammed and hammered into yokel skulls" by local preachers (*H. L. Mencken on Religion*, 189). For the young Southern man, following this archetypal masculine pattern of moving out into the world meant not only crossing the border out of the South and leaving Southern economic and racial oppression behind, but also struggling against a Southland that attempted to hold him tightly within its grip.

This journey across the threshold from Southern boyhood into adulthood in the world beyond Southern borders figures prominently in the creative literature of the twentieth century, particularly for writers who reached maturity in the 1920s through the 1950s. Success might have literally come from moving to New York City to work for the *New Yorker* as a writer as Truman Capote did or teaching at a Northern university like Robert Penn Warren, who referred to himself as a "dp" ("displaced person") and ultimately landed at Yale, but many writers who examined this narrative of the wandering youth found that liminal space many of them had experienced also provided them with the space to deal with recurring feelings of displacement and abandonment, a muse, and an impetus to practice their craft. Thomas Wolfe described this "eternal wandering, moving, questioning, loneliness, homesickness, and the desire of the soul for a home, peace, fixity, repose" as "the two things that haunt and hurt us" (Qtd. in Snyder 23), but that haunting is also what inspired him to write and in doing so to influence generations of other writers to wander. Of all the migrants who left the South, males—and generally that meant males of more privileged backgrounds or those who were able to assume that privileged aura—were the ones who were able to claim control of the liminal space and use it to great success. Liminal space was the site of creativity for the neophyte writer, yet ultimately, as the following chapter of this study suggests, liminal space was a masculine zone where women writers could not linger, and wandering was a masculine action—not a feminine.

When Thomas Wolfe began writing his novel *Of Time and the River: A Legend of Man's Hunger in His Youth* (1935), the theme of wandering and of placelessness had already become well established in his work. There's no doubt as well that he was influenced by the Lost Generation of American writers who, like Wolfe, fled to Europe in search of meaning and creative inspiration. Comparing the first section of his book to the Antaeus legend in correspondence with editors John Hall Wheelock and Maxwell Perkins, Wolfe identified the urge to wander as a masculine trait and the attachment to place as feminine. In *Of Time and the River*, he explained, "I tell why men go to sea, and why they have made harbours at the end . . . we all know we are lost, that we are damned together" (Wolfe, *To Loot* 46), for like Antaeus, they lose their strength when they are disconnected from the earth. Wolfe saw himself as akin to Homer's Odysseus, writing in 1924 to a friend that similar to Odysseus, he was searching for the "enchanted isles, or for the lotus, which if eaten could cause him to sink into a drowsy oblivion" (Qtd. in Snyder 22). He was inherently a wanderer, in fact, one from a long line of them, his mother, Julia, characterizing her husband and Tom's father, W. O. Wolfe, as from "a race of wanderers" (Qtd. in Snyder 21). Louis Rubin describes *Of Time and the River* as "a young American writer's flight from a very detailed and palpable social milieu . . . and his subsequent effort to discover a better place in which to live and write." "The place to write" was "anywhere on earth, so long as the heart, the power, the faith, the desperation, the bitter and unendurable necessity, and the naked courage were there inside him all that time" (101–2). In effect, Wolfe situated himself in liminal space, forever wandering, never finally reaching the other side of the threshold, using this as a literary strategy, one that held power and profit.

A mania evolved around Thomas Wolfe and his novels of departure and wandering. Wolfe's novels about Eugene Gant and then George Webber leaving home for life in the North created an obsession that has been said to have influenced writers—and not just Southern ones—as wide ranging as Jack Kerouac, David Madden, William Styron, Edward Abbey, Henry Miller, Ray Bradbury, Pat Conroy, and Truman Capote. David Herbert Donald, writing from Massachusetts in his preface to *Look Homeward: A Life of Thomas Wolfe*, described Wolfe's impact on an entire generation:

> As an adolescent, I really read *Look Homeward, Angel* and was certain that Thomas Wolfe had told my life story. . . . Like so many other teenagers, I was con-

vinced—without any just cause—that I too was misunderstood by my family and unappreciated in my community, and, like Eugene, I enjoyed writhing in romantic agony. Afterward, along with everybody that I knew, I was swept up in the turbulent rhetoric of *Of Time and the River* (1935). My friends and I were certain that we were unrecognized "artists," like Eugene Gant, and we believed that we also had Faustian appetites.... As a young man, packing to leave rural Mississippi forever to take up residence in the strange and terrifying North, I shivered appreciatively when I read: "We are so lost, so naked and so lonely in America.... Immense and cruel skies bend over us, and all of us are driven on forever and we have no home." But somehow, I gained reassurance from Wolfe's prediction: "I believe that we are lost here in America, but I believe we shall be found." (xi–xii)

Wolfe's influence runs deep. Jack Kerouac once said that Wolfe—"this dark-eyed American poet"—"made me want to prowl, and roam, and see the real America that was there" (Kerouac 75). In *Sophie's Choice*, William Styron draws clear ties between his narrator Stingo and Wolfe, identifying Stingo's father as sharing a birthday on October 3 with Wolfe and Nat Turner, the focus of another popular book by Styron (even though Nat Turner's was actually October 2). Styron's Sophie reads *Of Time and the River*, and Stingo describes the enthusiasm and popularity of Wolfe's story of leaving the South as a "Wolfe-worship" (16).

For male Southern writers and academics, the North represented a professional Promised Land, and thus, in effect, an economic one, too. Wolfe's Eugene Gant in *Of Time and the River* yearns for "the fierce, the splendid, strange and secret North," seeing himself as leaving "the enchanted, time-far hills" and crossing "out of the dark heart and mournful mystery of the South forever." Wolfe represents Gant much like his fellow Southerners: on "the road to freedom, solitude and the enchanted promise of the golden cities." The path that he follows on this journey is "now before him," "like a dream made real, a magic come to life," one that will soon be "speeding [him] world-ward, life-ward, North-ward" (24). But Gant's destination is different from the typical. He is, after all, headed to one of the icons of the American educational system: Harvard. (So, too, does Quentin Compson in William Faulkner's *The Sound and the Fury* and *Absalom, Absalom!* but Quentin's journey ends in a spiraling downward that isn't experienced by the characters discussed in this chapter.) Eugene also sees movement beyond the spaces of home as an education in itself. He is driven by an almost insane drive to read: "He simply wanted to know about everything on earth; he wanted to devour the earth, and it drove him mad when he saw he could not do this" (92), and he reads as much as he can, believing that this is the way to gain a better understanding of those places beyond home. Plotting a similar escape from the South, Jed Tewksbury in Robert Penn Warren's *A Place to Come To* (1977) turns up at the University of Chicago on the recommendation of one of his professors at a small college in Alabama, believing that he will be taken in and educated because of his love and deep desire to study the classics. Warren's novel picks up many of these same themes of wandering boyhood and the struggle to find a place to come to that are also at the heart of Wolfe's work.

In literary treatments of this Southern male coming-of-age story, oftentimes this narrator is a writer, sometimes professionally, sometimes not. In *A Place to Come To*, for example, Jed is a classics scholar, but he tells the reader about the process of recording his story as well. After he tells about his father's death after "tryen to jack off in the middle of the night on the gravel on Dugton Pike" (4), Jed says that the story came "rushing out, my ball-point pen rushing ahead—a new experience for me, who am accustomed only to scholarly and critical composition" (6). There is an urgency for Jed to get down his story, to record the narrative. Likewise, the unnamed writer-narrator of Truman Capote's 1958 novella *Breakfast at Tiffany's* has not been selling stories, but he finds success after he meets and gets to know Holly Golightly, another Southerner in flight from the South, who becomes a muse for him. As the novella opens, Capote's narrator tells readers that he lives in a New York apartment, "a place of my own, the first," where he has his books, and "jars of pencils to sharpen, everything I needed, so I felt, to become the writer I wanted to be" (3). But his stories of "negroes and children" (56) and another Lillian Hellman-ish story about "two women who share a house, schoolteachers, one of whom, when the other becomes engaged, spreads with anonymous notes a scandal that prevents the marriage" (15) aren't selling well. Holly tells the narrator that he should gauge his success as a "real writer" (19) on whether or not he sells his stories, and she promises to help him do that because he reminds her of her brother Fred. By the end of the novella—and the end of Holly's time spent in New York—the narrator is selling his stories and finding some success. Another writer-narrator, Stingo in *Sophie's Choice* needs the money that's been passed down to him through his family from the sale of a slave named Artiste so that he can survive in New York City as a writer. Stingo's father wants him to return home from the "barbaric North" to join "that great Southern tradition of writer-farmers" (109–10). There's also a good deal of handing round of books in the novel as Sophie reads Malcolm Cowley's *Portable Faulkner*, Stingo is patterning his work after Robert Penn Warren in *All the King's Men*, and Stingo refers to an unnamed novel that he published in 1967 and that "found hundreds of thousands of readers," which most probably is a reference to Styron's *Confessions of Nat Turner* (215).

Leaving the South meant escaping to a place like the Chicago that Warren's youthful Jed Tewksbury believes is a "land famed for the glory of horses and horsemen, where the nightgales sweetest sing," which leaves him "pouring out now . . . the great chorus from *Oedipus at Colonus*" (49) or the "secret North" where Eugene Gant felt "illimitable and exultant power, evoking for him the huge mystery of the night and darkness" (31). Wolfe says that "like a million other boys," Gant "had dreamed and visioned in the darkness of the shining city" (469). Over and over again, Wolfe tells of that desire to flee, to escape, to move out into the world and to keep going. The repetition suggests both the intensity of the young man's desire and the strength of this pull of the city and of life beyond the provincial hometown where a "country boy who is coming to the city with a feeling of glory in his guts" is able "to make money, to find glory, fame and love, and a life more fortunate and happy than any we have ever known" (506).

Generally, too, these young men can't wait to leave the South. The unnamed narrator of *Breakfast at Tiffany's* who shares a birthday with author Truman Capote mentions "having so recently escaped the regimentation of a small town" (69). Robert Penn Warren's Jed Tewksbury in *A Place to Come To* is a young man from Dugton, Alabama, who is torn between his intellectual studies in high school Latin and his desire for an education and a family background that has left him the joke of the community. Even before his mother tells him, "Ain't nothing here for you . . . Yores is waiting for you, somewhere" (26), Jed sees himself as a "wanderer," "trying to set eye to a mystic peephole that may give on a bright reality beyond" (23). After a particularly embarrassing moment at a high school dance, Jed proclaims, "I was through with Dugton and Dugton was through with me. . . . But spiritually I had already passed on toward my unspecifiable destination" (37). Jed leaves for the University of Chicago where he hopes to study, believing that he has arrived at a place as majestic as Oedipus's Colonus. In Wolfe's *Of Time and the River*, as Eugene Gant walks down the dark hallway of his mother's house, he hears whispering to him "all the lives and voices of the hundred others, the lost, the vanished people" and "far off, far-faint and broken by the wind, he heard the wailing cry of the great train, bringing to him again its wild and secret promises of flight and darkness, new lands, and a shining city" (404).

The train—so powerful to the narratives of African Americans escaping the South—became, too, a symbol of freedom for these young white men and boys, but a symbol layered with historical complexities. Within the context of Southern history, no other image was as potent to white Southerners in the postbellum years as that of train rails ripped from railway beds, heated over fires stoked from railroad ties, and then wrapped around tree trunks. Known as "Sherman's neckties," the rails were a visible, persistent reminder of Northern victory and Yankee capitalism (Millichap 8–9). For African Americans, the train was at once a symbol of "both escape and entrapment," both the Underground Railroad of the nineteenth century and the division of the races under Jim

Crow in the twentieth (Millichap 20–21). A border figure that provided passage between South and NotSouth, train cars were the site of the confrontation between self and "Other" as they transported people in small crowded spaces, but they also signaled change and oftentimes nostalgia for childhood and youth. If the wagon train was always moving in the nineteenth century, the image of the train shows the constant motion of the early twentieth. Especially for those who wanted to write, those "new lands" beyond the South were the lure and the train was the instrument of transportation, the way out.

The train whistle signaled that escape route. Warren spoke of his own personal experiences, the desires building within him to go out into the world and leave behind the provincialism of his hometown, Guthrie, Kentucky, and the urgency he felt as he lay in bed at night, listening to the sound of the trains coming through town. Thomas Wolfe associated the whistle with the adventure and freedom of flight from small-town life in Altamont in *Of Time and the River*:

> Trains cross the continent in a swirl of dust and thunder, the leaves fly down the tracks behind them: the great trains cleave through gulch and gulley, they rumble with spoked thunder on the bridges over the powerful brown wash of mighty rivers, they toil through hills, they skirt the rough brown stubble of shorn fields, they whip past empty stations in the little towns and their great stride pounds its even pulse across America. (331)

Railways course through *Of Time in the River* not only to suggest "a tremendous memory of space, and power, and of exultant distances," but also "a vision of trains that smashed and pounded at the rails, a memory of people hurled past the windows of [Eugene's] vision in another train" (412). Wolfe's description of the train is one of power on a grand scale, a reverence for a symbol of the industrialized, modern world. As his train races another, Gant sees "the great steel coaches, the terrific locomotives, the shining rails, the sweep of the tracks, the vast indifferent dinginess and rust of colors, the powerful mechanical expertness, and the huge indifference to suave finish." It is as if the people inside are transfixed by time, each having their own lives and stories, "all hurled onward, a thousand atoms, to their journey's end somewhere upon the mighty continent, across the immense and lonely visage of the everlasting earth" (410). The train played such a vital role in Wolfe's work that at one time he was planning an entire novel about a train journey northward. The working title of the book, *K-19*, was notably the number of the Pullman car on the Southern Railroad's overnight express from Asheville to New York (Millichap 44).

Other methods of transportation used to cross the South's borders appear as well. Although Robert Penn Warren was raised in Guthrie, Kentucky, a small town that sprang up because it was at the crossroads of two railroad lines, and trains figure prominently in his poetry about boyhood, in *A Place to Come To*, the youthful Jed Tewksbury instead hitchhikes to Chicago. Planes also represent motion and movement and wandering. In a sense fleeing into the West as Jack Burden does in Warren's *All the King's Men*, Jed finds himself engaged to Agnes Andresen, a fellow student at the University of Chicago, and headed to Ripley City, South Dakota, by plane for the wedding. Jed seems to have fallen into the marriage, perhaps from guilt, perhaps out of vanity because she had been engaged to another man and Jed had won out, but as they approach Ripley City, Jed sees the town as "a slight abrasion on the velvety vastness of the green and purple striped prairie" and feels a "new kind of loneliness" that "comes because the distance is fleeing away from you, bleeding away from you, in all directions, and if you can't stop the process you'll be nothing left except a dry, transparent husk, like a cicada's, with the ferocious sunlight blazing through it" (78). Jed describes this "bleeding away" as a Western type of loneliness and the Southern "kind" as a "bleeding inward of the self, away from all the world around, into an internal infinitude, like a pit." He identifies himself as the "original, gold-plated, thirty-third-degree loneliness artist, the champion of Alabama," directly tying his wandering throughout the book with introspection and the desire to find a place to come to (78–79).

This moving away from the area to look back at the past is part of the Southern experience, according to Warren, who said that in his own life, this physical separation had made him think more about the region. Of course the distance is significant, but the process of leaving, the wandering spirit that comes to the forefront in a number of Southern texts, focuses specifically on the complications of a sojourn that ultimately became permanent. Wolfe writes in *Of Time and the River* of Eugene "looking through walls he never had seen before, exploring the palpable and golden substance of this earth as it had never been explored, finding, somehow, the word, the key, the door, to the glory of a life more fortunate and happy than any man has ever known." Eugene ultimately recognizes that he "must escape not out of life but into it" and that language ("the word") can open the doorway for those opportunities before him (389). Shawn Holliday in his book *Thomas Wolfe and the Politics of Modernism* points to the influence of Homer's *Odyssey* on Wolfe's book, noting not only the similar uses by James Joyce, who out of all the modernist writers most influenced Wolfe's novel, but also suggesting that the allusions to Homer's story of Ulysses frame Eugene's journey as an "attempted catharsis—his constant striving to purge emotional distress by traveling out of the South" (22). Holliday explains that Wolfe "makes Eugene exile himself from Altamont to stand outside of the disparaging pressures of small town life" (23). Movement itself becomes a way for Eugene to shed his old self, remake himself, cleanse himself in a sense.

Such movement also becomes the focal point for the creative inspiration of Capote's narrator in *Breakfast at Tiffany's*. Capote's narrator observes that Holly Golightly, whose real name is Lulamae Barnes, is always running away from her past, but always trying to find something, a home. Even her mailbox identifies her as "Miss Holiday Golightly, Traveling" (5). Capote includes a number of references in the novella to taming wild things and to cages—settling down and being pinned in. When Holly finds out that the narrator has been admiring a $350 antique bird cage with "a mosque of minarets and bamboo rooms yearning to be filled with talkative parrots" (9), she buys him the cage for a Christmas present. He gives her a Saint Christopher medal (a sure reference to her wandering nature) that he has bought from Tiffany's, a place that represents the ideal life and security for her. Holly can never be caged in—never settle down. And neither can Capote's narrator, it seems. When they go out to celebrate the publication of one of his stories in a small university review, they avoid the zoo with its caged animals and end up stealing masks for the sport of it, a suggestion that neither ever shows a true face to the other. The narrator frequently hears Holly playing her guitar and singing on the fire escape, with her cat beside her. She sings popular songs of the day and what the narrator calls "harshtender wandering tunes with words that smacked of pineywoods or prairie," one with the lyrics, *"Don't wanna sleep, Don't wanna die, Just wanna go a-travelin' through the pastures of the sky"* (10-11). This particular song seemed to please her most. By the end of the novella, Holly has left for places beyond the North American continent, and the narrator seems convinced of the necessity of their both being far from the South—Holly from her roots in Texas where she was already wife and mother when she was "going on fourteen" (61). Capote's narrator now understands that to be a success, he must write with a passion that didn't seem to be coming to the forefront in his stories about Southern life. His success notably comes with Holly's story of displacement and wandering.

The spaces where these characters reside are temporary ones. Jed Tewksbury lies on his cot at the YMCA in Chicago, staring at the ceiling, feeling he "had no place to go to" (45). Capote's narrator describes his first apartment—his first place of his own—as one room with a single window that looked out on a fire escape. The room was "crowded with attic furniture, a sofa and fat chairs upholstered in that itchy, particular red velvet that one associates with hot days on a train." The walls were the color of "tobacco-spit," and "everywhere, in the bathroom too, there were prints of Roman ruins freckled brown with age." He says his "spirits heightened" every time he felt the key of the apartment in his pocket (3). The space is loaded with baggage of the past, including the archetypal trip out of the South on the train, but the space is his—a room of his own. After Styron's Stingo loses his job at McGraw Hill, he says he wishes he had told his boss, "Up yours, Weasel, you're firing a man who's going to be as famous as Thomas Wolfe." Finding he can't afford to live any longer in the University Residence Club in the Village, Stingo finds an apartment in what his new landlord calls Yetta's Liberty Hall. The outside of the building reminds him of a castle set from an MGM backlot, and the inside is painted all in pink because the owners had found a bargain on some navy surplus paint. Stingo is taken with the low rental price, the bidet that "lent a risqué note," and the freedom to have a girl in his room "once in a while" (34). Both Stingo and Capote's narrator describe their apartments as places that give them greater freedoms as young men, but the spaces also reflect a transient quality, spaces that give them a place to write and reflect, spaces that don't yet physically suggest the qualities of the young men who live there. Both apartment buildings are places that bring together people from all walks of life that the narrators haven't experienced before and represent a cosmopolitan, worldly setting. Perhaps, too, the "castle set" of Yetta's Liberty Hall signals that Stingo's apartment is still just a façade—not yet the full independence he craves, painted over with a shade that still veils him from the realities of human tragedy that he will ultimately face as Sophie's story becomes part of his own narrative.

Crossing the border into that new world and into that new life also comes with the complications of making that transition. By making this transition, these border crossers find themselves in the spaces in between, not only experiencing the enthusiasm and adventure of youth, but also confronting roadblocks that aim to keep these young men "Southern." Stingo's father, for example, tries to "preserve" his son "from going over to the Yankees" (294). For Wolfe, that "process of endless locating and undermining" was one that he referred to very specifically. Wolfe notes that he intended *Of Time and the River* to be "a coherent legend of the savage hunter and unrest that drives men back and forth upon this earth and the great antagonists of fixity [and] everlasting change, of wander and returning, that make war in our souls." He planned for the final section of the book "to conclude the fury of movement, unrest and wandering that drives men across the earth" (Donald 297). It is this ending that leads Wolfe to finally conclude that "you can't go home again." The wandering would find no resolution. Belonging to the place they have come from is problematic because of the baggage of history that's carried along by the very fact of their Southernness.

Styron and Warren equate the weight of the Southern past carried across the threshold with the weight of guilt carried by survivors of Hitler's Germany. They feel something akin to the "awful responsibility of time" that Warren referred to in *All the King's Men* and they carry it with them as they make the crossing. At first the story of a young writer who has fled the South for a future in the publishing world of New York City, *Sophie's Choice* is, for example, loaded with these sorts of parallels. In arguments with Nathan, Sophie's Jewish lover, who reminds Stingo again and again that "The South today has abdicated any right to connection with the human race.... No Southerner escapes responsibility" (71–72) for slavery and violence against African Americans, Stingo feels the weight of that past and is "suddenly sick with a past and a place and a heritage" (73). Stingo reflects on the relationship between the extermination of the Jews and slavery in the United States, Sophie compares anti-Semitism in Poland to racism in the South, and Nathan equates the racist Southern politician Theodore Bilbo with Hitler. Styron's book revolves around Stingo's struggles with his past as well as Sophie's own and the choice she was forced to make between her two children in the Auschwitz concentration camp. She lost them both when she was forced into making a decision about which child should survive. A Catholic Pole, Sophie was pressured by her anti-Semitic father to pass out copies of a pamphlet that he wrote on *"Poland's Jewish Problem"* (237) and interned in the concentration camp after she was caught stealing a ham for her dying mother. Working in the camp as a stenographer and typist for the commanding Nazi at the camp, Sophie cannot escape her past: her father's anti-Semitism, her choice between her daughter and her son, and her attempts to seduce the Nazi commander at Auschwitz in hopes that her son will survive. Ultimately, Sophie stays with Nathan, who is schizophrenic and abusive, out of guilt and trauma. "I cannot live without him" (335), she tells Stingo, and they ultimately commit suicide together. Describing the novel as about "the nature of evil in the individual and in all humanity," Richard Rubenstein asserts that the novel claims "It is no longer just the South that is grandly decayed, morally tortured . . . it is the world" (426).

While Styron portrays Stingo yearning for a physical and emotional relationship with Sophie as a way to overcome his loss and disconnection, Warren, as is quite typical in his writings, sees the displaced, fleeing Southerner in search of a father figure who can give direction and roots. In *A Place to Come To*, Jed looks to Dr. Stahlmann, who teaches at the University of Chicago, as a replacement, as a new guide. Raised on his father's stories about a valiant great-grandfather who had fought in the Civil War and left his sword behind for posterity as a mark of familial bravery and manhood, Jed learned from his mother that the stories were a sham and his great-grandfather probably fought not in battles of war but against the alcoholism that also inflected Jed's father, Buck. Arriving in Chicago as a gawky young man, Jed is rarely invited out for drinks with the other students, but when he starts telling stories about his father's death and his hometown Dugton, Alabama, with an Eskine Caldwell-like flavor, he is an immediate success. Yet, as is typical Warren, Stahlmann offers no comfort or guidance. Jed's flight from Dugton and the stories of his alcoholic father instead lead him into what is a life lived in continual movement from place to place. Dr. Stahlmann, a displaced German, is so lost himself that he can only hold on to his connections to the place he came from through "the stomach"—that is, food (54). Stahlmann carries with him the thought that even though his Jewish wife died in an American hospital, the Nazis were to blame for her death just "as surely as though they had put her in one of their camps" (59). Dealing with guilt about the place he came from, Dr. Stahlmann tells Jed, "I should have gone back to Germany, to claim my patrimony of honor. I should have gone back to offer the public testimony of my curse upon what my land had become. And to demand the consequences" (60). The book becomes a series of false hopes for a character who is consumed by his search. Warren ends the book with Jed returning to the graveside of his parents in Dugton, but even though he "had the wild impulse to lie on the earth between the two graves . . . and stretch out a hand to each," he was "afraid that nothing might happen . . . afraid to take the risk" (340). Jed remains the wanderer—continually facing his displacement and disconnection.

While Jed remains in constant motion, forever in the liminal space, looking for a father figure and a place to set down, Stingo's father visits him in Brooklyn and writes letters from home in Virginia with news about people Stingo knew in the past and with encouragements for Stingo to return to the South, specifically referring to Stingo's time in New York as a "sojourn" in the "barbaric North" (109). In another letter, he tells Stingo about the suicide of a young woman named Maria Hunt, a girlfriend from back at home who was living close by Stingo in his Manhattan apartment. Stingo tightly weaves together the deaths of Maria and his own mother, thinking about his mother's death when he hears the news that Maria jumped out of a window to her death and was buried in a pauper's grave. Memories of Maria and his mother flood in. Stingo says he "brooded" (44) over the news from his father of her death, wondering if he could have done something if he had known she was living just around the corner from him. He contemplates returning back home, thinking that perhaps he had "made a grave mistake" (45) by moving to Brooklyn, but soon after, he meets Sophie. Immediately taken with Sophie's "distant but real resemblance" to Maria, he "if not instantaneously, then swiftly and fathomlessly [fell] in love with her" (46). Clearly Stingo sees a relationship between Sophie and the dead Maria, who represents the dangers of the crossing that Stingo attempts into the North and New York. Her failure is symbolically represented with the window, the border figure through which she commits suicide. Thinking he should perhaps write about Maria's death, Stingo's search for a subject to write about ultimately lands on Sophie.

Creating a story that revolves around Sophie and her time in the Nazi concentration camp and her eventual death, Stingo finds success as a writer through the creative muse of a woman who is lost to him. Sophie's *choice* brings about the tragedy of the story—a past that Sophie is always trying to flee and a past that brings her to a destructive relationship with Nathan. Not long after Nathan's brother tells Stingo that Nathan is a paranoid schizophrenic who has been falsely representing himself as a Harvard graduate and a research scientist at Pfizer, Nathan begins to suspect that Sophie and Stingo are having an affair and threatens to kill them. Stingo tries to save Sophie by taking her southward on a train to Virginia where he hopes they can live on a peanut farm his father has inherited. Traveling in an inverse pattern to the journey he made to flee the South for the promise of New York, now he instead seems to believe there is some security for both of them if he returns South and takes her with him. Losing his virginity and fulfilling many of his sexual fantasies, Stingo makes love to Sophie, but she ultimately returns to Nathan, leaving a letter to Stingo that closes with "I love Nathan but now feel this Hate of Life and God. FUCK God and all his Hände Werk. And Life too. And even what remain of Love" (500). Like Maria, Sophie ends up taking her own life. Although Stingo cannot physically possess her and save her from Nathan and from herself and her past, she becomes an inspiration for a story of heartache and despair. "I did not weep for the six million Jews or the two million Poles or the one million Serbs or the five million Russians—I was unprepared to weep for all humanity—," Stingo says as he closes, "but I did weep for these others who in one way or another had become dear to me" (515). He, like Wolfe's Eugene realizes, can't go home again. And he ultimately recognizes that he can't "save" Sophie.

Although Holly Golightly does not die at the end of Capote's *Breakfast at Tiffany's*, she is just as lost to the novella's narrator as Sophie is to Stingo. In flight from the heart-wrenching news that her brother Fred was killed in action overseas, the miscarriage of her child fathered by José, and suspicions that she was involved in an international drug ring run by Sally Tomato, Holly leaves the country, first going to South America where she is seeing a "duhvine $enor" who has a wife and seven "brats" (110). When the narrator visits his old neighborhood, literally noting that for him, his old apartment was "haunted" (110) and that's why he left in the first place, he visits with Joe Bell at his bar. Joe has a photograph taken by Mr. I. Y. Yunioshi, who *happened* to be in Africa and *happened* to take a photograph of a tribal wood carving that *happened* to strike the very appearance of Holly. For the narrator, whom Holly calls "Fred" after her brother, the tribal statue is a tribute to an iconic figure that ultimately helped him to become a true writer, one whose stories actually sold.

At the end of Capote's novella, "Fred" seems to believe that he has claimed a sense of peace at the end of the narrative. Before he left his haunted apartment, he tracked down Holly's cat, finding him sitting in the window of an apartment building, but one framed by signs of the domestic and of connections with people. "Flanked by potted plants and framed by a clean lace curtain" in what appeared to be a "warm-looking room" (110–11), the cat has found a new home. The narrator hopes that Holly has, too. Although the narrator expresses an uncertainty about Holly, he seems secure in his role as writer, maturing because of the story that she has given to him, the narrative of her own searching and wandering. Jed Tewksbury ends his story with more uncertainty. He has written to Dauphine, hoping to reconcile and to build a relationship with their son, Ephraim, but Jed remains unable to come to terms with his past in Dugton. Although he is compelled to fall on his parents' grave and physically reach out to them, he doesn't follow through. Warren describes Jed's "fantasy" of showing his son "all the spots that [he] had dreamed of pointing out to him" (341), yet that fantasy leaves readers with a feeling that Jed is a "perpetual wanderer." Stingo, on the other hand, represents a more successful journeying. Richard Rubenstein points out that within the first several pages of Styron's *Sophie's Choice*, Stingo asks the reader to "Call me Stingo," a line that reverberates with allusions to Ishmael's opening, "Call me Ishmael," in Melville's *Moby Dick* (432–33). Stingo, like Ishmael, is a "survivor-narrator," one who says that he has awoken to a new morning, "excellent and fair," after "being split in twain by monstrous mechanisms, drowned in a whirling vortex of mud, being immured in stone, and most fearsomely, buried alive" (515). He has made the decision never to return to the South again.

Reflecting a parallel narrative of wandering and placelessness, Jewish characters appear in Styron and Warren's novels. Styron's Stingo spends long passages in *Sophie's Choice* equating Jews with Southerners, describing himself as in part drawn to Brooklyn because of "an unconscious urge to be among Jews," for after all, "the Jew has found considerable fellowship among white Southerners because Southerners have possessed another, darker sacrificial lamb" (39). In *Two Covenants: Representations of Southern Jewishness*, Eliza McGraw describes the movement connected with the Wandering Jew as especially pertinent in both Warren's fiction and his personal biography. Portraying himself as a "southerner who shares the Jewish ability to internalize identity even while wandering" (McGraw 80), Warren explicitly states in his book *Segregation* that because he has gone through the experience of leaving the South, he knows "the relief, the expanding vistas" that it can bring. The relief, he says, is "relief from responsibility" (51). "Motion can save a beloved home," according to McGraw, "rendering it a valuable memory rather than an onerous one" (79).

Wolfe, on the other hand, more specifically draws his wanderer as an American figure, reclaiming an American narrative of wandering for the Southerner. Wolfe's Eugene Gant has made the journey from Altamont to "the tower-masted island of Manhattan," a journey that is not particularly long, but one through which "one may live a life, share instantly in 10,000,000 other ones, and see pass before his eyes the infinite panorama of shifting images that make a nation's history" (25). Wolfe ties this journey to Americans, a people he describes as "seeking always on this earth" (90). He claims that as Americans, "We walk the streets, we walk the streets forever, we walk the streets of life alone" (155). In contrast to the ex-patriot writers who fled eastward, back to the European roots of Western culture and literature, Wolfe turns the movement on itself, stating that although the "great" ships, the engineering marvels that were built not long after World War I, were designed and built by Europeans, "without America [those ships] have no meaning." Wolfe places greater worth on the journey itself that has given those ships significance: "These ships are alive with the supreme ecstasy of the modern world, which is the voyage to America. There is no other experience that is remotely comparable to it, in its sense of joy, its exultancy, its drunken and magnificent hope" (906). Such journeying is also patterned in the flow of American rivers, which, as Wolfe writes, run "deep as the tides of time and memory" (510).

Essentially, then, what binds Eugene Gant and the other wanderers discussed in this chapter is their journey to redefine themselves, a journey outward from the South that is propelled not only by society, but also by the individual's desire to lay claim to the borderlands and to reclaim self. In a very real sense, they become powerful shapers of their own lives and in most cases at least dabble in reclaiming an Americanness that might have been pushed aside by a Southern upbringing. Although Thomas Wolfe lamented in a letter to his mother that "you can't go home again. . . . I found that out through exile, through storm and stress, perplexity and dark confusion," and "for a long time I grieved" (Nowell 707), the tendency among Wolfe's male characters is to define the migratory journey as one where they are able to make their own choices to stay in the borderlands and not pass on to the other side. Warren's Jed, Styron's Stingo, and Capote's narrator share similar experiences as border crossers. Although they can't go home again and in fact, never become fully adjusted to the new place, the border country offers more possibility, and in that border country, they find potential for a new definition of self, a model of Southern manhood that holds on to and is still haunted by the past, and the promise of a new voice as a writer.

Such a journey, however, is dramatically different when the threshold a Southern male must cross is one conflicted by racism. If Eugene, Stingo, Jed, and Capote's unnamed narrator all left the South because of their own choice, the unnamed narrator in Ralph Ellison's *Invisible Man* (1952) is still controlled by the system of racism in the South and in the nation at large. Ellison's narrator is pushed out of the Southern black college he desperately wants to attend as punishment for letting a white patron of the college, Mr. Norton, talk with Jim Trueblood, a man who has disgraced the black community. Jim is one of "the black-belt people, the 'peasants'" who "did everything it seemed to pull [the rest of the black community] down." He makes "crude, high, plaintively animal sounds" (47), and his daughter is pregnant with Jim's child. Although Mr. Norton insists that the narrator stop the car that the narrator is using to chauffeur Mr. Norton, Dr. Bledsoe, the president of the college and a man who was "the example of everything" the narrator wants to be (101), sends the Invisible Man to New York City to work for the summer. He expects to return South to his college, but Dr. Bledsoe cuts him off with letters to prospective employers that keep him from returning. The Invisible Man's departure from the South is not on his own terms—but on someone else's. After he leaves Dr. Bledsoe's office, he feels as if he has been through "almost a total disembowelment" (146), although he does not recognize until he reaches the North how Dr. Bledsoe has manipulated his reference letters.

Perhaps there is no more memorable confrontation with the "Other"—a confrontation largely shaped by race—than Ellison's description of his narrator's first New York City subway ride after he arrives in the North. Crammed into a car "so crowded that everyone seemed to stand with his head back and his eyes bulging, like chickens frozen at the sound of danger" (157–58), the Invisible Man says that as the door to the car shut, he was thrown against a smiling woman dressed in black who just shook her head as he "stared with horror at a large mole that arose out of the oily whiteness of her skin like a black mountain sweeping out of a rainwet plain" (158). He is terrified by the closeness of her body—a certain reference to the dangers of lynching that he would have known in the South—but no one around him seems at all distressed, even though he is close enough to her that he could touch his lips to hers. All he wants to do is raise up his arms and show her that he had not meant to get so close to her. He feels the train heading downhill to its next stop, "feeling like something regurgitated from the belly of a frantic whale" when the train "lunge[s] to a stop that shot [him] out upon a platform" (158). For Ellison, the train becomes a symbol of spiraling change—out of control and off the tracks.

The Invisible Man's arrival in the city reflects both the promise that the North represented for him and the clouded vision he had of the possibilities he could achieve there. His first night in the Men's House, he turns to the book of Genesis in a Gideon Bible that he finds in his room. The next day, as he looks around the city, he sees the Statue of Liberty at a distance, "her torch almost lost in the fog" (165). His first job in the North is at a paint factory, notably called Liberty Paints, where he mixes Optic White, "the purest white that can be found" (202). He's sent to a new assignment after he mixes a batch of the Optic White paint intended for a national monument that ends up with a gray tinge—a symbol of the prejudices and racism that taint American democracy and nationhood. The Invisible Man lives at the Men's House in

Harlem until an explosion in the boiler room of the paint factory leaves him in the factory hospital where he is subjected to electric shock treatments. The medical personnel discuss castrating him, but decide against it and continue with the shock treatments that are interspersed with racist comments. Trying to wipe clean his brain of any racial memory, they release him, telling him that "you're cured" (246) after a long series of questions, including "Who . . . are . . . you?" and "What is your mother's name?" (240). "I tried to remember how I'd gotten here, but nothing came. My mind was blank, as though I had just begun to live" (233). Trying to hold on to who he is, trying to reclaim at least part of himself, he finds himself coming out of the subway in Harlem, with his head aching and "with wild, infant's eyes" (251). A black woman named Mary Rambo finds the Invisible Man and takes him to her home where she gives him a bed to sleep in and cares for him as a mother might do. When he returns to the Men's House, he finds that he has been barred from the building because he has "lost his prospects and pride" (257), so he returns to Mary's to rent a room. Reminding him continually that "something was expected of me, some act of leadership, some newsworthy achievement," the Invisible Man says that he didn't think of Mary as a friend, but as "something more—a force, a stable, familiar force like something out of my past which kept me from whirling off into some unknown which I dared not face" (258).

Back when the Invisible Man first arrived in New York and began his search for work, he decided he should shed that past, his Southernness. He must "slough off [his] southern ways of speech" and have "one way of speaking in the North and another in the South. Give them what they wanted down South, that was the way" (164). For much of the book, the Invisible Man believes he must put on the appearance of someone he is not. After ordering at a diner in New York where the counterman asks if he wants the special—a plate of typically Southern foods including grits and biscuits—the Invisible Man seems exasperated when he asks, "Could everyone see that I was southern?" He notes, soon after, that he had better be careful not to speak like a "northern Negro" when he returns to his Southern college (178). Perhaps the first point in the novel where he at least begins to recognize and understand the implications of this divided self is after he has moved in with Mary and he is wandering the streets of the city and comes across an old man who is selling baked yams. The smell of the baked yams immediately brings "a stab of swift nostalgia"; he is "struck by a shot, deeply inhaling, remembering, [his] mind surging back, back." At home in the South he had eaten yams hot out of the fireplace or cold in his school lunches, and he remembers them, eating them behind the pages of a large book, hiding the yam from his teacher as he and the other students "munched them secretly, squeezing the sweet pulp from the soft peel" (262). Now he feels an "intense feeling of freedom" as he walks down the street, eating the yam in full view of everyone. Wishing someone from back home could see him, the Invisible Man feels he "no longer had to worry about who saw me or about what was proper" (264). At once he seems aware of the divisions within himself and willing and able to accept that he is situated in the spaces in between. In effect, this space frees him from his past because he recognizes that past as part of the person that he is.

Similar to other Southern border crossers, the Invisible Man "tries out" different fathers in this journey across the border of the South and into the city beyond. Looking back as he tells his story, the Invisible Man says that "All my life I had been looking for something, and everywhere I turned someone tried to tell me what it was" (15). His grandfather, who had been a slave, "an odd old guy" that the narrator is told that he takes after, was the one that the Invisible Man claims "caused the trouble" (16). On his deathbed, he called up the Invisible Man's father and told him, "Son, after I'm gone I want you to keep up the good fight. . . . Live with your head in the lion's mouth. I want you to overcome 'em with yeses, undermine 'em with grins, agree 'em to death and destruction, let 'em swoller you till they vomit or bust wide open" (16). The grandfather closes with "Learn it to the younguns" and then dies, leaving the family perplexed and secretive because Grandfather was a "quiet old man." The narrator says that what left him confused was that what left him praised by "the most lily-white men of the town" was defined by his grandfather as "*treachery*" (16–17).

Other potential father-figures or guides appear in *Invisible Man*, including Dr. Bledsoe, who is superintendent of the college the Invisible Man attends, a man he describes as "of more importance in the world than most Southern white men. They could laugh at him but they couldn't ignore him" (101). But Dr. Bledsoe ultimately sells him out, writing in his reference letter to Mr. Emerson, "Please hope him to death, and keep him running" (194). Farah Jasmine Griffin argues that throughout Ellison's novel, the Invisible Man rejects safe spaces that are offered to him by figures who represent connections to his past: in the South, the grandfather and the veteran, and in the North, Mary, Petie Wheatstraw, and Brother Tarp (130). Instead of recognizing the value of the "ancestral figures" he encounters, the Invisible Man is guided by Bledsoe and Brother Jack (130). Although Dr. Bledsoe puts up a façade that the Invisible Man can't recognize as such until after he heads north and has some distance between himself and the South, Mary offers the Invisible Man a safe space. Griffin notes that the narrator believes any part of the South he retains "inhibits his personal growth and development," while Ellison unmistakably judges the Invisible Man's attempt to push himself away from his past as proof of his overconfidence and lack of awareness (124). Ellison's wanderer ultimately lands in a basement room where he lives and writes, lighting the underground space with 1,369 light bulbs powered with electricity he has siphoned off illegally from the electric company. Griffin concludes that although the Invisible Man is farthest from the ancestors in his underground room, he is, in fact, most psychologically connected to them while he is in that space (134).

This threshold from boyhood to manhood that the Invisible Man passes across does not liberate and empower in the same way that it does for the white Southern male who crosses. This basement room might offer a safe space—what is, in fact, one aspect of a liminal space between South and North—where the Invisible Man may write his story and reflect on his experiences as a Southern man coming into adulthood in the North. But this space also keeps him unnamed and closeted away, still not able to call himself by name and still marginalized by American society. Even though he can look to the strength of the ancestors, the act of retelling his story has tormented him in ways that white male narrators don't encounter. Ellison's narrator describes the deep anguish of writing down his story, asking, "why do I write, torturing myself to put it down? . . . The very act of trying to put it all down has confused me and negated some of the anger and some of the bitterness" (579). Calling himself an "exile" (170), he sees Harlem as "not a city of realities, but of dreams" (159). Explaining at the end of the novel that he has "sometimes been overcome with a passion to return into that 'heart of darkness' across the Mason-Dixon line," he says that he then reminds himself that "the true darkness lives within [his] own mind, and the idea loses itself in the gloom" (579).

Ultimately, however, there is hopefulness in the Invisible Man's "hibernation" (580). While his invisibility is often read as a way to control him and to push him into conformity, his time in this basement room can also be read as empowering. Shelly Jarenski explains that the Invisible Man "comes to embrace that invisibility and claim it as a site of power." Emphasizing the importance of looking at the novel through the lens of intertextuality, Jarenski claims that the "'invisibility as disempowerment' argument overlooks the fact that matrices of power are rooted in the visibility of bodies rather than in the erasure of agency that 'invisibility' implies." Pointing to the publication of the novel during the early civil rights movement when "a crossover music industry fused with the emergence of television," Jarenski notes that the representation of African Americans was controlled by whites who decided when black bodies should be visible—"when they performed the role of 'other' for white culture." According to Jarenski, "invisibility allows Ellison to create a black male subjectivity that is fully outside of visually constructed white, hetero-male hegemony" (85). And in claiming that space in the basement, the Invisible Man is ultimately able to say at the end of the novel that his "hibernation is over. I must shake off the old skin and come up for breath. . . . I'm shaking off the old skin and I'll leave it here in the hole. I'm coming out, no less invisible without it, but coming out nevertheless" (580–81). He is able to make the decision to leave, recognizing that he has "overstayed" his "hibernation," knowing "there's a possibility that even an invisible man has a socially responsible role to play" (581).

Yet even as the Invisible Man leaves his basement room and as Richard Wright ends his autobiographical novel *Black Boy* (1945) resolute in using his writing as a way to reach the world and determined to "wait for an echo," the liminal space between South and North—in effect, the threshold into the freedoms of American democracy—remains a space tainted by the prejudices that still linger in the nation as a whole. The case of African American Henry Louis Gates, born in West Virginia and now a Harvard professor, brought that to our attention when he was arrested for trying to enter the doorway of his own home. In 2001, literary scholar Houston Baker wrote of "Battling the Ghouls of a Southern Boyhood," the living nightmare of the Blue Man, who was "stealthy, yet ferocious, fanged and vicious in pursuit of young black men," "a pure product of black Southern boyhood rumor, a sinister function in a continuous narrative that was always enhancing itself." Even though Baker's parents reassured him that the ghoul did not exist, he could not shake the fear of this narrative, "a grab bag containing snatches of colorful adult conversation, grim details of an Illinois black teenager mutilated and killed in Money, Miss., flashes from the Negro newspaper (the Louisville Defender) about police beatings and tavern brawls in black communities."

In a similar fashion, Capote's narrator in *Breakfast at Tiffany's* remains unnamed, invisible, and veiled just as Ellison's Invisible Man is because he, too, shares some of these complications—not because of race, but because he is marginalized by society because of his sexuality as a gay man. Essentially, then, these crossings experienced by male characters and male writers are as much about the entering on the other side as they are about the leaving. The threshold is, in actuality, a doorway, with passage through still controlled by societal prejudices. Even a man who is said to have all the rights and privileges to pass through is still controlled by societal views on race, class, and sexual orientation. Although departure from the South leaves the Southerner dealing with the complications of memory and identity, perhaps the greater struggle is crossing into the other side, dealing with not only their marginalization but what it means to be marginalized in America.

CHAPTER 4

Southern Womanhood and "The High Cost of Living and Dying in Dixie"

Claiming her own more contemporary reasons for departing the South while also recognizing the legacy the Grimké sisters left behind for women like her, Shirley Abbott frames her 1983 essay "Why Southern Women Leave Home" in *Womenfolks* with the story of Angelina and Sarah, two sisters born in Charleston, South Carolina, who were able to "shed the ladylike ethic" to become important figures in the abolitionist and early women's rights movements *because* they left the South. Abbott seems fascinated by the lives of these two women who were raised in the privileged home of their father, a lawyer and judge who served on the supreme court of South Carolina and who was a wealthy slaveholder. The sisters grew up among what Sarah described as the "butterflies of the fashionable world," carefully tended to be Southern belles, whose primary goal in life was expected to be marriage. Twelve years apart in age in a family of 14 children, the sisters were incredibly close, with Sarah assuming a mothering role to Angelina. Sarah was determined to educate herself, but their father refused to allow his daughters to use his library or to study Latin or the law. As devote Christians, the girls grew to abhor slavery as they saw firsthand the treatment of slaves in both their parents' home and in the homes of others in their Charleston community. They heard the cries of slaves after they had been beaten, saw families broken apart when their father's slaves were sold, and knew of the sexual abuse of slave women by white men. Determined to speak out against slavery, but unable to do so in the South, Sarah, who had become a Quaker, made the decision in 1821 to leave Charleston for Philadelphia. Angelina followed her north in 1829. Joining the Female Anti-slavery Society, the two sisters began traveling throughout New England, lecturing in support of the abolitionist movement. Seeking to effect change and driven by their "saintly motives," according to Abbott, the Grimké sisters saw a clear relationship between the causes of abolitionism and feminism. Angelina once wrote, "Woman ought to feel a peculiar sympathy in the colored man's wrong, for, like him, she has been accused of mental inferiority, and denied the privileges of a liberal education" (Lerner 114). Although the women's convention in Seneca Falls, New York, would not be held until the following decade in 1848, the Grimké sisters, who found their voices outside of the South, were speaking against the oppression of women even earlier, in the 1830s.

In effect, what Abbott gives credence to as she relates the story of the sisters is a shared legacy for many Southern women of movement and flight. Noting that the sisters were "probably not the first women to flee the Southland," Abbott emphasizes that "they were the first to leave any coherent record of their reasons" (193). "The journey northward set them free," Abbott proclaims (198). Although she points out that her own experiences influenced her decision to leave the South, nevertheless, like the Grimké sisters, Abbott roots her reasons in feeling disenchanted with the South, unable to bring about change from within the South, and unable to live her life as she had hoped. She very specifically identifies not only her kinship with the Grimkés but also with Willie Morris and William Styron. Referring to Morris, who made the decision to leave as he stood naked after having been abandoned by his fraternity brothers in a hazing incident, and William Styron's "émigré" in *Sophie's Choice* (180), Abbott explains that after all, the South's biggest "export" has always been people (190). At first believing that she was on her own in her desire to depart from the South and in leaving, Abbott came to discover that she was actually a part of what she calls "a vast northward exodus" (189). Seeing in herself some of the same thoughts and feelings that Bessie Smith expressed as she sang, "I ain't good-lookin', and I doan dress fine, but I'm a travelin' woman with a travelin' mind," Abbott explains that Smith's words point to an image of womanhood that Abbott felt she herself could not fulfill and the desires for a freedom "with portents both spiritual and sexual." Describing the northward exodus as having "special meanings for women," Abbott says that "Every year—and long before Bessie—the South has produced its small quota of travelin' women who dread the high cost of living and dying in Dixie and find they have to depart" (189–90).

Because Southern cultural traditions and practices aligned and to a large degree still align women in a gender framework that traps them in identities intended to perpetuate racism and sexism, crossing the border can also signify freedom from that framework. Crossing a border can signal an opportunity for a woman to remake herself in much the same way as her male counterpart, but as the narratives covered in this chapter suggest, Southern women face challenges as they negotiate the border that are clearly linked to highly prescribed images of what black and white Southern women are expected to be. Even though Victor Turner describes the border crosser—the initiate into a new space—as having nothing, not even gender, gender and race are always carried, and especially in a Southern context. And while Abbott represents herself as one of Bessie Smith's "travelin' women," the gendered borders and borderlands navigated by women like Smith and Abbott were obviously vastly different because of race and racism in the South. While the overt border consciousness of Southern society figured (and still figures) in explicit male/female dichotomies and historically deep-riven boundaries between races and classes, the intersectionality of race and gender created a very different life experience for black women than it did for white ones.

Borders that outline nations and communities are gendered. Historically and across cultures, women have stood as "the 'inviolate centre' (of the nation, the region, the community, the family) and as 'symbolic border guards,' upholding and reaffirming the demarcation between that which they represent and the 'other.'" Woman's "duty" is literally "to embody the line" that identifies difference for the nation or community and sets it off from others, and Woman represents what needs saving when outside aggressors threaten (Abrams and Hunt 193). While such a role generally suggests passivity, the effects of this symbolic identifying, however, have very real and tragic effects when women's bodies literally become the site of warfare. The rape of women by soldiers from conquering armies, for example, has been used not only as a tool to denigrate and subjugate women, but also to symbolically conquer and assert power over a less powerful nation or community. Woman's embodiment of the line has also been used as a strategic tool to stop the flow of migrants and refugees across borders of nations and regions. Nations make claims that the movements of people across borders endanger women, in particular, as recent language used to describe Mexicans as "rapists" and fear of a "migrant rape crisis" in Europe testifies. Women's bodies have literally been secured as tools to keep people out.

In the South, woman's "duty to embody the line" divides along the lines of race. White women in the South because of their race came to represent the Southern "nation" itself, the motherland "Dixie" to protect. White womanhood was placed upon a pedestal as something to be venerated, something that needed to be fought for and safeguarded. Yet while the antebellum Southern slave system elevated the white plantation mistress as a marker of Southern nationhood, African American women's bodies were viewed as ones that could be transgressed, as possessions that marked white power over black. Within this plantation mythology, black womanhood came to be represented in the figure of the mammy and then in the postbellum and twentieth-century Souths as the devoted black female domestic worker who unselfishly cared for white children at the expense of her own. The image was solidified in books and films like Margaret Mitchell's *Gone with the Wind*, which identified the mammy figure in Southern mythmaking as a stalwart upholder of tradition:

> Her [Mammy's] eyes lighted up at the sight of Scarlett, her white teeth gleamed as she set down the buckets, and Scarlett ran to her, laying her head on the broad, sagging breasts which had held so many heads, black and white. Here was something of stability, thought Scarlett, something of the old life that was unchanging. (575)

It was this image of womanhood that came to represent the African American woman's "duty to embody the line"—what whites pledged to fight for as well because it allowed whites to keep African Americans "in their place."

Navigating the border, passing on across thus suggests very different complications about the nature of women's crossings than it does for men. What happens if the "symbolic border guard" leaves her post? What happens if women are the border crossers? Are women's bodies figuratively crossed in the process? Can a woman claim difference from the place she left behind, show she is not complicit with the values of the place from which she came? Or what if she desires like Zora Neale Hurston to "claim the horizon"? What happens when the Southern woman leaves the home place? Or, more drastically, leaves the South? What happens when the woman wants to cross on her own? Are African American women freer to cross? Like women's physical bodies that can help men mark a place as their own, the borderland thus becomes a contested site, one that some—especially the white, heterosexual Southern men described in the last chapter—can claim with ease, but one that others find difficult to navigate because of the limitations and continued obstructions that they encounter there. Likewise, there are also societal expectations of how both genders should negotiate the border and thus how Southern women should act "on the other side." Although most of the writers covered in this chapter reached their prominence and popularity as writers in the early half of the twentieth century, the border crossings they examine in their work are framed by societal expectations that still impact and scaffold the lives of girls and women across the United States but even more intensely in the South. Any study of Southern women's border crossings also entails recognizing the tightly bound relationships among gender, race, and class, that is, looking through the lens of intersectionality. And although I am hesitant to label all the writers included in this chapter as "feminists," I would define their responses to and embracing of borders as "feminist practice," what Glenda Tide Bonifacio describes in *Feminism and Migration* as "the 'doing' in the daily lives of (im)migrant women that questions, alters, compromises, or resists commonly accepted normative practices" (6). Here in my study of border crossing narratives I would use not the specific phrase "(im)migrant women," but instead identify them as women who make physical passages from one place to another. For Southern women, border crossing has and continues to signal such questionings, and picking up the pen (or sitting down in front of the keyboard) to write about the experience validates the significance of the passage and points to the contesting identities that women face.

Abbott's narrative, for example, carries patterns shared by many other Southern narratives of departure, but it shows more specifically the weight of gender that Southern women carry with them beyond the borders of the South. Only nine years old when she left the South for the first time, Abbott moved with her family from Arkansas to San Diego where her father took a job during World War II as a machinist on a navy dry dock. Describing San Diego as an "easy port city of no discernible seasons or traditions, a tepid harbor accustomed to the ways of soldiers and sailors and the rootless and the drifting," Abbott explains that her family "wore the mark of [their] origins too clearly," and Californians were "just ordinary folks hating Southerners for the sport of it, back in the days before anybody cared what whites were doing to blacks." The family spent weeks looking for a place to live because landladies would not rent to them. They were called "Arkies, Okies, clay eaters, hicks, tramps," and "cracker folks." At school, Abbott was checked for head lice by the principal and a boy asked if she had hookworm and if the shoes she was wearing were her first pair, despite the fact that she was dressed neatly with ribbons in her hair and wore clothing that was meticulously ironed. When she was finally invited over to another girl's house to play, the girl's mother was appalled to find out that her daughter had let Abbott—that "little hillbilly"— use their bathroom. Overhearing her friend's conversation with her mother, Abbott realized she had soiled the guest towels left out in the bathroom and ran out of the house without saying good-bye. Abbott adds, however, that "any self-respecting hillbilly would have gone in the kitchen and beat the lady up" (181). Experiences like her mother's bouts with hives and her own nightmares sent Abbott's family back to Arkansas. Nevertheless, Abbott explains, moving was "not a wholly destructive experience." She learned from seeing an outside perspective that "the South was alien, and you paid a price for coming from it." Finally concluding that "it costs something to be what you are," and "being a hillbilly was better than having no identifiable origins at all," she "began mainlining Margaret Mitchell," ordered *The Clansman*, and read "partisan stuff, local colorists by the peck." She became "a blind Southern chauvinist beyond the wildest hopes of [her] father" (181–82).

In Abbott's case, she ultimately says that "the glorious Southland was not what I had taken it to be." She was not what she had believed herself to be either. Struggling through her attempts to understand what she was seeing in the South around her, she was particularly troubled by the injustices against persons because of their color. One day as she watched a marching band on the street of her hometown, she saw that the African Americans in the band did not have uniforms and some of them did not have instruments. Although she had been carefully studying the work of Mitchell and Dixon, she tells the reader, "Right there on the sidewalk my regional identity started to unravel.... I could see I wasn't turning out right. Or else the South wasn't turning out right. I began desperately trying to figure out which. The conclusion I finally reached—ambiguous as it was—drove me out of my homeland forever" (183). An equally important reason Abbott claims for leaving the South is because of the image of the Southern woman that she wanted to escape. Struggling to find what she calls "a place for myself in Southern life," Abbott tells of being encouraged to pursue a career in teaching because it was "the perfect career for a wife" who would want to "help her husband out" and spend her time at home when her children were there (187). In her own family, she recognized, too, that she did not want to follow the traditional route of a woman: marrying and having children. She was so determined to avoid following this pattern that, despite her feelings for the women in her family—women she describes as loving "in my body and bones"—she decided she needed to "seek my people in another country." That was "the only solution." Such a drastic turn was necessary because she saw herself living a life of "desolate boredom, more frightening than the Sahara, illimitable as the Empty Quarter of Arabia." After finishing her last final exam at school—completing her responsibilities—and telling the women in her family that she did not intend to "be next in line to supply an heiress for this society and a back yard for it to meet in" (189), she bought a round-trip ticket to New York, where she cashed in the return ticket as a concrete symbol that she was not planning to return.

Living in the North was unusual for a white Southerner during the 1950s. When people at parties heard her accent, they were always quick to assume. One comment she claims she finally got used to people saying was "My God, I never met anybody from Arkansas before in my life." At first the attention was a novelty to her, but she came to find that New Yorkers jumped to the conclusion that all Southerners were "lynch-mob veterans" (208). She found herself automatically responding with her "little loyalty oath": "no, I had never been to a cross burning, and yes, my sentiments toward black people were entirely correct." Her vision of the North as a place of freedoms for all races was also corrected as she quickly noticed that the publishing house where she worked and where everyone supported civil rights did not employ any African Americans. When she visited an exhibition of photos of Harlem at the Metropolitan Museum of Art, she found herself among white people who were eager to see what Harlem looked like—not in person, but through the photos. Even though they were New Yorkers, they had never been there. Because Abbott was so determined to stay in and become part of a place where being single and educated were "not crippling disqualifications for a woman," she tried to hide her Southernness (209). While Californians had believed she and her family were "diseased," New Yorkers thought of Southerners as "stupid." She tried to recreate herself, to represent herself as disconnected from that place, as she intentionally lost her Southern accent. Trying to sound like a Vassar graduate, she hoped no one would ever discover her deception.

Although Abbott identifies herself as one of a long line of Southerners who left the South, the representation of that departure did not play a substantial role in writings by Southern women until the early twentieth century. If the Grimké sisters were "the first to leave any coherent record of their reasons" for leaving the South, other Southern women didn't pick up that theme until much later. The early twentieth century saw Southern women writers experimenting with the narrative of women leaving the South in order to find individual freedoms and to make their own choices—a narrative the complete opposite of the nineteenth century that paired Southerners with Northerners who moved to the South and were swayed over by pro-slavery arguments. In *Life and Gabriella* (1916), for example, Ellen Glasgow—essentially attempting to redefine Southern womanhood—creates a central character for her novel who is Southern by birth and upbringing, but who finds freedom in both occupation and marriage in the North. Seeing the difficulties of marriage through the experiences of her sister who is separated from her husband, Gabriella nevertheless finds herself in an unsuccessful marriage to George Fowler, who is self-centered, a drunk, and a womanizer. George is the one who actually takes her North, but it is also in the North that she is able to divorce him. Supporting herself as a milliner, she ultimately becomes a successful businesswoman and falls in love with a man from the West, whom she plans to marry. As Glasgow "voices her revolt against the old ideal of chivalry," according to one early reviewer (Reely 176), Gabriella has the "will to grow, to strive and to conquer" and moves beyond those "empty rules of the past" (527). In a similar vein and published within just a few years of *Life and Gabriella*, Mary Johnston's feminist novel *Hagar* (1913) focuses on a central female character who leaves the South and falls in love with a non-Southerner in large part as a way to escape her own Southern past. Both Johnston and Glasgow notably had strong ties to the suffragist movement.

In the case of African American writers such as Zora Neale Hurston, the empowerment that might come in encapsulating and retelling stories of movement is also situated in an institutionalized framework of racism. Crossing the boundary between the home place and the world beyond the South is particularly significant for Hurston in her autobiographical writing

Dust Tracks on the Road (1942), a text in which she seems fascinated and drawn to crossings. Focusing on the frontier and settlement of Florida as she opens her book, she tells the story of this "dark and bloody ground," her birthplace and the setting for years of unrest. Native Americans had fled into the "wilds of Florida" to escape being forcibly removed westward on the Trail of Tears and lived there until whites decided that there was something there that they wanted. The beauty of Lake Maitland—Hurston's home region in Florida—soon began to draw settlers from New York State and the Midwest. Railroad lines were laid and roads were paved. Maitland became "a center of wealth and fashion," Florida boomed, and settlers—black and white—rushed in. Hurston says that African Americans were drawn from the cotton fields of Georgia and west Florida for the promises that the boom held (or at least they hoped): "No more back-bending over rows of cotton; no more fear of the fury of the Reconstruction. Good pay, sympathetic White folks and cheap land, soft to the touch of the plow" (5). When Eatonville was incorporated in 1886, the town made history on the "raw, bustling frontier" as an experiment in self-government for African Americans (6). Hurston is also taken by the story of Cudjo Lewis, who was enslaved in Africa and among the last group of slaves transported to the United States. When she met him, it had been 75 years since he had been taken from his homeland, but Hurston explains that "he still had that tragic sense of loss. That yearning for blood and cultural ties. That sense of mutilation." Understandably, she adds, "It gave me something to feel about" (168). The title of *Dust Tracks* reflects as well the journeying aspect that it takes as its focus. While Hurston notes in the text itself her humble hope that those "who play the zig-zag lightning of power over the world [will] think kindly of those who walk in the dust" (232), the tracks imprinted in the dust also signify the impressions, the physical signs of movement.

Early in the autobiography, Hurston writes about her childhood wish to reach the "horizon" (27) and of seeing herself "astride of a fine horse," "riding off to look at the belly-band of the world" (28). When one Christmas, Hurston's father asked his children what they wanted Santa Claus to bring them, Zora says that "a beautiful vision came before me." "Two things could work together," she decided. "My Christmas present could take me to the end of the world" (28–29). Attaching her dreams to a literal horse, she was crushed when her father told her that she could not have a riding horse because she "ain't white." Hurston adds in a note that the "Negro saying" meant "Don't be too ambitious. You are a Negro and they are not meant to have but so much." Her father describes her as "always trying to wear de big hat!" and different from the rest of the family. She received a doll. So instead of riding out into the world, Hurston explains that she "was driven inward" (30). That desire to ride out into the world, however, still remained. Will Brantley describes Hurston as creating an image of herself as a "wanderer," pointing to her rejection of her father's opinion that she should know her place in society. Instead, as Hurston says, she would "wander off in the woods all alone, following some inside urge to go places." Referring specifically to a story Hurston relates from her childhood about a sow, Brantley notes that Hurston identified an "angry sow" with first encouraging her to "get off her feet and go." Hurston's actions so upset her mother that she failed to recognize her husband's own wandering personality in his daughter, thinking instead that some sort of adversary had "sprinkled 'travel dust' around the door" when Zora was born (Brantley 195).

Although Hurston's father associates his daughter's inability to ride a horse with race, Hurston herself clearly links the roadblocks to riding out into the world with gender. She describes herself as a girl who was able to "take a good pummeling without running home to tell." Although she wanted to play with boys, her family believed that was "unlady-like." "No good could come of the thing," she was told, "no matter how young you were." Instead, she was expected to find satisfaction in sitting still and playing with her dolls (30). Hurston, similar to her character Janie in *Their Eyes Were Watching God*, would sit on the top of the gatepost, watching "the world go by" (33). As Janie grows into womanhood and dreams of a love relationship, she stands behind the front gate as her grandmother has told her to do, waiting for love to come to her. "Looking, waiting, breathing short with impatience," she "wait[s] for the world to be made" for her by the man—or boy—who comes up the road to her (11). Janie's grandmother admonishes her when Janie leans across the gate for her first kiss.

Looking at the structure of Hurston's *Dust Tracks*, Will Brantley points to a series of visions represented in the memoir that "punctuate [Hurston's] belief that she is someone extraordinary, and provide a mythic, larger-than-life structure for her wanderings—for her quest" (194). Such a framework—traditionally assigned to the white man figuratively set upon the riding horse—defines her journey as a challenge to the status quo, in effect, an act of heresy. Hurston describes herself as starting to have visions when she is "not more than seven" (41), visions "just disconnected scene after scene with blank spaces in between." She claims that she "knew that they were all true, a preview of things to come" (41):

I knew that I would be an orphan and homeless. I knew that while I was still helpless, that I would have to wander cold and friendless until I had served my time. I would stand beside a dark pool of water and see a huge fish move slowly away at a time when I would be somehow in the depth of despair. I would hurry to catch a train, with doubts and fears driving me and seek solace in a place and fail to find it when I arrived, then cross many tracks to board the train again. I knew that a house, a shot-gun built house that needed a new coat of white paint, held torture for me, but I must go. I saw deep love betrayed, but I must feel and know it. There was no turning back. And last of all, I would come to a big house. Two women waited there for me. I could not see their faces, but I knew one to be young and one to be old. One of them was arranging some queer-shaped flowers such as I had never seen. When I had come to these women, then I would be at the end of my pilgrimage, but not the end of my life. Then I would know peace and love and what goes with those things, and not before. (42)

Reflecting that same wandering spirit that I discussed in the previous chapter on Southern men, many of the visions described in this passage suggest displacement, loneliness, confusion, the heart-wrenching failure of family and relationships. Driven from her home in large part because of the death of her mother and her fights with her stepmother after her father remarries, the sense of disconnection Hurston experiences is accentuated by the time she spends away at school and the abandonment she feels when her father suggests that the school adopt her. She also seems continually torn between her desire to learn and her evolving hopes to be a teacher and the types of jobs she is pushed into in order to provide for herself. Several times she works in homes, including that of her brother, as a domestic servant, caring for children, helping in the house, but the tension between the roles connected to the domestic are in sharp conflict with her own desires for education and enlightenment. Her intense desire for a home leaves her struggling between accepting the female role of domestic and leaving that role behind.

What Hurston describes as the "end of [her] pilgrimage" comes with a job working as a lady's maid for Miss M——, who is a singer in a traveling theatre group, a job Hurston explains actually gave her "an approach to racial understanding" (118), perhaps in part because the job gave her the ability to move more freely in the same ways as Bessie Smith, who is discussed in chapter 5 of this book. At once drawn to the excitement of the stage, to "the sounds, the smells, the back-stage jumble of things" (102), Hurston says that at first she is treated as "a new play-pretty" (104) in large part because of the novelty of her Southern accent, and she is tirelessly teased and stuffed with ice cream sodas and Coke. Ultimately, she learns through such "a communal life" (117) she describes as represented by "all branches of Anglo-Saxon, Irish, three Jews and one Negro" that gave her a racial perspective she explains left her no longer race conscious. "I took a firm grip on the only weapon I had—hope, and set my feet. Maybe everything would be all right from now on. Maybe. Well, I put on my shoes and I started" (119). Finally tired of "nickeling and dimering along," Hurston decides to attend night high school in Baltimore after Miss M——marries and leaves the stage. Describing her high school English teacher as "a pilgrim to the horizon," she says, "He made the way clear" (123) for her to begin her journey in becoming a writer, especially as he read *Kubla Khan* to the class: "Listening to [the poem] for the first time, I saw all that the poet had meant for me to see with him, and infinite cosmic things besides. I was not of the work-a-day world for days after Mr. Holmes's voice had ceased. This was my world, I said to myself, and I shall be in it, and surrounded by it, if it is the last thing I do on God's green dirt-ball" (123). The text—the words of the poem—thus set her free. She continues her wanderings, but this time without the restraints of gender, and this time she heads to New York where she hopes to become a writer.

When Hurston does finally leave the South, her travels make it possible for her to find her identity and to find her vocation. Inspired by teachers at Howard University and concluding that she herself should be an English teacher, Hurston soon turns her studies to anthropology at Columbia University, working under "Papa Franz," Dr. Franz Boas, whom she refers to as "the King of Kings" (140). It's through a fellowship that was arranged through Boas that Hurston returns to the South to begin fieldwork. Her return home not only reconnects her to family members, but also returns her to her work. Not having been able to experience that "warm embrace of kin and kind" since her mother's funeral when they "huddled about the organ all sodden and bewildered, with the walls of our home suddenly blown down," once again, Hurston says, "We could touch each other in the spirit if not in the flesh" (142). Research into her Southern past, collecting folklore and songs, ultimately is what helps her to recognize the power of the language she once heard on the front porches of the South. Although Hurston's Janie can't join in the talk on the porch in *Their Eyes Were Watching God*, Hurston does, in fact, record and join in that talk through her work in folklore. The North offers her the ability to join in a community in which she has been marginalized because of gender and race, and represents education and vocation for Hurston. As for many other writers, New York, in particular, is where she believes she must relocate if she is to join the profession. The South is home and family, but it is in the North, it is through her vocation that she is able to return home, recognize the value of that home, understand her relationship to it, and reestablish her relationship with the South. Crossing the boundary gives her a new perspective, and by crossing that border she is also able to reconnect with her African American past, in large part because of her studies with Boas and because of where her studies take her for her research. Hurston not only aimed to collect and record the African American folk past, but she also wanted "to show what beauty and appeal there was in genuine Negro material, as against the Broadway concept" by creating performances for the stage that she hoped would reach a wide audience in the North (158).

Experiencing the highs and lows of life—the "sharp shadows, high lights, and smudgy inbetweens," Hurston has "been in Sorrow's kitchen and licked out all the pots." At the very heights in her life, she has "stood on a peaky mountain wrappen in rainbows, with a harp and a sword in [her] hands" (*Dust Tracks* 227). Hurston interrogates the border in ways similar to what Alma Jean Billingslea-Brown describes in her book *Crossing Borders through Folklore: African American Women's Fiction and Art*. Focusing on Toni Morrison, Paule Marshall, Faith Ringgold, and Betye Saar, the book offers a framework that can certainly be applied to Hurston as well. The folk aesthetic was for Hurston—as it was for Morrison, Marshall, Ringgold, and Saar—a way to "revise and reverse meanings." Calling it "the boiled down juice of human living," folklore was for Hurston a means to "establish differential identity, resist dominance, and affirm group solidarity," a way to "transgress borders and locate sites of intervention" (2). If *Dust Tracks* is, according to Nellie McKay, Hurston's "statue," then "it celebrates a black woman who wanted us to know that very early in her life she decided to ride to the horizon on the finest black riding horse with the shiniest bridle and saddle she could secure" (Qtd. in Brantley 212). McKay suggests the book represents Hurston's desire to move beyond the regions assigned to her—whether that be spaces assigned because of race, gender, or regional background—to claim "the horizon" on her own terms.

For a woman like Hurston, writing did, quite obviously, become an essential part of gaining control over her own life and asserting the value of her place in the world because through it she could map out her life, assign significance to it, and delineate the fact that boundaries can be crossed and that pathways do lead outward into the world. Describing women as having been "mapped and colonized" because of their gender, Susan L. Roberson claims writing as "itself a location, a site for the construction of further spaces of power and knowledge" (7). It has been well established that writing is recuperative—a way for women to gain control over their lives because they can use it to interpret where they have been and where they are going, yet Roberson's analysis also gives me the opportunity to look at this role of writing in relation to bordering. Pointing out that we all "make maps and plot our lives cartographically," Roberson explains that by creating cognitive maps, we are able to navigate through our lives and through space. A cognitive map holds power because it represents our journeys, because it is "something that I make up to represent the way I see or react to my environment." Because it is a representation, it may not—and most probably is not—factual or absolutely truthful or even the only map that could have been created to represent a particular space. What is ultimately most important is that this map is a self-made way to locate self-identity in a self-crafted framework: "*where* I am and *who* I am." After all, Roberson notes, "'[The] sense of place is essential to any ordering of our lives'" (9). Mapping spaces thus becomes a powerful way for women to recognize their abilities to cross boundaries, to enter new space, to take control of their *own* lives. Although Hurston described herself as having "the map of Dixie on my tongue," that map exists *because* of Hurston's desires and attempts to search outward, across the boundaries of the South.

For Eudora Welty, creating a cognitive map and mapping out spaces plays a role in her autobiographical work *One Writer's Beginnings*, and like Hurston, the trajectory on that map leads her home, but in a significantly different way. Focusing on the evolution of self as a writer, Welty, similar to Hurston, points to a childhood spent on the gatepost, wishing for the time when she might move beyond the limits of home. *"Pear tree by the garden gate, / How much longer must I wait?"* went the line that she says she remembered from one of her nursery books. Clearly, this is not a unique experience of childhood, but it is one with more particular implications for a writer and a persona who are female. Such musings show not only the significance of passing over boundary lines, but also the necessity of moving beyond the home place in order to mature as a person and as a writer.

Welty's *One Writer's Beginnings* is structured in three parts: Listening, Learning to See, and Finding a Voice. Equating the chronology of our lives with the chronology of fiction, Welty explains that our lives may be composed as a sequence of events, but those events find their own order according to the significance that we place on each of them. "The time as we know it subjectively," Welty explains, "is often the chronology that stories and novels follow: it is the continuous thread of revelation" (75). The section of the book entitled "Listening" focuses on experiences in Mississippi growing up, from the Christmas presents such as Tinker Toys, trains, and kites that represented her father's "fondest beliefs—in progress, in the future" and were always gender appropriate to the books her mother read and the opportunity to read and to be read to in any room of the house. Welty describes her father as a "pretty good weather prophet," who hung a barometer on the wall of the dining room. He even told his children what they should do if they found themselves, according to Welty, "lost in a strange country": "'Look for where the sky is brightest along the horizon,' he said. 'That reflects the nearest river. Strike out for a river and you will find habitation'" (4).

The second section of the book, entitled "Learning to See," opens with Welty's reminiscence of the many car trips her family took to Ohio and West Virginia in the summertime to visit family. Taking the route through the country, they typically traveled a week each way. Welty says that although her father knew every mile of the route by train, on the car journey, her mother served as the navigator, sitting beside her husband "at the alert," with a copy of the AAA Blue Book and usually with Welty's baby brother, Walter, on her lap. Eudora and her brother Edward sat crammed in the back seat with suitcases at their feet, with more cases strapped to the outside runners of the car. Their mother acted as the guide, keeping a record of their mileage, the time they spent on the road, the route they took each day, and their expenses. "That kind of travel made you conscious of borders," Welty notes. Perhaps in large part because of her mother's modeling, Welty says, "You rode ready for them. Crossing a river, crossing a county line, crossing a state line—especially crossing the line you couldn't see but knew was there, between the South and the North—you could draw a breath and feel the difference" (48–49). Even as a young girl, Welty seemed aware of the lines drawn between places and the distinctions between the places that lines divided.

For Welty, crossing boundaries became an education that helped her to evolve into a writer. As Welty looks to the similarities between fiction and the passages of our lives, at the chronologies that actually occur and the chronologies we create in our minds, so too does she see in movement across distances a connection with the way in which stories evolve. The summer trips by car and by train to Ohio and West Virginia—to points northward and across lines—were "wholes unto themselves. They were stories." She explains that they were stories "not only in form, but in their taking on direction, movement, development, change":

> They changed something in my life: each trip made its particular revelation, though I could not have found words for it. But with the passage of time, I could look back on them and see them bringing me news, discoveries, premonitions, promises, I still can; they still do. (68)

Welty explains that when she began to write, "the short story was a shape that had already formed itself and stood waiting in the back of my mind" because of those summer journeys. Yet the influence of movement outward became not only the shaping element of her short stories, but also an important part of the creative process of composing her novels. Welty states in *One Writer's Beginning*, "Nor is it surprising to me that when I made my first attempt at a novel I entered its world." In her example that follows, she specifically connects this entrance to the novel *Delta Wedding* to trains and the Delta landscape, where as a child, Laura rides into the "mysterious Yazoo-Mississippi Delta." Looking out of the train window with her head between her hands and her elbows planted on the windowsill as the landscape of "endless fields glowed like a hearth in firelight," Laura comes to this place feeling "what an arriver in a land feels," according to Welty, with "that slow hard pounding in the breast" (68).

Born and raised in West Virginia, Welty's mother hoped, in part, to instill within her daughter some of the spirit of independence of the mountaineer by taking Eudora to visit her family's mountain home. "It seems likely to me now," explains Welty, "that the very element in my character that took possession of me there on top of the mountain, the fierce independence that was suddenly mine, to remain inside me no matter how it scared me when I tumbled, was an inheritance. Indeed, it was my chief inheritance from my mother, who was braver" (66). According to Welty, her mother attempted to guard her from and caution her about the troubles of such an independent spirit. Nevertheless, such an inheritance was impossible to halt. Such an independent streak, according to Welty, at once both brought mother and daughter together and created tense moments between them. Welty's mother would play a recording of the song "The West Virginia Hills": "'A mountaineer,' she announced to me proudly, as though she had never told me this before and now I had better remember it, 'always will be *free*'" (67). This freedom in a sense, for the West Virginian, comes because of living on the line, on the border. Gaining statehood because it broke off from Virginia during the Civil War because of the antislavery sentiments of the population, the state remained in Welty's lifetime a region that has gone its own way—not quite Southern, but not quite Northern.

The final section of *One Writer's Beginnings* focuses on the achievement of voice, the obvious final goal in the evolution and development of Welty as writer. This section begins, similarly, with a description of Welty sitting on a train with her father beside her. Welty points to the familial ties she has to this train, which carried back and forth the letters of her parents when they courted and were separated by the miles between West Virginia, where her mother was teaching, and Mississippi, where her father had settled to work in Jackson for the Lamar Life Insurance Company. For Welty's parents, the train was the line that connected them before they married and settled in Jackson. Her imagination, Welty writes, "takes its strength and guides its direction from what I see and hear and learn and feel and remember of my living world" (83). The passage reiterates her parents' role as travelers, but Welty also uses the train and movement to show how the world beyond home became the fundamental part of her inner life as a writer.

Welty identifies these journeys outward and into the world—specifically the ones she writes about as clearly connected to the process of becoming a writer—as ones in which she was guided by a parent. In the train ride that opens this section, readers never clearly know the purpose of the journey Welty takes with her father. Is it to see relatives? To join her mother and siblings in West Virginia for a visit? The details suggest they have left the Delta for West Virginia as the train encounters "walls of mountains" and train tunnels. Of course it is important that Welty connects this physical journey with her journey as a writer, but a key element that doesn't usually appear in the narratives of male writers headed north on a train is that Welty is accompanied and guided by her father. Daddy shares his traveler's drinking cup with her when it's needed, and she fills it with the water from the cooler at the end of the Pullman car. The porter readies their berth for them, turning down their beds, standing up their fluffy pillows, and switching on the reading light. Welty says that her father over the course of the journey "put it all into the frame of regularity, predictability, that was his fatherly gift," but her imagination also took over as they passed landscapes of houses, roads that turned out of view as they curved around hills, and people who were perhaps picking blackberries or plums looked up to watch the train go by and to wave. "I dreamed over what I could see as it passed, as well as over what I couldn't," Welty says. She was "proceeding in fantasy" (81), as her imagination wove together new stories.

Welty was, after all, a child of 10 who needed the guidance, but she identifies her growth as a writer with this childhood journey—not departure for New York as an independent young adult. She next traces her formal education, first at Mississippi State College for Women where she encountered William Alexander Percy's poem entitled "Home," which was written in New York City. According to Welty, it didn't matter to her that the poem was entitled "home," but that it was "about somewhere else, somewhere distant and far." In many ways this passage recalls Hurston's *Their Eyes Were Watching God* and the possibilities for journeying, discovering self, and finding an authorial voice. Welty writes that "in the beautiful spring night, I was dedicated to *wanting* a beautiful spring night. To be *transported* to it was what I wanted" (85–86). There were a few literary opportunities that showed themselves in Mississippi, but it was not until she transferred to University of Wisconsin-Madison that Welty says she made a "discovery" for herself that "fed" her life from then on.

It is passion that Welty discovers in her time in Madison. Recalling a scene from one of her short stories about a middle-aged Midwestern man who is walking with a woman through the streets of New Orleans, Welty explains that this man is a teacher of linguistics who has reached a pivotal moment in his life. He tells the woman of an experience at the University of Wisconsin that Welty says was similar to one of her own. Reading in the library stacks he discovered the poetry of W. B. Yeats, was struck by Yeats's poem "Sailing to Byzantium," and pictured himself as being able to "go out into the poem the way [he] could go out into the snow" that was falling outside. Welty says that for her, the poem that "smote me first" was "The Song of Wandering Aengus," a poem whose influence runs through her stories in *The Golden Apples* (87–88). Yeats's poem is the story of a wanderer, a traveler who spends his life in pursuit of a "little silver trout" that changes into "a glimmering girl / With apple blossom in her hair," calls his name, and then runs away. He is Aengus, the Irish god of youth and poetry, who "Through hollow lands and hilly lands," says he "will find out where she has gone, / And kiss her lips and take her hands; / And walk among long dappled grass, / And pluck till time and times are done / The silver apples of the moon, / The golden apples of the sun." But Welty's narrative of pursuing those golden apples—her journey to education and to experience—is shaped by "supportive parents" who "willingly agreed" that she could go. The setting for her scene of discovery in the library stacks in Madison, Wisconsin, is one that had been influenced, too, by her father's "choice" of the university because of its "high liberal-arts reputation." Although Welty decides she wants to pursue graduate work at Columbia in New York City, she says she is "sent" by her parents (89). Certainly Welty's parents are represented in the narrative of her growth as a writer as people who always had the best intentions for their daughter and the greatest love and respect for her, but the narrative of movement—one that could have ended with Welty living in New York City as a writer—is one shaped by the influences of family and of home, and societal expectations of a Southern woman.

Other Southern women writers—like Katherine Anne Porter and Evelyn Scott—did make more dramatic departures from their home places that were intended to signal the permanency of their leaving. Porter said in 1974 that she left Texas because she did not "want to be regarded as a freak. That was how they regarded a woman who tried to write. I had to make a revolt, a rebellion . . . so you see, I am the great-grandmother of these bombers, and students beating each other up with bicycle chains" (Allen 165). Janis P. Stout notes the similarities between Porter's travels and those of Evelyn Scott, who each "signaled their departures" by changing their names. Elsie Dunn became Evelyn Scott. And with Porter's travels taking her to Chicago, Los Angeles, Denver, New York, and Mexico, on what Stout calls Porter's "ill-defined search . . . for personal freedom and a vocation" (17), Callie Russell Porter became Katherine Anne, renaming herself after her grandmother Catherine. The difficulties of birthing a new identity (like the ones that Porter and Scott attempted to craft) are ever-present in the stories of the lives of numerous Southern women writers throughout the twentieth century. But that birthing is perhaps most thoroughly woven throughout the text of Evelyn Scott's autobiographical narrative entitled *Escapade*, and probably no other writer captures so fully the Southern white woman's desire to escape the South as does Evelyn Scott.

Born Elsie Dunn in Clarksville, Tennessee, Scott was raised in a home of wealth and privilege. She later described herself as "not a beautiful child, but neither was I stupid, except as I reacted with blind impressionableness to demands made by Southern custom upon the vanity of womanhood" (Qtd. in Thomas 411). Relocating to New Orleans with her parents, Elsie enrolled as a student at Sophie Newcomb College when she reached college age. Finding the life of a young white Southern woman in New Orleans to be restrictive and limiting, Elsie found a way to leave New Orleans and her family when she met the 40-year-old Frederick Creighton Wellman, who was then dean of Tulane University's School of Tropical Medicine. Wellman, a friend of her father's, was a married man with a burning desire to return to the tropics where he had worked previously. The two "eloped," traveling first to New York, then to London, and finally to Brazil where they lived for six years in poverty and harsh conditions. In remaking their lives, they also decided to remake themselves, and their first step was to rename themselves as Evelyn Scott and Cyril Kay Scott.

Threading through Scott's novels is a narrative of escape and movement. Scott focused in her 1927 novel *Migrations* on the story of her great-aunt Eliza, who migrated westward to California with her husband; Scott's next two books, *Background in Tennessee* and *Escapade*, deal specifically with her own migrations, her own flight from the South. The story of Scott's early life that sets the early stages of flight, *Background in Tennessee*, according to Martha E. Cook, is "encoded in images and symbols of entrapment." "Rather than simply setting herself against her background," Cook says, "Scott reveals herself in conflict with it" (53). Scott opens *Background in Tennessee* by setting up the conflicted relationship between being both a Tennessean and a "voluntary exile" from the state (2). Her book is, as Scott explains, her attempt to understand how the place from which she has come has influenced her life, including an assessment as to why she tries to conceal her Southern roots. Scott even wrote of her own childhood desire to dig through the earth to China, for she felt "like a trapped rat, forging a way through obstacles with a new burrow! Like a convict frenziedly employing a pocketknife as he seeks freedom through ten yards of solid masonry with a guarded continent beyond! I wanted to get out, and be able to arrive somewhere else—on the other side of the strange taboos and inscrutable injunctions which hedged and hemmed me in" (Cook 57). Scott's novel *Escapade* details her own escape from entrapment in the story of the Scotts' flight from New Orleans and their time in Brazil, including the birth of their child and the extended visit of Evelyn's mother, who is represented by Nannette, Evelyn's aunt, in the novel.

Escapade echoes these same desires to escape a code of conduct for Southern women that is bound up in societal constructions related to, in large part, a woman's value in relation to monetary wealth and prestige. Evelyn also wants others to be more tolerant of difference, a difference in attitudes about marriage and as she states, "at everything else." She doesn't want to force her opinions on other people, but she recognizes that her relationship with Cyril/John is "considered dangerous" back at home in the United States—not just in the South. Evelyn says, "I have no wish to force myself on the world," but she claims she won't take anyone's criticism of her actions. "Because I alone of all the world can understand and pity myself," she explains, "I am God. I alone of all the world can offer equality to myself" (186–87).

The social constructions of the South are notably exemplified in the novel by women characters: Mrs. Beach, the wife of an American doctor who lives in Brazil, and Nannette, the narrator's aunt. Described as possessing a tone that is "cold and blunt," Mrs. Beach has a manner that is "frigid, but tolerantly humorous, and her precise gestures are somehow full of self-congratulation" (105). She quickly tells Evelyn that she is a Southerner and intends for Evelyn to understand that she is an aristocrat. Finding the secretiveness of their life in Brazil difficult, Evelyn holds off telling Mrs. Beach that her own grandparents are from Maryland and Virginia. Although Evelyn tries to convince herself that she should not be bothered by Mrs. Beach's mind-set and high opinion of herself, Evelyn nevertheless ends up struggling with depression because of the poisoned environment that Mrs. Beach perpetuates. Likewise, the impending arrival of Nannette leaves Evelyn anxious and fearful that she and John will once again be judged. Although Nannette's trip to Brazil is identified as a way to help right the wrongs that Evelyn has committed, in fact, it is a ploy by Evelyn's uncle Alec to push Nannette out of their household so he can divorce her. The narrator indicates that even at the age of 15, she knew that there were problems in the relationship and encouraged them to separate. Uncle Alec believed Evelyn's opinions on marriage were "strange" ones that were the result of her age. After all, he frequently told her, "nonconformity was a symptom of youth"; she would outgrow it (144). Such independent attitudes put her in sharp conflict with Nannette, even though Nannette is a victim of Uncle Alec's manipulations.

Nannette's memories are filled with images of a girlhood lived in privilege and comfort. It is especially after illness that Nannette recalls those icons of wealth and perfection that have always defined her. Her memories are, in large part, constituted by images of riding horses she had as a girl and dresses—of outward appearance. Made of satins, the dresses are hand painted or embroidered with nature scenes—butterflies (similar to the ones the Grimké sisters hoped to escape), birds, and pond lilies. A toque trimmed with ostrich tips and an ermine coat measure out the remaining memories set alongside recollections of a phaeton with a rose-colored canopy, a fountain on the lawn of their home, and strangers who come to town asking who lives in the stately mansion. Nannette's memories point to a value system that is based in judgments from the outside world about her sense of worth. Worth is measured in monetary wealth, but additionally, that wealth comes from others. It is what has been given to her.

Although Evelyn notes that Nannette's "self-pity"—the tears she sheds because of her situation—do not affect her, she indicates, too, that they all share this same attitude of self-pity. Although Evelyn portrays Nannette as unable to fully grasp her circumstances, passages in the text indicate otherwise. When Nannette sees a group of female prostitutes, she is taken aback by their shamelessness, but she is also as fascinated with them as is Evelyn. "She watches them furtively," Evelyn explains, "Observing them in their profession stirs the dim fleshliness which propriety has submerged. Her shame only adds nuance to her appreciation" (140). On the one hand, Nannette seems taken with the sexual freedoms of the prostitutes, but she is aware of her own sexuality that she has been forced to suppress. Nannette has also been compelled throughout her life to depend upon other people to support her, telling Evelyn about their current situation in Brazil, "I am dependent on you and John for everything, for the very air I breathe!" Choice seems to have been taken out of the equation for Nannette. She explains, too, "At least you chose the thing you wanted and you have each other, while I have no one—nobody on earth!" Evelyn blames Nannette's education for Nannette's dependence, but she believes, too, that Nannette will never change (211). Evelyn also "blames" Nannette's dependence on others on her attitude that men like John are "capable of the miraculous." According to Evelyn, Nannette thinks that "everything which is wrong with us now can be righted by John" (185).

Facing the truth of her own situation seems confusing and at times impossible for Evelyn. The text of Escapade itself seems a way for the narrator, and perhaps even the author, to deal with the harsh situations of her life and the psychological implications—an attempt at a recovery narrative of sorts. She wishes for "a world without contours, without relations!" and says she is trapped in a cycle that will only allow her to "gather this huge thing [her life?] together and rearrange it in its old form, even though I am so fatigued with it" (74). What has compelled her to escape the female role in the domestic world now becomes her goal: "I do not wish to escape," she writes initially of the life they have created at the ranch. "I want to stay here forever and ever behind the wall that enfolds our peace" (188).

Even though Evelyn left New Orleans with Cyril as a way to free herself and to formulate a self closer to the person she had hoped, their escape to Brazil seems to further blur the lines of identity for her: "We are fading, fading away in the depths of isolation. We are only memories now. Everyone has forgotten us. Perhaps we are already dead" (199). Although there seemed to be freedom in escape, this migration appears to end in self-annihilation. Ultimately, their survival is based on the societal labels that Evelyn tries to free herself of. John tells everyone that Evelyn's father is rich. According to John, if anything happens to him, then Evelyn, Nannette, and the baby will more likely be helped by the community to find their way back to the coast and their way home if they believe the family has resources. When their situation becomes desperate, Evelyn sends out a plea to the world for help. She states that she has "written to everyone—to those who have insulted us. To those who have been most unkind." Explaining that she realizes there is an "ecstasy of bitterness" in her letters, she asks for money—any support that can help them. Her behavior is brash and inconsiderate: "I am too proud to be proud any longer. . . . I give them all the opportunity to despise me if they will send us a little money." She writes to an American woman who is a social worker and to a Swedish writer who is supportive of women's rights. Noting that she has "no claim on either of them and perhaps there will be no response," Evelyn suggests that it is not so much the money that she struggles for, but instead reaching the world with her words and her feelings. She wants confirmation that this is not the way that women should lead their lives. "I want my words to live," she writes. "I want to poison the whole world with my own suffering. I want to infect people with the disease of our defeat." Indicating that she might be able to pressure them for help because they may be willing to "buy off their Christian consciences," she recognizes, too, that her words may bring "not sympathy but resistance." She is confounded when she sends her poetry to a woman editor at an American magazine and receives a reply that she should "live more" before she begins to write (222–23).

The book ultimately outlines the condition of femaleness—not just in the South, but in far reaches of the world as well. Although at one point Evelyn wishes for a second child, she recognizes the common bonds of women when Dona Isabella says to her, "The senhora is blessed by the saints. What happiness! To be married four years and have only one child." Considering woman's situation in a more historical framework, she thinks about the significance of items such as tin cans and earthen pots—simple objects, yet ones that suggest woman's "gradual liberation from the slavery of necessity." They represent the increasing freedom of women from an environment strictly grounded in the domestic to one that offers "a little time to indulge one's curiousness as to what one may be, a little time for idleness and rest" (224). The animals on the plantation reflect as well Evelyn's feelings about woman's condition. In many ways, the situation with the sheep that they raise seems similar to what Evelyn believes is woman's plight. Their sheep die mysteriously, one every day. They do not appear to be ill, she notes, for their bodies are not swelling and their wool looks just fine; they simply just keel over dead. Bleating out their "shrill questioning," the newborn lambs "cling close" to their dead mothers and continue their bleating. Surprisingly, the mothers, "with their filmed quiet gaze, have a dim look of peace" (230). Evelyn notes, too, that her relationship with her pets, including birds and an armadillo, is one that reflects her own desire for control—control that she believes men have over women. She says that she recognizes "the cruel element in [her] passion for pets. I love them because they are subject to me, because I cannot be hurt by them, and it flatters me to give to them without anticipating a response" (244). Stating that, in fact, this might be how she feels around other people, she claims she would rather be around animals.

If the end of the novel should offer some hopefulness, it doesn't. Evelyn claims she would like to "retreat" into Portuguese, a language she explains she has no relation to, but she hopes will give her some escape from her present: "I prefer not to think of seeing white faces again, and I was stirred unpleasantly by that one word of English" (251). A man named Jose Marinho will take them back into the city, where they must remain in hiding until they have the proper clothes to "make a decent appearance." Nannette isn't surprised that John was able to free them from their life at the plantation and to deliver them back into civilization. "Her faith in man is more than I can conceive," Evelyn explains. Nannette "talks of New York as if we were already there, dwells on gowns, on places to live, on the things we will eat" (256). Evelyn, on the other hand, leaves the plantation drugged on morphine to dull the physical pain.

Responding to Evelyn's claim that she made the choice to elope with Cyril/ John and was not "taken" across state lines for "immoral purposes," Janis Stout, who describes Evelyn as "a good colonel subject," points out that the real-life Frederick Creighton Wellman was the one who actually chose Brazil. He was fluent in Portuguese, and he was the one who had the opportunity for a job collecting insect specimens for the British Museum—insects that Evelyn found disgusting. "She is subjected not only to a sexual possession that she seems to have desired," according to Stout, "but also to medical blundering, the encroachments of dirt and vermin in an unfamiliar environment, prolonged pain, and surgical invasion in the course of which she is scorned by her openly misogynist physician for being female" (28). When at the end of the book the train begins to descend to its destination, Evelyn sees washerwomen bending down over their work at the river. One woman has rolled her skirts to her waist, and Evelyn sees her "fat buttocks immersed in the stream." As the train's heavy door of iron opens for their departure, it is as if the door "rolls back from one world's end to another, and lets me out" (259). This vehicle of movement and motion may open for her departure, but she is only trading one world for another similar one. Or perhaps the masculine world she originally believed she was entering by escaping with Cyril wasn't all it was cracked up to be. If this is a recuperative narrative, then it is through the process of writing that Scott herself must have achieved it, for this Evelyn of the novel seems to be presented with little chance of mending or recovery.

Other Southern women writers relate comparable stories of the challenges and sometimes devastating effects of border crossings, but perhaps the most well-known example is Harriette Arnow's *The Dollmaker*, which focuses on the Great Migration of Appalachian Southerners to Midwest industrial cities, the implications of a husband's move for work, and the societal and familial pressures on a wife to follow. While the book revolves around the trying circumstances and consequences of movement, it also expresses the unifying aspect of a newly discovered community of women and the recuperative elements of those relationships. Gertie Nevel, the mother of five children, clings to the hope of returning South, building up enough savings so that she and her family can move back to Kentucky and purchase a piece of property. Although the novel was influenced by Arnow's own life in that she, like Gertie, lived in a Detroit housing project in the 1940s because of her husband's work in the city, Arnow stated that she herself actually had no desire to return to the South except for visits.

Writing *The Dollmaker* became for Arnow a way of expressing the losses experienced by Southerners—especially those from Appalachia—in making their journeys northward and the implications of that movement on the communities that were left behind. In an interview with Barbara Baer, Arnow explained the magnitude of the events that she saw at work in the story itself:

> At an early age I saw my work as a record of people's lives in terms of roads. At first, it was only a path, then a community at the end of a gravel road that took men and families away, and finally, where gravel led to a highway, the highway destroyed the hill community. I was aware that nothing had been written on the Southern migrants, of what was actually happening to them and to their culture, of how they came to the cities the first time in the 1920s, leaving their families behind. I began writing during the depression, which had sent hill people back home again. And then, as I was still writing during the Second War, I witnessed the permanent move the men made by bringing their wives and children with them to the cities. With that last migration, hill life was gone forever, and with it, I suppose, a personal dream of community I'd had since childhood and have been trying ever since to recapture in my writing. (Qtd. in Chung 53)

Although she explained in another interview that she did not like using the word "adjust" to describe the transition that Appalachian people were forced to make in leaving their home places for new locales, her interest in writing about their journeys came from her own speculations and questions about why and how they made decisions to leave and how they were able to survive making the transition (Chung 266). Similar to many other sojourners, Gertie plans for her family to make enough money in Detroit so that they can return to Kentucky to purchase "one a dem big bluegrass farms" (Arnow 146).

Arnow chooses not to show the actual departure of Gertie and her children from Kentucky; she begins in the middle of the train ride from Cincinnati to Detroit. Trying to sleep in a coach seat, wriggling her "big body" (129) to get comfortable, Gertie falls asleep and dreams that she has slept past sunrise, and the cow Lizzie is "bawling" because it is "way past milking time." Struggling to move her legs, she dreams she can't get out of her bed. Her leg muscles throbbing, Gertie feels cold on one side of her body and "steamy hot and sweaty" on the other. Deciding she should build a fire, she moves quickly to her feet—hitting her head on the metal luggage rack above her. It is only then

that she realizes she is on the train with her children headed to join Clovis in
Detroit. Recognizing where she is, she tries again to sleep, pushing her body
back as far as she can into the seat and pressing against the window, "where,
in spite of two thicknesses of glass, the cold, like water trickling, seeped into
her hip so that it ached from the cold as her arms ached from weariness" (129).
Feeling disoriented and very far from home, Gertie is overcome by the smells of
vomit in the car—from the babies and the "red-faced, red-eyed soldiers"—the
cigarette smoke, "wet babies," and the "stale soda biscuit from Alabama, fried
fresh hog meat from Georgia" (130). Pressing her face to the window, all Gertie
can see are "lights, streaks of dirty snow, roads, telephone poles, a few cars, and
earlier in the little towns the cold shapes of hurrying people, and once, across
what had seemed to be a vast reach of palm-flat land, smudged lights that might
have been stars" (134). Unlike Thomas Wolfe's Eugene Gant, who can see the
blur of people in the other cars that his train passes, Gertie's vision is clouded
by the filthy windows of the train. She can only see shapes and once she just
barely can make out the stars—a symbol of the rural landscape she left behind.

Arnow's Kentuckians are met by a guide when they arrive in Detroit. The
Alabama-born-and-raised taxi driver described as "a little weazened black-eyed
man" at first frightens Gertie and her children when they believe he will put
them out because they cannot tell him how to find Merry Hill—their destination (144). They don't recognize he is a migrant as well until after Enoch asks
him what he learned in his second reader. Reflecting on his own passage into
the North long ago, he tells them, "When I went through that second reader
forty years ago down in Alabam, they didn't teach us how to live in Detroit
like they do little Kentuckians now" (146). The migration process seems to
have become so frequent and so standardized for Kentuckians that migrating
Kentucky children are "schooled" in the transformation process. Although,
of course, the process isn't the subject of school lessons in the South, the taxi
driver suggests that the South is complicit in expelling its people—claiming
some as Outsiders even before they cross the border. When Clytie responds
to the driver with "How'd you know where we was frum?" he quickly replies,
"I've met youse atta station through two world wars. I oughta know" (146).

Not long after their arrival, Gertie takes the children to school for the first
time, carrying a basket that holds the children's birth certificates and "shot
papers from County Health." Although Clytie is embarrassed that her mother
is carrying the old-fashioned basket—a marker that tells others that the Nevels
are outsiders—the "familiar feel of the basket dangling from her arm was a
comforting thing" for Gertie (172). At the school, one of the teachers—a "little
bald-headed man" (183)—admires the basket, asking Gertie about its origins.
He can only imagine that it must be foreign, Polish, in particular. Gertie replies
that the basket "come frum back home," where it was made by Ole Josiah Coffey,

one of the last baskets he made before he died. When the teacher asks where "back home" is, Gertie replies, "My country is Kentucky" (183). What proceeds after this is a discussion between the two about the "adjustment" of Gertie's children. The teacher reassures her that "This school has many children from many places, but in the end they all—most—adjust, and so will yours. They're young" (184). Gertie's response, "I want em to be happy, but I don't know as I want em to—to—" (185), suggests the disconnection she feels and her inability to control the fact that her family has landed in the liminal spaces, holding on to the place they have come from but ostracized and manipulated because of it.

Gertie's migration is characteristically feminine. On the one hand, it is a forced migration that Gertie shares with others from the South who are pushed out of the region in order to find support for their families and a way out of the depressed conditions of Appalachia, but it is also a migration impacted by her experience as a woman. Even after Gertie has saved the money to buy land and has been working on the deal, Gertie's mother persuades her to move to Detroit because as the Bible says, a woman must "Leave all else an cleave to thy husband" and follow the teachings of Paul, who called for wives to "be in subjection unto your husbands, as unto th Lord" (124). Rachel Rubin calls it a "coerced" migration that is "both paralleled and prefigured by the ravishment of Gertie as a woman colliding with the larger male institutions of society." Linking the family's move specifically to the functions of industrial capitalism in their lives—and the need to make money to support themselves and to spend money on commercial products in Detroit—Rubin also points to the ways in which relationships between men and women in marriage—even ones viewed as "relatively successful"—"are chillingly emblematic of larger control-submission schema of industrial capitalism" (179). Gertie's means of sustaining her family through providing for them through her farming the earth has been replaced by a world in Detroit that is driven by a capitalist market economy. Gertie's tasks within their household in Detroit are shaped by these new commercial products and by the capitalistic drive that they represent. While Gertie is forced off the land that she cultivates to raise her family, the appliances in her Detroit kitchen suggest, too, what has happened to her ability to reach the earth and to look to it for sustenance, according to Rubin. Called the Icy Heart, the refrigerator is not a modern convenience, but instead an "unwelcome present from husband to wife." With a name that suggests "the soullessness of the war economy," the refrigerator has "the power to ruin the nourishment that the land and the woman offer" (182). Gertie also has little understanding of how the oven works and serves her family a raw Christmas turkey because the bird is too large for her oven: "Hemmed in as it had been in the too small oven, the turkey had burned on the outside, scorching the breast meat, but they all came near gagging when Clovis cut into a thigh joint and blood ran out" (Arnow 259). Perhaps most importantly, Gertie's "whittlin' foolishness," her desire to draw art from the wood, is for Clovis a useless goal. Instead, he wants her to mass produce dolls for quick sale and profit.

Gertie loses two of her children because of the disastrous results of the pressures of assimilation. On the one hand, Gertie encourages Reuben to assimilate by urging, "Honey, try harder to be like th rest," while at the same time, "She choked—she was no rabbit to beget rabbits" (309–10). Ultimately, Reuben returns to Kentucky, and to his grandmother. At least from Clovis's perspective, the blame for Reuben's difficulties lays squarely on Gertie's inability to "adjust." Clovis tells her, "You've got to git it into yer head that it's you that's as much wrong with Reuben as anything" (308). Gertie also shifts this blame on to herself, recognizing that "most of the trouble with Reuben was herself—her never kept promises, her slowness to hide her hatred of Detroit" (334). Rubin argues that by novel's end, Gertie's remaining children laugh at a picture of a woman with a mule because they have been assimilated by a culture in Detroit that belittles the hillbilly. The woman in the cartoon is Gertie, who at the opening of the novel was set astride a mule, and the children's laughter is symbolic of the "intersecting processes of hegemonization" that sever their ties to Kentucky. Gertie's place on the mule, that is, her life "in transit," is what "marks her as an object of ridicule." The novel ends tragically because "What's gone stays gone; landscape and homespun wisdom, as Arnow lamented, 'cannot be excavated or re-created'" (Rubin 189).

If there is any hope for Gertie, it is in the bonds she forms with the women she meets in Detroit. Arnow herself experienced similar relationships when she lived in a multiethnic community in a Detroit housing development. There she came to recognize, as she once said, that "most of us, regardless of our backgrounds, have a common bond. . . . Most women I met were like myself in that they, too, were wives with children, all of us because of the war uprooted to follow our husbands to Detroit. . . . We grew to know each other better than those who study 'the immigrant' by statistics built on direct questioning can ever know" (Qtd. in Goodman 49). Arnow stresses the bonds among women and the support they provide for each other that is in sharp contrast to the antagonistic relationships she represents as characteristic of men. According to Haeja Chung, Gertie's "final act" in cutting up the wood figure of Christ or Judas (Christ in Kentucky, but Judas in Detroit) is "the rite of passage she must perform on her way to self-redemption" (Chung, "Harriette" 220). Whittling helped her relax and it connected her to Kentucky, but Chung points out that Arnow herself said in an interview that "Gertie didn't think of her whittling as art":

> Externalizing her suffering helps Gertie take the final step. As Arnow says, she
> has learned that "she was only one among the many women who had their troubles and suffered." Because Gertie is inarticulate, she needs to objectify her con-

fused thoughts in similar situations, just as she has visualized her guilt in the block of wood. In an unexpected revelation, she sees herself in the weeping Mrs. Anderson who accuses her husband of stealing her "birthright" . . . In another parallel, Gertie sees herself in the "cactus woman," who, evicted from her unit, is concerned only about the loss of her cactus. . . . Gertie realizes then that she does not need to single out one face for Christ. . . . However painful it may have been, Gertie has finally learned what to give. (Chung, "Harriette" 220–21)

Even though we might accept Arnow's assessment that Gertie would not have elevated her whittling to the level of "art," her craft does become a very personal expression that is recuperative and restorative. It is, after all, through her whittling that Gertie becomes able to cross boundaries that separate her off from others, from those who are different from her. And in doing so, she builds relationships that help her to heal.

The female community at Merry Hill is certainly not a utopian one, but it does represent a type of community that the male characters are incapable of forming. When Cassie is killed by a train, it is the women who help Gertie cope with her loss. After the United States bombs Hiroshima and Nagasaki, Mrs. Daly hears her Japanese neighbor, Mrs. Saito, crying. Mrs. Daly gathers flowers for her. Despite the fact that Mrs. Daly believes "it ain't like them Japs was good white Christians," she can still recognize their common humanity: "yu still gotta say, people is people. Why them Japs lives something like this . . . all crowded up tugedder inu towns; little cardboard houses kinds like what we've got; and maybe lots—you—know—kids" (454). Ethnic names among the women such as Saito as well as Bommarita, Schultz, and Anderson show the women's ability to move beyond the barriers of cultural background. Elizabeth Harrison situates these female relationships within a pastoral framework, one that is rooted in the rural and characterized by cooperation and equality. According to Harrison, although the husbands' lives revolve around competition and survival in an industrialized, money-focused community, "the women learn to care for each other and each other's children and to share emotional burdens." While the women of the housing development come together as a community, the men are broken down and broken apart by arguing and fighting (92).

Women's relationships grow and are highlighted in the novel because of the act of movement—because of migration. In part, the relationships among the women at Merry Hill develop because the women share a common narrative, a common story that binds them. Not only do they share the story of woman's second-class status in American society, but they also find a common bond because their lives have been ones of movement. They have been pulled to the city, uprooted from homes because of the war, because of their husbands' search for jobs. Likewise, the novel is similar to John Steinbeck's *The Grapes of Wrath* and Dorothea Lange's Migrant Mother series of photographs, which helped to popularize the myth of the mother during the Depression era. Mothering takes a pivotal role in the liminal space—giving the only sense of stability and guidance, even as women's lives and families are broken down and torn apart.

Despite the pitiful nature of the lives of Gertie, Ma Joad, and the Migrant Mother, woman's courage and strength are represented as key for the survival of humanity. The female nature of bonding—of family and community—is ultimately what is necessary for modern humans displaced from rural life, according to Arnow. But if the narratives of Southern white male border crossers tell of Odysseus-like journeys out into the world that are symbolic of maturation and growth, the narratives of black and white Southern women writers show the complexities of gender that continue to follow them. Even the journey itself is manipulated and controlled by elements beyond a woman's control. The journey itself remains loaded down with the burdens of parental apron strings, husbands' self-centeredness, and society's gender expectations.

And if a Southern woman writer returns southward after a sojourn in the regions beyond the South, coming home has additional complications. Arnow only wanted to visit—not stay. The Grimké sisters would have been arrested if they had attempted to go home again to South Carolina. Hurston returned South to live her final years in poverty and when she passed, she was buried in the unmarked grave that Alice Walker went in search of decades later. In returning to Florida to collect folklore in her younger years, Hurston was confronted by a home community that she described as "a featherbed of resistance." "They didn't know how to take Zora," Hurston's niece said of her. "They—I think they guarded what they had about their community because it had previously been held up to ridicule. And you could even look at it and say it's a control issue, that they wanted to keep what was theirs. So they were leery about the fact that she could, in fact, dance between these two worlds" (Hansen). In effect, Hurston and the other women discussed here remained in that liminal space, dancing a dance that gave them a rare slant on the South and an inspiration for their work, but one that forever left them in the margins, forever conflicted because they embodied that line.

CHAPTER 5

Rescripting What It Means to Be Southern: Musical Performance as Border Narrative

Sitting atop the icebox where the beer is cooling in the 230 Club, tilting her head to one side as she surveys the room, Memphis Minnie appears to be the very picture of a "colored lady teacher in a neat Southern school" who is about to proclaim to her students, "Children, the lesson is on page 14 today, paragraph 2." As she plays the blues on an electric guitar that is amped up to "machine proportions—a musical version of electric welders plus a rolling mill," Memphis Minnie's slender legs work like "musical pistons" and a "deep and dusky heartbeat" fills the space. It's New Year's Eve 1942 on the south-side of Chicago, and "the rhythm is as old as Memphis Minnie's most remote ancestor." For Langston Hughes, who was sitting in the audience that night and who wrote this description of the performance for his column in the *Chicago Defender*, the music flooded in memories of a complicated past for African Americans who had migrated from the South:

> Through the smoke and racket of the noisy Chicago bar float Louisiana bayous, muddy old swamps, Mississippi dust and sun, cotton fields, lonesome roads, train whistles in the night, mosquitoes at dawn, and the Rural Free Delivery, that never brings the right letter. . . . Big rough old Delta Cities float in the smoke, too. Also border cities, Northern cities, Relief, W.P.A., Muscle Shoals, the jooks. (14)

Pulling the bar patrons into the borderlands, the music is so powerful that some in the audience "holler out loud" (14). At once in Chicago and back in the rural

South, the aura in the bar mixes the solitude of a rural landscape with the slow drain of a mosquito bite and unfulfilled expectations as the smoke overcomes bar patrons in a dream-like experience of remembering.

As Hughes's description suggests, the psychological and societal borderlands that Southerners confronted as they left the South were difficult, complex, and varied. Physical places like the 230 Club in Chicago became sites where displaced Southerners gathering in communal spaces could confront and navigate the borderlands. But they also became important creative sites. Whether consciously or subconsciously, migrating Southerners and their music, especially in the first half of the twentieth century, were becoming something in-between. In his classic book *The Story of the Blues*, Paul Oliver recounts a story about Big Maceo Merriweather and Tampa Red, the ways blues music was being reshaped by the migration of African Americans to Northern cities, and the rapidity of those changes that sometimes left musicians unaware of the transformations that were taking place. Best known for his *Worried Life Blues* and his *Chicago Breakdown*, Merriweather was born in Texas in 1905 and was 35 years old when he arrived in Chicago. Characterized by his roaring boogie bass that was in sharp contrast to his soft voice, Merriweather was determined to see that his fellow musicians remembered their roots in the South. After hearing Merriweather play, Tampa Red asked, "What kind of jive d'ya call that?" Merriweather replied, "Man I call this—is the *Texas Stomp*," as he pounded out the notes with the "propulsion of an express train." Merriweather urged him on, saying, "Come on Tamp, show me what you do in your home." Even though, as Oliver explains, Tampa Red answered with his guitar "singing against the piano rhythms" of Merriweather's playing, exclaiming, "This is the way we do it back in my home, Macey—listen here . . . !" it really wasn't like "back home." They were instead playing in the "brash, confident manner of Chicago" (Oliver 115). Hillbilly/country singers experienced similar shifts—perhaps ones they themselves could not name, but they knew were real. Trying to identify the differences, Rose Maddox, who with her family migrated to California and performed as part of the highly popular Maddox Brothers and Rose from the 1930s to the 1950s, described hillbilly/country music that had migrated from the South to California as having "more get up and go" (Rubin 94).

While the previous two chapters in this book focus on the interior lives of Southerners writing autobiographically about their own border crossings, this chapter shifts direction to look at the collective experiences of bordering and border crossing that are represented in Southern roots music. Because Southern roots music is a music of the masses, these collective narratives give voice to communal experiences. Looking at these sorts of texts emphasizes the important roles that performance and public memory play in creating and perpetuating communal identities. In this chapter, I want to emphasize the process by which communities are built through the performance of musical texts and by the literal movement of musical genres from out of the South. As a broad range of genres, including gospel, blues, country music, zydeco, Tejano, and pow wow, roots music is, according to music historian Charles Wolfe, "a powerful and unacknowledged folk literature." Focusing on the lives of everyday people who are oftentimes dealing with societal conditions that limit them because of their race, class, or gender, roots music not only honors the lives of common people, but also deals with the difficulties people face when they encounter oppression and societal change. As a result, American roots music as both a form of expression and as a means to bring about societal change often takes up the theme of Freedom ("American Roots Music"). In Southern roots music, in particular, these characteristics are primary to songs about and by migrating Southerners.

On a more general scale, American popular music from the late nineteenth century through the world wars evolved because of the movement of Americans from rural to urban regions. But the migrations of Americans, especially from the rural South to the urban South or to the urban North, not only produced much of the music that can be called crossover, but also much of the music of the twentieth century that can be specifically identified as American. The music that evolved, in fact, was not only the product of migratory peoples, but also was instrumental in stabilizing and reinforcing American culture as it migrated from country to city. Music itself blended the rural with the cityscape. Especially during the 1920s through the 1940s, when the sounds of what were called "race" music and "hillbilly" music were popular, the venues in which they were played underwent changes as migrants moved to metropolitan areas and artists straddled the line between the rural and the industrial. Instrumentation was increasingly amplified with the use of electric guitars and microphones. Music was a reflection of the lives of those in transition as they held on to a rural impulse of the past (a mix of real and imagined) or reflected upon the hardships that Southerners had escaped. Songs about American migrations have long seen wide popularity in the United States, including songs such as "Ho! For California!" but music that came from the migrations of Southerners has special implications and intricacies because of the nature of the experiences of those who moved. Westward expansion was a national movement—part of fulfilling the "promise" of Manifest Destiny—but migrating Southerners carried "baggage," and music that told of their journeying reflects upon that baggage and the "otherness" of those Southerners caught in the liminal spaces. In studying movements of Southerners, border crossing narratives in music offer a unique window because they reflect both individual identity and collective identity. Music, in general, according to musicologist Simon Frith, "offers so intensely a sense of both self and others, of the subjective in the collective"

(110). Music can sustain a culture, be the site of cultural change or shift, create new communities, bind communities together and pull them apart, and it played all these roles as migrants and their music left the South.

My intent here is to look at music from the South as it was carried to other parts of the country and how that music rescripted what it means to be Southern. I'm also concerned with Southern borders as the site of culture and the evolution of Southern musical forms on this line. I want to look at Southern music as it was first being more widely consumed by the general American population but as it was still marginalized, while it was still in large part being consumed by those who had been marginalized because they had crossed over from South to NotSouth. My interest here is specifically in the blues and in country music because both genres are closely linked to the migrations of Southerners out of the South, and both genres have had tremendous impact in the music world and beyond. LeRoi Jones (Amiri Baraka), in his classic 1963 book *Blues People*, for example, identifies the blues as the music that is most closely identified with "the *path* the slave took to 'citizenship'" (ix). Blues songwriter Willie Dixon, known as the "poet laureate of the blues," once described the blues as "the roots and the other musics are the fruits. . . . The blues are the roots of all American music" ("Willie Dixon Biography"). Bill C. Malone calls country music "America's truest music . . . [L]ike no other musical form in our culture, country music lays bare the uncertainties that lie at the heart of American life" (*Don't Get Above Your Raisin'* 13). Although I look back to earlier periods to examine the background of these genres, my focus here is primarily on the 1920s through the 1960s, the period when Southern music first became more widely marketed with the advent of the recording industry and radio, and as increasing numbers of Southerners left the region. The blues evolved from rural to urban and then to rhythm and blues, and "hillbilly" music to country and then to country western *because* Southerners were on the move. I focus here on music as well because performance can be interpreted as a liminal space and because performance plays a key role in transformation, not only in the ritualistic movements of crossing but also in the public nature of transformation. In looking at music, the role of performance is important because of its specific connections to liminality.

Identifying performance as "reflective" and "arousing consciousness of ourselves as we see ourselves," Marvin Carlson, for example, claims the "image of performance as a border, or margin, a site of negotiation" as a key concept in performance theory (20). Basing his argument on the work of van Gennep and Turner, Carlson explains that performance "can work within a society . . . to undermine tradition, to provide a site for exploration of fresh and alternative structures and patterns of behavior" (15). Thus musical performance can be a liberating creative site for the border crosser not only because it builds connections with others who share the same experience, but also because liminality opens up a space for looking at the world from the margins with the complications that living on the border brings with it. Performance can be recuperative as well—a site of healing.

Up until the commercialization of music in the 1920s, according to music historian Patrick Huber, music in the South had for three centuries been "profoundly and inextricably multiracial," a "vibrant cross-racial exchange" (22). Southern vernacular music that was performed in communal spaces at dance parties, fiddle contests, and tent shows was transformed as records and radio changed the ways people experienced music. By the 1920s, the number of bands and musicians that played Southern rural music had increased dramatically, and those involved in the music industry of the time were keen on finding a label to identify the music. As music became more widely consumed through commercial enterprises such as the recording industry and radio, Southern music became more racialized and segregated. Scholars differ on what occurred to make this happen. Music historians have explained the identifiers of "race" music and "hillbilly" music that were used in the recording industry as the product of racial segregation in the South, but Huber sees the development of these labels as the result of a recording industry that believed racial classification was the best way to market and advertise their products. In effect, they assumed that consumers made purchasing decisions according to their race and that salespersons and retailers would be better able to sell records if they fit into specific categories. Thus the terms "race" music and "hillbilly" music (23).

These would be the labels given to the blues and to country music until after World War II when the identifiers rhythm and blues and country western would become commonly used. Race recordings were first produced in 1920 and included blues, jazz, and gospel. Although the word "hillbilly" has long been used to refer to backwoods Southerners, it wasn't until the mid-1920s that the term was commonly applied to music and began to replace the identifier "hill country tunes," according to Bill Malone. The folk qualities of music were identified with labels such as "old familiar tunes" or "old-time music," and the "southernness" of music was represented in images of mountain feuds or African Americans working in cotton fields. The first band to be identified on their label as "hillbillies" was a string band whose members came from Virginia and North Carolina and recorded with Okeh Records. Supposedly, one of the group members commented as they searched for a name to call themselves, "Call the band anything you want. We are nothing but a bunch of hillbillies from North Carolina and Virginia anyway." Malone describes the history of the word as a "curious one," commenting that the term was rarely used by record companies or radio stations, but was used by the musicians, fans, and "detractors alike." According to Malone, when he published his *Country Music,*

U.S.A. back in 1985, at that point, Waylon Jennings, Loretta Lynn, and Tammy Wynette were still using the term to speak of themselves, but they did so in private, looking at the term as derogatory when others used it to refer to them (*Country Music, U.S.A.* 39-40).

Rural blues was rooted in the West African tradition of the "griot," an oral tradition that was carried on in some regions of Africa through a hereditary line. The griot preserved cultural traditions and communal narratives through song and story. Composing songs that celebrated powerful tribes and tribal leaders, the griots also composed complaint songs, which typically resulted in their being labeled as rebels by tribal leaders. As persons who had special insight because they were believed to be the companions of evil spirits and false gods, they were venerated by the other members of their tribes. Although griots typically remained connected to one particular tribal community, oftentimes they wandered from tribe to tribe, providing entertainment and educating people in other villages in the region. Because they were part of an oral tradition, the griots became "libraries" of a sort for their communities and cultures, preserving the customs, the traditions, the culture of their people. William Barlow describes the earliest blues musicians in the South as "descendants of the griots, carrying forward the historical and cultural legacy of their people even while they were setting a new agenda for social discourse and action." Borrowing from folk traditions of African American culture and looking through the lens of their lives in the postbellum South, early blues musicians both broke with and returned to the past. "It was this tension between innovation and tradition," according to Barlow, "that endowed the blues with a capacity to illuminate the emotional life and social consciousness of the African-American people" (8-9). While the blues was a highly individualistic means of expression, blues music was also intended to be shared. The blues was a way to voice internal group problems, a way for listeners to cope and identify. When Fae Barnes, also known as Maggie Jones, sang of "Going North, child, where I can be free / where there's no hardship, like in Tennessee," listeners understood her anguish and many recognized themselves. Boogie woogie artist Cow Cow Davenport found similar success with songs with words such as "I'm tired of this Jim Crow, gone leave this Jim Crow town / Doggone my black soul, I'm sweet Chicago bound."

The road out of the South and heading for Chicago not only was the theme of song, but also the actual physical route that changed the music. "The man who moved the blues north from the Delta and made it electric," according to *Rolling Stone* magazine, was Muddy Waters ("Muddy Waters Bio"). Waters, who was named McKinley Morganfield at birth, grew up in the Mississippi Delta hearing the music of Son House and Robert Johnson, and was renamed "Muddy Waters," perhaps in recognition of the waters of the Mississippi River region where he was raised or perhaps because he loved to play in the mud as a child—the stories differ. As a musician in the Delta, Waters played the acoustic guitar for audiences at dances and house parties and in juke joints. While still in the Delta region, his talent caught the attention of Library of Congress field researchers Alan Lomax and John Work, who recorded several of his songs for their recording project. Deciding to head northward, Waters first lived in St. Louis and then in 1943 moved to Chicago, where during the day he worked in a paper plant and in the evenings played acoustic guitar in the same types of venues where he had played in the South. In Chicago he experimented with his sound and became increasingly popular as an artist. Drawing larger and larger audiences into small city spaces, he decided to shift from acoustic to electric guitar. "When I went into the clubs, the first thing I wanted was an amplifier. Couldn't nobody hear you with an acoustic," Waters explained. "You get a more pure thing out of an acoustic, but you get more noise out of an amplifier" (Filene 81). Reaching national prominence in the recording industry in the 1950s, his songs frequently made the *Billboard* charts and he reigned over the Chicago blues scene. In the 1970s, his work saw a resurgence in popularity and he was recognized with half a dozen Grammy awards. When he passed away in his home in the Chicago suburbs in 1983, *Rolling Stone* wrote a tribute to him, recalling his Southern roots:

> Hot red and green chili peppers, okra, turnip greens, cabbage and tomatoes grow in immaculate, carefully nurtured rows all around the foundation of Muddy Waters' house. . . . Muddy planted them himself, and when his crowded touring schedule permitted, he could often be found pruning and weeding his little gar-den, crouched on his hands and knees between his house and driveway, working the brown earth and enjoying the way it felt between his fingers. Some country people who move to the city can't wait to get away from the mud and dirt. But Muddy Waters, who transformed the Delta's back-country blues into electric blues, always liked feeling the earth, crumbly and moist against his skin. (Palmer)

The tribute, though, also recognizes the route backward. The road was not just the trajectory outward of Muddy Waters's own life from out of the South and the evolution of blues music and culture from out of the region, but also the route back, to the roots of Waters's music—roots that had a lasting impact on not only the blues, but also rock bands and rock guitarists including Eric Clapton and the Rolling Stones.

Like the blues, country music also evolved as it literally moved. Rooted in a British musical heritage, the music of the white settlers who crossed the Appalachian Mountains and moved farther west was dramatically reshaped by the diverse populations that the settlers encountered. "As they inched their way across the southern frontier," says Bill C. Malone, "British immigrants came in contact with other peoples, whom they often fought, traded, and worked with, made love to, and sang and danced with." These populations included Native Americans, Mexicans, Germans who had settled in Virginia's Great Valley, the Spanish and French of the Mississippi Valley, and especially African Americans (*Country Music, U.S.A.* 4). Like the blues, country music evolved because of people's movements. Rachel Rubin traces these patterns of influence and cross-pollination in her discussion of the Bakersfield Sound of the twentieth century, as Bakersfield evolved into "Nashville West" (although California became a recording center before Nashville). "In general the instrumentation is considered to be more sophisticated than in other country music, manifesting a strong jazz influence that reached the music by way of western swing, a big-band dance music favored by the cowboys and oil-rig workers in Texas," says Rubin. "West Coast country is also marked by its heavy reliance upon steel guitars and its high, tight vocal harmonies" (94). Similar to the blues, country music breaks with and returns to the past, especially in the music as it was carried from the rural South to urban areas outside the region. Both musical genres speak to the human condition of everyday people and the struggles and joys they experience because of their displacement.

Migrant pathways into cities outside the South were firmly wrapped around the promise of industry. While the train appears throughout literary and musical texts by men as a way to freedom, for African American women in the South, however, the sound of the train was, according to Farah Jasmine Griffin, "a mournful signal of imminent desertion and future loneliness" as their men left the South to migrate northward (Griffin 18). For Southern migrants moving northward to Detroit, the image of the automobile represented the journey down the road to success. The promise of opportunity made its way into song narratives such as "Say, I'm goin' to get me a job now, workin' in Mr. Ford's place" (98), and the mechanization and industrialization of the city influenced and shaped the sound of the blues as the rural blues was transformed by electric instrumentation. The Ford company and Ford automobiles were the focus of a number of blues songs because of the jobs the company offered in Detroit, but in part, too, because the Ford Model-T, which was labeled "the poor man's car," was one of the first cars that African Americans purchased in large numbers (Jones 97). As more and more Southerners took jobs in the automobile industry in Detroit, word spread throughout the South that jobs were to be had. Other Midwestern cities held similar promise. Cow Cow Davenport, who went to Chicago in the mid-1920s, was inspired to write his signature boogie-woogie piece "Cow Cow Blues" by the movement and sound of a railroad engine. He says, "I'm goin' up north where they say money grows on trees, / I don't give a doggone if my black soul leaves, / I'm goin' where I don't need no BVDs." Kid

Cole's 1936 song "I'm Going to Cincinnati" proclaimed that "the times is good" there. Bobo Jenkins, who moved to Detroit in the 1940s, worked 26 years in a Chrysler plant, and was popular in the local jazz scene in Detroit, said of the new sound and the influence of his work in industry: "That whirlin' machinery gives me the beat. It's like hearin' a band playing all day long. Every song I ever wrote that's any good has come to me standin' on the line" (Smith 12). Yet his music, which oftentimes referred to his life and work in Detroit, also reflected the difficulties and hardships of factory work:

> Please, Mister Foreman, slow down that assembly line,
> Will you please, Mister Foreman, slow down that assembly line,
> I don't mind workin', but I do mind dying.

Another song, "24 Years on the Wrong Road," also describes the economic plight that workers often faced: "Cut my gas, baby, stole my speed, / I said they cut my gas, baby, stole my speed, / Now I'm paying double for everything I need."

Musicians seemed to understand that their words and music could have lasting effects on those who listened, while others recognized that music was one of the few cultural signifiers that migrants carried with them. John Lee Hooker, who grew up on a sharecropping farm near Clarksdale, Mississippi, moved to Detroit in 1943. Working at factory jobs and playing in local clubs, Hooker ultimately found national success in the late 1940s with his hit rhythm-and-blues song "Boogie Chillum." When asked where his songs came from, Hooker once said, "I write songs about life in the present day and in the past. That's where the blues come from: life, people, how they're living and how some of them are suffering. It hits everybody in the audience because they know it's the real thing. . . . It's the truth about things. . . . I don't get my songs from books, they come from the way I feel down here" (Barlow 286). Blues artist Henry Townsend, who was born in Mississippi, grew up in Cairo, Illinois, and moved to St. Louis, explained the impetus for his music, saying, "Maybe it wasn't exactly then but I had the experience of these things. You find it's easier to tell the truth about your life so you sing about it" (Oliver 105). Likewise, country music star Loretta Lynn understood the significance of her life story that she retold in her song "Coal Miner's Daughter" (1976), "knowing how powerfully," according to James Gregory, "that origin story would resonate in the world of country music" (178).

Despite the willingness of some to see themselves as speaking for and to the migrant experience, many felt an intense conflict between their attachments to the place they came from and the circumstances, such as racism, poverty, and sexism, that prompted them to leave in the first place. Many distanced themselves from their Southern roots as a coping mechanism. Rose Maddox once said that she and her brothers began learning to play instruments and sing professionally because her brother Fred "hated picking cotton" back at home (Rubin 107). Buck Owens typically told interviewers who asked about his days as a youth that he couldn't remember that time of his life very well because he had so much hatred for it. Owens explained, "I think we laughed at ourselves because we didn't want to address . . . how hard the work was, and how little we got from it" (Rubin 108). He took ridicule of his background to a high level through his work on the cast of television's *Hee Haw*, a variety television show that aired from 1969 to 1993, first on CBS and then in syndication. The show left many viewers forgetting about his successful recording career and remembering him for his trademark image as a country hick. Creating this sort of hick persona was a way to leave a Southern past behind. For performers and viewers alike, according to Rachel Rubin, "Laughing at the silliness of a country hick on television rescues a viewer from likeness to that figure" (107). Folklorist Archie Green explains this internal conflict as one more generally American: an escape from the rural and the consequent looking back to that place with nostalgia. "We flee the eroded land with its rotting cabin," according to Green, and "at the same time we cover it in rose vines of memory." This "national dualism," says Green, "created the need for a handle of laughter and ridicule to unite under one rubric the songs and culture of the yeoman and the varmint, the pioneer and the poor white" (Qtd. in Malone, *Country Music, U.S.A.* 40).

For African Americans, that relationship between the place of the ancestors in the South and the new place in which they found themselves was obviously a much more complex relationship because of the lingering history of slavery, the intensely racist society of the South, and the racism that African Americans encountered in regions outside of the South. LeRoi Jones describes the South as "*home,*" "the place that Negroes knew, and given the natural attachment of man to land, even loved." The North, he says, was a place "to be beaten, there was no room for attack. No such room had been possible in the South, but it was still what could be called home." Arriving in the North, African Americans were quick to acclimate, according to Jones, as they found themselves the focus of jokes that labeled them as "country." Despite the popularity of lyrics like Big Maceo's "My home's in Texas, what am I doin' up here? / Yes, my good corn whiskey, baby, and women brought me here," new transplants quickly adapted, shedding their Southern markings, hoping to avoid greetings like "Hey, Cornbread!" (Jones 105–6). Musical space itself also became a site of acclimatization for African American migrants who, as Paul Oliver describes, "wanted to feel in touch with their friends and at the same time be urban and sophisticated." Pointing to the work of Lonnie Johnson as one "who met their needs," Oliver sees Johnson's ability to play a wide variety of instruments and his "unending stream of blues themes" along with his "clean, limpid guitar and

sweet-toned voice with a Louisiana vibrato" as producing "the fortunate combi-
nation of southern inflections with an urbane, disarming delivery" (Oliver 99).

Nevertheless, other songs proposed leaving the North and returning back
home to the South, such as Jazz Gillum's "Down South Blues," a song about
a migrant who lives in an apartment building that is slated to be torn down
by a WPA wrecking crew. Without any money to pay the rent, the weather
turning cold, and with "no place to go," the persona sings about "goin' back
down South where the chilly winds don't blow." Similarly, in "Creole Queen,"
Little Bill Gaither wrote about a persona who lived near New Orleans "a good
many years ago" who has been sleeping on the floor of a bar since he arrived
in the North. He has "been on relief in Chicago and soup lines in Kokomo," but
now he is "goin' back down South" where he says he won't be "driven from door
to door." Questioning a life of displacement and dislocation, one anonymous
blues lyric asked, "What Am I Doing Up Here?" Another song questioned,
"my home's in Texas, what am I doin' up here?" (Jones 106). Huddie Ledbetter
(Leadbelly) warned in his song "Bourgeoisie Blues," "Don't try to buy a house in
Washington, D.C." Recognizing the migrants' need to deal with the difficulties
of crossing the border and leaving home, Muddy Waters wrote songs with titles
ranging from "Southbound Train" to "My Home Is in the Delta" and "Feel Like
Going Home." But despite the popularity of these songs, the vast majority of
migrants stayed.

In effect, communal spaces where migrants gathered acted as liminal spaces
where they could also find connections that helped them to cope with navigating the borderlands. The places where border narratives were recounted
quickly became the literal and figurative spaces where migrants could connect
with others who were facing similar circumstances. Pianist James P. Johnson
remembered dancers at Southern migrant gatherings in Manhattan calling
out "Let's go home." He would respond by answering with music that helped
to recreate the South (Griffin 55). The literal spaces where "race" and "hillbilly"
music were performed were carved out as places where Southern migrants
sought and generally found freedom. Rent parties, after-hour joints, barbecues,
and gut parties were frequent gathering places for urban blues musicians. Big
Bill Broonzy gives a vivid description of those Saturday-night blues parties on
the south side of Chicago in the 1920s:

> I came to Chicago and the people asked me to come to their house. Some of
> them had known me at home and they knew I could play and sing the blues.
> So I went to their houses and they had fried chicken and pig feet and chittlins
> for seventy-five cents a plate, and if you could play and sing you got all the eats
> and drinks free. . . . All of them was from some part of the South and had come
> to Chicago to better their living. And these people started to give parties and

some Saturday nights they would make enough money to pay the rent, and so
they started to call them house rent parties because they sold chicken, pig feet,
home brew, chittlins and moonshine whiskey. (Qtd. in Barlow 300–301)

These sorts of parties, according to LeRoi Jones, were "a form of acclimatization" (106), a chance to give musicians a venue to play, a way to raise money to
pay rent for an apartment as the hat was passed, and a communal setting that
helped the migrant in making the crossing. Essentially, these spaces offered
what Marvin Carlson describes as a "site of negotiation" (16), "a site for social
and cultural resistance and the exploration of alternative possibilities" (19).

In sharp contrast to the solitary experience today of listening to music on a
cell phone or an iPod, historically, American popular music was shaped by this
assembly tradition. Since its beginnings, American music has revolved around
public performance on a stage, however rustic or informal that stage might
have been. Communities gathered together to hear local musicians perform
and sing, and more formalized productions such as vaudeville and orches-
tral concerts were popular long before the advent of the recording industry.
Although phonographs transformed musical performance into a recorded
version, listening at home to the phonograph still tended to continue to reflect
the assembly tradition as families gathered around to listen. Even with the
advent of radio, shows such as the *National Barn Dance* and the *Grand Ole
Opry* brought the assembly tradition into homes, with a listening and dancing
audience who were part of the show itself. According to Chad Berry in *The
Hayloft Gang*, WLS and the *National Barn Dance* met with tremendous success because the show was able to recreate the assembly tradition, and singers
attempted to portray themselves as "friends who had come into your home
to visit" (36). Communities of Southerners who had migrated from the South
were as small as pockets of neighborhoods in Chicago and Detroit, and as
large as the listenership of a major radio show. Southerners living outside the
South were at once of the region, but displaced from it.

Music was a safe space. African American migrants found a "scheme for
survival" in the music of blues artists, according to Farah Jasmine Griffin, which
helped them in making the transition from South to North (55). While song
lyrics might suggest a fragmented new life for the migrant, performance offered
"order, stability and community," "a transitional space making the transformation from migrant to urban dweller a little less harsh," "a means to negotiate
the 'here'" (54). The blues was a personal type of musical form typically written
and performed for a black audience as a way to voice group concerns and
work through experiences group members faced. Urban blues was performed
in spaces like the 230 Club where whites had less control over the music, in
comparison to the classic blues, which was performed for black and white

audiences in tent shows and theaters owned by whites. While black migrants were "healed, informed, ministered, and entertained" in safe spaces that music offered (Griffin 55–56), so too were white migrants. Music was also crucial for the white migrants who settled in California. Country music of the 1930s, for example, "by and large belonged to Okies," according to James Gregory (223). Yet while music helped Southerners make the transition from back home to new homes beyond the South, it also communicated the distinguishing markers of a migrant people to the larger population around them—and generally those markers led to further prejudices and stereotyping of them. Nevertheless, music became a coping mechanism. "In a social situation that is itself fragmented," that is, in a new city setting, Griffin says, the blues "begins to provide some narrative coherence and order. The blues performance fills a void" (54).

In reclaiming and preserving African traditions, blues musicians also rebelled against white society in both the musical forms they used and in the lyrics of their songs. Calling them "proselytizers of a gospel of secularization" that equated freedom with mobility, William Barlow says the early rural blues placed value on the individual and the struggle against social oppression. Typically from poor farming communities, rural blues musicians, by the nature of their chosen profession, were "cultural rebels." Not tied to traditional jobs that kept them in one place, rural blues artists were often vilified by more conservative, older African Americans as "the Devil's disciples" because of the value they placed on the freedom and independence of the open road and the choice to play music rather than to labor in the fields (5–6). The improvisation of the blues allowed musicians more room for individual creativity—more personal reflection and expression. But as the blues moved to the city, the music became more narrative in format, more structured than the rural. As the numbers of instruments increased and amplification was used, openings and closings of songs became more standardized, instrumental sections became longer, diction became clearer and less nasal, and a wider variety of tempos was used (Keil 54–55). Yet the city blues, like the rural, was shaped by the freedom of the road, with Big Bill Broonzy, the "male archetype of Chicago-style blues from the late 1920s until the Advent of Muddy Waters and Howling Wolf in the postwar era" (Barlow 300), singing of having "got the key to the highway, and I'm billed out and bound to go / I'm gonna leave here runnin', cause walkin' is most too slow. . . . I am due in West Texas, and I've got to get on the road."

Perhaps it is that quality of searching, then, that most clearly links the blues and hillbilly/country music as Southerners left the South. The man on the road—and note, that's a man—also played a key role in hillbilly music and can be traced through later country music as well. Often referred to as the "ramblin' man," one of the earliest examples in recorded music is Henry Whitter's 1924 "Lonesome Road Blues," which was followed by Woody Guthrie and his

"Goin' Down the Road Feelin' Bad." In hillbilly and then country music, the wanderer was a displaced worker, a hobo on a train, then a cowboy, and more recently a trucker on a long haul. "Sometimes happy and fulfilled on the road," according to James Gregory, "more often they are lost souls trying to sing their way back home" (73). More recently this pattern has continued in songs such as Waylon Jennings's "I'm a Ramblin' Man," Hank Williams's "Ramblin' Man," Merle Haggard's "Ramblin Fever," Willie Nelson's "On the Road Again," Bobby Bare's "When Am I Ever Gonna Settle Down," and the Allman Brothers' "Ramblin Man." For the musicians themselves, commercialization made movement more important—from radio station to radio station, and also gave them more exposure to other musicians and their work. Some artists even sang of going back home after the rambling and longing to go back to "the one I love so well" and "building a little ole log cabin on a hill" in songs like Flatt and Scruggs's "I'm Gonna Settle Down."

The songwriter perhaps best known for capturing the experiences and becoming the voice of the white Southern migrant on the road was Woody Guthrie, who early in his career was called the Homer of his people. Guthrie was born in Okemah, Oklahoma, a town which experienced a boom in 1922 after the discovery of oil in the area, but the boom became a bust when the oil dried up after several years. Seeking employment, Guthrie moved to Pampa, Texas, where he married and had three children. Guthrie began his music career in Pampa, but the Great Depression and the Dust Bowl conditions in the region made supporting his family exceedingly difficult. Following the westward trek of thousands of destitute farmers and unemployed workers, Guthrie decided to head to California in search of work. Hitchhiking, riding freight trains, and walking, Guthrie made his way westward by working jobs painting signs and playing his guitar. Although the journey was one that left him surviving on hand-to-mouth wages and dealing with the uncertainty of the future, it also left him with an intense desire to take to the open road—something he would have the urge to do again and again throughout his life.

Guthrie also responded to the conditions of migrant Southerners by providing a common voice for them on the radio. First partnering with his cousin Jack Guthrie singing country-western in Los Angeles, the duo promoted their act on KFVD radio. After Jack took a break from performing, he teamed up with Maxine Crissman, whom Guthrie dubbed "Lefty Lou," for *The Woody and Lefty Lou Show*. The partnership was a highly successful one. Although the job was in large part a way to make a living, Guthrie also spent much of his life working in activist roles. On KFVD, Guthrie sang traditional songs that the migrants would have recognized, such as "A Picture from Life's Other Side" and "Boll Weevil," and new songs of his own. Performing with Crissman, Guthrie garnered widespread success in the California camps. Guthrie understood the emotional turmoil and upheaval of migration that broke apart his native Okemah and the conditions of the road that the migrants had traveled and the desperation that they faced. His song "So Long, It's Been Good to Know Yuh" quotes the frequent line of migrants as they got together to say their good-byes: "We talked of the end of the world, and then / We'd sing a song an' then sing it again. / We'd sit for an hour an' not say a word, / And then these words would be heard: / So long, it's been good to know yuh." Guthrie's songs about Dust Bowl refugees typically tell the stories of families pushed off their land and making the westward trek on, as he says in "Dust Bowl Refugee," a "never-ending highway."

Although Guthrie never lived in one of the California migrant camps, known as "Hoovervilles," he did perform in them. During the spring of 1938, he traveled around California, singing in the camps, trying to give the migrants some hope for the future, accompanied by his friend the actor Will Geer, who was also an activist working to improve the conditions of the migrants and who years later played Grandpa Walton in the popular 1970s television show *The Waltons*. Guthrie sang with nostalgia of a home that the migrants had left behind, even though that home had left them in desperate straits. His music provided not only a release from the day-to-day concerns, but also a voice for social justice. His increasing concern for the working rights of the people and his desire to speak out against corruption in politics and business helped mold an image of Guthrie as an outsider, a position that would help him to situate himself as a voice for the dispossessed and displaced. From 1937 to 1940, Guthrie wrote some of his best-known songs about the migrant situation, including "I Ain't Got No Home," "Goin' Down the Road Feelin' Bad," "Talking Dust Bowl Blues," "Tom Joad," and "Hard Travelin'." Many of Guthrie's songs about the migrant experience are characterized by a mix of the promises of a better life in California after the desperation of the Dust Bowl, a sharp rebuke of that promise in clear references to the realities of the difficult situations in California that the migrants actually encounter, and a nostalgic view of life back home in the places they left. In one of his best-known songs, for example, entitled "Do-Re-Mi," Guthrie refers to the image of California as a "sugar bowl" that drew thousands of migrants westward from the Dust Bowl region. Rather than the promise and prosperity they had hoped for, the migrants instead find the policemen at the border of the state numbering the migrants who enter—and the number is now up to 14,000 just for the day. The qualification for leading a good life in California (or at least finding the "sugar bowl") is bringing the "do-re-mi" along with you. "If you ain't got the do-re-mi," that is, if you don't have money, according to the song, then you'd "Better hang on" back at home.

The migrant in Guthrie's songs is characterized as honest, hard-working, supportive of family, persistent, religious, and patriotic. In "Hard Travelin'," for example, the narrator says to his "lord," "I thought you knowed / I've been havin' some hard travelin." God doesn't seem to be answering, but the migrant still prays. He's been "Cuttin' that wheat, stackin' that hay . . . tryin' make about a dollar a day. . . . working that Pittsburgh steel . . . dumpin' that red-hot slag . . . a blasting . . . a firin' . . . pourin' red-hot iron." The song harkens back to the promises of America. The migrants travel the Lincoln Highway and Route 66, highways that represented the new possibilities for movement across the country via the automobile, and one with a name that also recalls the promises of emancipation that looked to American democracy as freedom for the dispossessed. Similarly in "Pastures of Plenty," written in 1942, a first-person narrator tells of the seemingly invisible American workers who "come with the dust and . . . go with the wind." He recalls harvesting the landowner's crops, gathering his hops, digging his beets, and cutting his grades for the "light sparkling" wine that the owner will serve at his table. The song closes noting that the persona, who wandered like the river "All along your green valley," "will work till I die / My land I'll defend with my life if it be / Cause my pastures of plenty must always be free." The reference here at the end of the song is to World War II, yet the persona even claims the landowner's property as his own. Because they "must always be free," he'll give his life for "my pastures of plenty" that he has tilled and harvested even though they are someone else's.

Guthrie claimed a persona for many of his songs that validated and in some cases glorified the role that many in his audience also saw themselves as assuming. His song "Pretty Boy Floyd" specifically portrays the outlaw as outsider and helped to solidify the folk hero status of the bank robber Pretty Boy Floyd. Although Floyd began his robbery career as a young man, Guthrie focuses in on the Floyd of legend: a Georgia native known for valuing family and a career gangster who was glorified as a Robin Hood figure in Oklahoma where the Depression had hit earlier than in other regions of the country. When he robbed banks, the story goes, he would destroy any mortgages he came across on the chance that they had not yet been recorded. Floyd would also casually throw money out of the windows of his escape car after a heist and give money to people he knew were suffering through tough economic times. Floyd's defiance of the wealthy establishments of business and banking left him a folk legend among the people. The song obviously downplays Floyd's often careless and meaningless acts of murder, in favor of an image that displaced and dispossessed migrants would have seen as reaffirming their own value as human beings.

While songs sung by other artists, such as the traditional hymn "I Can't Feel at Home in This World Anymore" by the Carter family, encouraged migrants to think about their heavenly reward rather than a better life on earth, Guthrie inspired the migrants to see the road as tying them together in a shared earthly relationship. The words of the Carter family's "I Can't Feel at Home in This

World Anymore" describe heaven as the goal and an acceptance that "This world is not my home, I'm just a-passing thru." The persona can claim ownership, possibility, hopefulness, and a home only in the hereafter: "My treasures and my hopes are all beyond the blue; / Where many Christian children have gone on before." Guthrie's version of the song entitled "I Ain't Got No Home in This World Anymore" addresses more specifically the plight of the migrant and a clear dissatisfaction with the conditions of their lives. Guthrie explained in the liner notes for *Hard Travelin'* that "this old song to start out with was a religious piece . . . but I seen there was another side to the picture. Reason why you can't feel at home in this world anymore is mostly because you ain't got no home to feel at" (Logsdon). The "wandrin' worker" of Guthrie's song "ain't got no home in this world anymore" because the wealthy have driven him out. The persona points to the sharecropping system that has held him in poverty and made him in debt to the bank. He has also lost his wife, who "took down and died upon the cabin floor." In his ramblings and wanderings, the worker finds his life made even more difficult by police officers who harass him. Alone, without family, he wanders, with no sense of direction and no dreamed of promises of a final reward in heaven.

While the Carter song points to personal salvation and the promises of heaven, Guthrie's words directly pull together a community facing the here and now. Writing in a letter to folklorist and ethnomusicologist Alan Lomax, Guthrie noted that using language that tied the listener to the song's narrator helped "to make one part of the community feel like they know the other part and one end of it help the other" (Qtd. in Garman 89). In "I Ain't Got No Home in This World Anymore," Guthrie refers to fellow migrants as "My brothers and my sisters" and identifies their common path, "A hot and dusty road that a million feet done trod," whereas in the Carter song, the Christian journey heavenward is what links the persona to other Christians who have already reached heaven. The final assessment of the song's last stanza suggests a stepping back, an intentional appraisal of what has happened in the life of the persona and the lives of fellow migrants. On the one hand, there is a hint of the positive in the persona's view of the world as "such a great and a funny place to be," but he concludes, as he says, "Now as I look round, it's mighty plain to see," that "the gamblin' man is rich and the workin' man is poor." The irony of life leaves the persona with a sense of the unfairness of his living conditions and his recognition that he is homeless and marginalized—but he is not alone on the migrant's road.

The injustices and hypocrisy of American capitalistic society are at the core of many of Guthrie's songs such as "Jolly Banker" (1939) and "Vigilante Man" (1940). In "Jolly Banker," Tom Cranker "safeguard[s] the farmers and widows and orphans" as he sings, "I'm a jolly banker, jolly banker I am." Speaking

directly to the audience for the song, using the pronoun "you," Cranker the
Jolly Banker appears to be helping the dispossessed and the suffering as he
says he will "check your shortage" and "bring down your mortgage." Instead,
he "plasters your home with a furniture loan," expects double the return on a
loan, forecloses on your property, and takes all that you own. He hits the farmer
and his family when they are at their lowest, when mouths need to be fed, dust
storms settle on the farmland, and crops fail. If the "bugs get your cotton," then
the Jolly Banker will "rake you and scalp you." Showing his own disdain for
the banker and the entire system, Guthrie reinforces here in this song what he
wrote in one of his *Woody Sez* columns: "A policeman will jest stand there an
let a banker rob a farmer, or finance man rob a working man. But if a farmer
robs a banker—you wood have a hole dern army of cops out a shooting at
him." Communal ties and the importance of communal action come to the
forefront in "Jolly Banker," as well as in "Vigilante Man," in which the persona
asks if listeners have "seen that vigilante man," who he is, and what it means
to be a vigilante. The vigilante man is the one who chased "us" out of shelter
from the rain and other harsh weather conditions when we were "sleepin' just
as still as a mouse." Vigilantes populate the landscape, taking responsibility for
enforcing order, but using brute force to do so and in the name of corporate
America and big business rather than for the sake of humanity.

Audiences might have seen their own plight in the words of Guthrie's songs,
but he also gave them a chance to relieve the stresses and complications of
migrant life in his use of humor. As Guy Logsdon says in the liner notes to *Hard
Travelin'*, "through it all [Guthrie] never lost his sense of humor—he probably
survived because he could laugh, a personality trait that too many fans and
scholars seem to forget" (5). Undoubtedly, migrants not only saw themselves in
the struggles Guthrie wrote about in songs such as "Talking Dust Bowl Blues,"
but they also found some relief and camaraderie in Guthrie's retelling of the
migrants' trip westward. After he "swapped" his farm for a "Ford machine,"
the narrator of the song tells of his family's journey over the mountains westward, of gaining speed and then not making a hairpin turn. The fiddles and
guitars fly as the Ford careens out of control "like a flying squirrel." The car
flies "halfway around the world," flinging wives and children "all over the side
of that mountain." Ending with a political statement by noting that the thin
tater stew his wife feeds to the kids when they reach California is thin enough
that "Some of these here politicians / Coulda seen through it," nevertheless,
the song carries a mixed tone of suffering and hardship along with an ability
to survive that's rooted in comradeship and connection.

Wanderers, however, even for a composer or musician as politically and
socially progressive as Guthrie, were still men or accompanied women. As I've
pointed out in previous chapters about the ability of men to cross borders, to

move out into the world with stereotypical freedom and without the confine-
ment faced by women in the domestic world, in music, too, this same pattern
continues. As one of the earliest country music stars Jimmie Rodgers sang
in "Train Whistle Blues," "When a woman gets the blues, she hangs her little
head and cries, / But when a man gets blue, he grabs a train and rides." In the
blues tradition, however, women were challenging this narrative pattern and
beginning to strike out on their own. Women blues artists were identified
with the urban blues—not with the rural—and migration made this possible.
Bessie Smith, for example, who was described as the "high priestess" and the
"undisputed 'Empress'" of the blues in the 1920s who introduced mainstream
America to the blues (164), was an "unabashed rebel" who resisted the music
industry's attempts to commodify and misrepresent African American music,
according to William Barlow (165). Yet while male blues artists were viewed
as "free men," female blues artists were typically labeled as "fallen women"
(Barlow 180). Given traditional models of womanhood, for both black and
white women, being on the road was in sharp contrast to the domestic realm
that women were expected to inhabit. Unconventional for the times, particularly in her attitudes about intimate relationships, Smith challenged the
dominance of white culture in American society.

Born in Chattanooga, Tennessee, in 1894 into a poor family, Bessie Smith
was one of nine children. Her father, a Baptist preacher, died not long after
she was born, and her mother died before Bessie reached her teens. Smith
started singing on street corners to make tips and entered show business when
her brother, who was working as a comedian for a traveling minstrel troupe,
returned home and got her an audition for his troupe, where she started as a
dancer. Ma Rainey was also a member of the troupe and became a strong influence in Smith's life. First moving to Atlanta and then Philadelphia for work, she
then toured the South and the Atlantic seaboard, but ultimately sang to an even
wider audience as she toured Northern and Midwestern cities. Always faithful
to her Southern roots, Smith was described by jazz guitarist Danny Barker, who
was from New Orleans, as able to "bring about mass hypnotism. When she was
performing you could hear a pin drop. . . . When you went to see Bessie and
she came out, that was it." Her music also recalled for transplanted Southerners
the life they knew back in the South. "If you had any church background, like
people who came from the South, like I did," Barker said, "you would recognize a similarity between what she was doing and what those preachers and
evangelists from there did, and how they moved people. . . . Bessie did the same
thing on stage" (Qtd. in Barlow 170–71). According to gospel singer Mahalia
Jackson, who was from New Orleans, "When I was a little girl I felt [Smith]
was having troubles like me. That's why it was such a comfort for people of
the South to hear her. She expressed something they couldn't put into words"

(Qtd. in Barlow 171). Singing a song like "Young Woman's Blues," with the lyrics "I'm a young woman and ain't done runnin' around. / Some people call me a hobo, some call me a bum," Smith was a new type of celebrity—a black female powerhouse. The persona of the song says she's "gonna drink good moonshine," she "ain't gonna marry, ain't gonna settle down" (Barlow 175). Like Ma Rainey, Smith represented a new image of womanhood that gained power for women blues artists. Women urban blues artists reached star status, while male performers were relegated to roles as backup singers and musicians.

Because of movement across the borders of the South, a new site of identity was opened for women African American blues artists like Smith. That liminal space offered freedoms that women had not experienced in the South and a connection to roots and Southern blues culture. In her landmark study *Blues Legacies and Black Feminism*, Angela Davis points out that even though after emancipation African Americans were still dealing with oppressive poverty and political inequality, their lives were changed radically in three areas: they had greater freedom to make decisions about their own movements (e.g., whether or not to stay in the South), increased educational prospects, and sexual freedoms. "The new blues consciousness," according to Davis, "was shaped by and gave expression to at least two of these three transformations: travel and sexuality." Although women were more limited in their movements because of their gender, Davis says, blues women were able to overcome this obstacle (8). Smith was able to do this very intentionally and deliberately with her appropriation of a train car that she used as she toured. Made for her personally by the Southern Iron and Equipment Company of Atlanta, the luxurious 78-foot car was brightly painted a yellow color and showcased green lettering. Two stories high, the car contained seven staterooms and could lodge up to 35 people who might be touring with Smith. As she traveled South and North and across the borders between regions, Smith's train car gave her freedoms that other African Americans would not have experienced. She was able to travel freely, without concern for the prejudices and oppressions that would have limited her in her lodging in particular communities or in public train cars (Braziel 14–15). In effect, borders were blurred for Smith as she was able to pass over them with ease.

Music unlocked new sites for charting out both personal and communal identities. "The blues, as a musical genre and as a performed cultural art form," according to Jana Evans Braziel in "'Bye, Bye Baby': Race, Bisexuality, and the Blues," "opened new spaces of travel and autonomy not only for women, but also for queer artists, musicians, and writers" (Braziel 14–15). Smith, who was bisexual, was married twice to male partners, had a long-term relationship with her second husband's niece and openly sexual relationships with two women dancers who toured with her, and a number of casual sexual relationships.

Describing bisexuality as in itself residing in "a liminal, deeply ambivalent space" (9), Braziel argues that the blues "offered an audible, if not always heard, site for mapping queerness within blackness." Perhaps Isaac Julien explains this even more clearly, as Braziel quotes from him in an interview with poet Essex Hemphill: "Blues is very important in relationship to black culture and specifically in relationship to black gay identities because blues songs were some of the first spaces where one could actually *hear* black gay desire." "Bessie had the beat. . . . It's that *tone*, that sound, which is in me," expat James Baldwin said in an interview with Studs Terkel (Braziel 15). Instead of the emptiness of the road and feelings of being pulled two ways, this site in the liminal space contained new sounds that resonated.

Although marginalized communities were better able to cultivate new spaces of identity through the blues, in general, as the music of this period evolved into a commercialized commodity imprinted on records, musical reflections on those liminal spaces and representations of the South and the migrant experience also became more contained, more standardized and regularized. In the blues, the blue note itself provided a liminal space "betwixt and between" for both the artist and the listener. Characterized by flatted third, fifth, and seventh notes in a key, the blue note expresses intensifying emotions with a falling pitch that bends the notes on the scale. Identifying the blue note as "the repository of the 'ancestor,' of 'home,'" Farah Jasmine Griffin suggests that the blues "infused urban music with the secret ingredient of the 'blue note,'" and in that site, "at the level of content, the falling pitch of the blue note acts as the space where the absence, the terror, the fear, and the tragic moments of black life reside . . . truly the site of history and memory" (56–57).

In discussing country music, Rachel Rubin describes something similar—perhaps not musically but thematically—in terms of an iconic image of the South she sees developing. The nostalgia that many migrants experienced in leaving the South became a deeply ingrained pattern. "Explicit homesickness" became a key element of the song lyrics and performances of many country singers, with the birthplace branded as "home." At the same time that large numbers of migrants were leaving the South, the life stories of country music performers became an increasingly significant part of the marketing and performance strategies used to sell records and tickets to performances. Telling their own stories of migration—indeed, stories similar to those that their listeners had experienced—the country music singer became the "new ethnic hero," and in the process, their stories of relocation became "public property" (Rubin 99). The Maddox Brothers and Rose, for example, gained popularity in part because they spoke to a common Southern experience, no matter where in the South the Southerner lauded from. Finding fame with songs such as "In the Land Where We'll Never Grow Old," "Do-Re-Mi," and "Dust Bowl Blues," the Maddox family of seven hitchhiked and rode the rails from Boaz, Alabama, to California looking for work during the Depression. Eleven years old when her family started performing, Rose Maddox told years later that the family headed west from Alabama because her mother had read about the "promised land" of California by reading dime westerns. When they arrived in Oakland, California, the local *Oakland Tribune* covered their journey with a story and picture of the family with the headline "Family Roams U.S. for Work" (Rubin 99). Ultimately, they became known as "America's most colorful hillbilly band" (Rubin 105). Family members described the transition for them from homeless family to singing stars as so abrupt that many of them learned to play their instruments as they played on-air. They saw performance as the way to get out of poverty (Rubin 99).

Although the Maddox Brothers and Rose became popular because their songs spoke for the masses, the "iconic South" of their music was something new, and something that can be specifically attributed to the Great Migration of Southerners westward and to Northern cities. Rubin points to "The South," a song the Maddox Brothers and Rose recorded between 1947 and 1951, as an example:

> Down below that old Dixon line
> There's a place that really is fine
> Where the sun is happy to shine
> Where the bees make honey all day
> And the folks are happy and gay.

Because it did not name a specific geographical location and was "remarkably unburdened by any concrete details," the song had particular meaning for a broader cross-section of migrants from the South. "Dixie" songs popular during the era of Tin Pan Alley and minstrelsy tended to reflect an individual persona's specific relationship to the South or projected emotional connections to the South onto an "imagined black narrative voice," whereas songs such as "The South," according to Rubin, conceptualize a "remembered place," "a sense of roots and pride" (101). The voice is a communal one that speaks of shared experience.

Music during this time period was also solidified as a voice for the dispossessed and displaced and made a new space for them in American democracy—whether in reality or perhaps in the imagination. Thousands of people wrote to Woody Guthrie in response to his songs on the radio in California, saying that he spoke for them (Jackson 25). Feeling compelled to respond to Irving Berlin's "God Bless America" because he saw so many people for whom this song did not speak, Guthrie wrote his second wife, "this world I've seen is alive and interesting, not because it's perfect and pretty and eternal, but because it needs my fixin', I need fixin', so does the land" (Jackson 28). Hearing

Kate Smith's version of the song again and again as he crossed the country, Guthrie answered with his "God Blessed America for Me," which eventually was retitled and revised as "This Land Is Your Land." Gaining its own popularity as a patriotic song, "This Land" was originally intended by Guthrie as a comment on capitalism and private property, and questioned the equality and promise of American citizenship. National recognition for a singer also meant recognition for the plight of the migrant and a hero for the migrants. Singing the words of a song not only helped to internalize feelings of longing, loss, and perseverance, but the musicians and singers themselves also gave migrants a visual image of someone not unlike themselves who had gone through similar struggles but had found success.

By World War II, the music industry had long recognized the buying power of Southern migrant populations. As Southerners flooded into urban areas, *Billboard* magazine became increasingly attuned to the migrant market. Noting the popularity of clubs that featured "hillbilly jazz" and western swing, *Billboard* ran headlines such as "Coast Orks Go 'Billy'" ("ork" meaning orchestra) and "Khaki and Overalled Oakies Make Metropolitan Maestri Feed 'Em Down Home Tunes." Southern war workers and servicemen insisted on hearing "their kind of music," and even Louis Armstrong felt pressed to play "ditties with a Texas-Oklahoma flavor to please the dancing Oakies." Armstrong was quoted as responding that "those cats in slacks (war workers) and all the servicemen don't want to hear anything else" (Gregory 182). American urban centers were influenced not only by the influx of new workers who moved there from the South, but also by the musical art forms that found their way as well. Chicago, for example, was not only the heart of a Midwest movement that saw the evolution of a new kind of American blues, but also the location of WLS, which aired the widely popular *National Barn Dance*.

Music ultimately became both an agent and a symbol of change in the United States, a sign that lines between races were being crossed during the civil rights movement. Although Elvis Presley, for example, might not have intentionally considered his work as taking a stand on civil rights, the early Elvis was, as Bobbie Ann Mason says in her biography of Elvis, "making music that was the voice of the Southern poor—both black and white working-class groups." At first mistaken by some as a black musician, Elvis was indebted to rhythm-and-blues artists, especially the songs of Big Bill Broonzy (28–29). When Buck Owens performed the blues singer Leadbelly's song "Cotton Fields" on his 1962 album *On the Bandstand*, white migrants from the Dust Bowl "could easily recall . . . the farms they had left behind," according to Rachel Rubin. Yet while Leadbelly performed "Cotton Fields" on an acoustic twelve-string guitar, Owens reimagined the song with the help of a lead electric guitar, pedal steel guitar, electric bass, and drums (98). Certainly, this crossover as both musical and social wasn't the norm in 1962, but it wasn't new either. My intent here is not to paint a rosy conclusion, but instead to show that navigating this line between musical genres did, in fact, encourage American audiences to at least look across the racial divide.

Well into the 1980s and 1990s, musicians were still dealing with the implications of crossing out of the South—and so were their audiences. Dolly Parton sang of Smoky Mountain memories and Glenn Campbell of a country boy who "had his feet in LA," but his "mind's on" Tennessee. Michigan-born Stevie Wonder's song "Living for the City" told the story of a boy born in "hard time Mississippi" who as a young man migrates to New York City. Although he may be "living for the city," he is "almost dead from breathing on air pollution." He "tried to vote but there's no solution." The migrant's path across the border, the metaphorical roadway that crosses the border, is essentially what redefines the individual. For many it was the road itself that branded them with new identities, whether they wanted that branding or not. Border narratives in music served as individual and communal voices that shaped the migrant experience, giving meaning and an outlet of expression. The shared story of movement and the liminal space that story defines can offer security and safety or terror and grief, and figure remarkably and deeply in evolving new conceptions of the South, Southernness, and what it means to be at once of and not of the South—somewhere in between.

CHAPTER 6

And Then They Drown?: Faulkner's Quentin Compson Lost in the Borderlands

Deacon greeted Quentin at the train station as he had all the other young men arriving at Harvard to start their freshman year. Everyone said that Deacon hadn't missed a train at the beginning of the school year in forty years. Dressed in "a sort of Uncle Tom's cabin outfit, patches and all," Deacon "could pick out a Southerner with one glance" and identify a student's home state as soon as he heard the student speak. Making sure that a young man's luggage was delivered directly to his dorm room, Deacon was "guide mentor and friend to unnumbered crops of innocent and lonely freshmen." He was "in or out of your room, ubiquitous and garrulous" until a student was "completely subjugated" to him. Deacon tells Quentin—the border crosser who looks to Deacon as a guide—"I've tried to treat all folks right. . . . I draw no petty social lines. A man to me is a man, wherever I find him" (123). With a name that suggests he serves as a sort of spiritual guide as well, Deacon is, of course, the African American porter who meets incoming students at the train station when they first arrive at Harvard in Faulkner's *The Sound and the Fury* (1929). Quentin's train ride north is symbolic. Cheryl Lester has written on the Great Migration of African Americans in *The Sound and the Fury*, focusing on the ways the journey north "produces an awareness of Southern racialism" for Quentin and for Faulkner, too, as he traveled in 1918 from Mississippi to New Haven, Connecticut, where he stayed with Phil Stone and worked for the Winchester Repeating Arms

Company after his childhood sweetheart, Estelle Oldham, married someone else. Lester points to the "experience of sitting beside the racial Other on these northbound train rides" as "a longstanding *topos* in the literature of migration" (130–31). Recounting Quentin's tumultuous freshman year, including his struggle to tell roommate Shreve why he "doesn't hate it," *The Sound and the Fury*, alongside Faulkner's *Absalom, Absalom!* (1936), portrays Quentin as a border crosser who is set into a downward spiral and suicide *because* he sees himself and his own family in the story of another border crosser, Thomas Sutpen.

Would Quentin have committed suicide if he had attended college in the South? Would he have committed suicide if he had stayed at home and never attended college in Boston? What if he had not been a border crosser? Of course, it's impossible to definitively answer these questions, but Faulkner's choices for Quentin seem highly intentional. Quentin leaves the South in the same way as other male characters I write about in chapter 3 of this book. Rosa Coldfield even surmises—perhaps to lay some guilt on him—that because he is leaving the South for college, he will probably never return home. Quentin, Rosa speculates, will perhaps pick up the pen as well to become a writer: "I dont imagine you will ever come back here and settle down as a country lawyer in a little town like Jefferson since Northern people have already seen to it that there is little left in the South for a young man," she says. "So maybe you will enter the literary profession as so many Southern gentlemen and gentlewomen too are doing now and maybe some day you will remember this and write about it" (5). Quentin's journey north is not unlike that of Stingo or of the Invisible Man or Eugene Gant or Jed Tewksbury, except that he isn't one of those survivor-narrators at the end of his story. Essentially, Quentin's story shows what happens if a border crosser doesn't read the "guidebook" correctly, doesn't see the dangers along the route. According to Barbara Ladd, "Quentin's is a failure of the imagination, an inability to rewrite the old stories" (154). I would assert that Quentin's failure is directly related to his refusal to recognize that Sutpen's story of crossing is his own story as well.

Faulkner emphasizes this pattern of crossing by surrounding Quentin with other border crossers: the Canadian Shreve, the little immigrant girl who reminds Quentin and Faulkner's readers of Caddy his sister and follows him around as he struggles with his suicide, and especially Thomas Sutpen, who left the Virginia mountains for the Tidewater, then the West Indies, and finally Yoknapatawpha County. Quentin's story ends tragically because he cannot successfully come to terms with himself. He doesn't survive the passage; instead, he drowns in his past, unable to create a frame of reference that will move him on into the future. Quentin is a reader of a border text: the story of Sutpen's early life in western Virginia, his time in the Tidewater and in Haiti, and finally his arrival and years spent in Yoknapatawpha County. And it is

Quentin's retelling of the story of Sutpen's border crossing and his ultimate conclusion that sends him into his frenzied declarations that he does not hate the South and ultimately to his suicide.

The story of Thomas Sutpen and his "grand design" is a communal one, first reinterpreted by grandfather General Jason Lycurgus Compson II, father Jason Richmond Lycurgus Compson III, and Rosa Coldfield, and finally by Quentin and Shreve, who attempt to fill in the gaps of the story as they sit in their Harvard dorm room. Sutpen's story is meaningful to Quentin not only because it is the epitome of the tragedy of Southern history and cuts to the core of the myth of Southern exceptionalism, but also because the narrative in many ways parallels Quentin's own. Success for both the young men Thomas Sutpen and Quentin Compson was defined by their individual abilities to cross borders. For Sutpen, making the crossing meant leaving behind his upbringing in a poverty-stricken family in western Virginia and chasing the dream of money and success in the West. For Quentin, leaving the South to study at Harvard had been a part of his family's desires for him since he had been born, but crossing the border meant having to face not only his own vision of the South as represented by his sister, Caddy, but also the history of the South that ultimately drowns him.

Faulkner represents a Yoknapatawpha County that is itself liminal space when Sutpen arrives in 1833. Mississippi had been a state for only 16 years, and the county seat was renamed Jefferson that year. Framing the county's history in the actual, Faulkner makes specific reference in his appendix to *The Sound and the Fury* to Andrew Jackson, "A Great White Father with a sword" who "patented sealed and countersigned the grant with his own hand in his gold teppe in Wassi Town, not knowing about the oil either" (404), a reference to the Indian Removal Act of 1830 that ultimately led to the forced migration of the Chicksaw Indians out of Mississippi and into the American West. (Perhaps Sutpen sees himself as following in Jackson's footsteps?) In the short story "A Courtship," Faulkner refers to Jackson as General Jackson, who met with Issetibbeha and "burned sticks and signed a paper, and now a line ran through the woods, although you could not see it . . . straight as a bee's flight among the woods, with the Plantation on one side of it, where Issetibbeha was the Man, and America on the other side, where General Jackson was the Man" (361). At the opening of *Absalom, Absalom!* Faulkner explains that "in the long unamaze," Quentin in his mind sees Sutpen and his slaves "overrun suddenly the hundred miles of tranquil and astonished earth" that he has claimed as his own to "drag house and formal gardens violently out of the soundless Nothing and clap them down like cards upon a table beneath the up-palm immobile and pontific, creating the Sutpen's Hundred, the *Be Sutpen's Hundred* like the oldentime *Be Light*" (4). The Yoknapatawpha County where Sutpen arrives in 1833 is a place that is still very much frontier.

Although situating Yoknapatawpha County within the context of actual Mississippi history doesn't neatly tie up an interpretation of Faulkner's fiction, specific references to Jackson and the removal of the Chickasaw Indians identify a history for Faulkner's county that is grounded in the actual. Yoknapatawpha is in the transitional stage from frontier to plantation culture as Sutpen enters the community. Native Americans have been pushed off the land and into the West, and Sutpen is described as "playing God," in effect, taking the virgin earth and recreating it in an image that he believes will bring him power and control. Early Yoknapatawpha County was in many ways like the frontier Mississippi that historian David J. Libby describes as "more western than southern, and more colonial than antebellum"—a "borderlands" (xiii–xiv). Libby's study reminds us that when Sutpen arrived, he didn't find a fully established plantation system. He was, in many ways, like those who left Eastern regions to move westward in order to start a new life, leave the past behind, and find prosperity in new lands. He was like many Americans who moved westward in the nineteenth century in the massive move to settle the continent from coast to coast.

The two community men that Sutpen is identified as having more specific relationships with are Quentin's grandfather, Jason Lycurgus Compson III, who befriends him and is the one who listens to Sutpen tell his story, and Goodhue Coldfield, father to Ellen Coldfield Sutpen and Rosa Coldfield. Grandfather Compson is one generation removed from settlement, as his father arrived at the Chickasaw agency in 1811 and two years later traded a racehorse to a Chickasaw chief in exchange for the square mile in the center of what would become Jefferson. Compson is referred to as "a young man too then" when Sutpen arrived in Yoknapatawpha (25). According to the story that Quentin's father tells him, Coldfield was "a man of uncompromising moral strength, coming into a new country with a small stock of goods and supporting five people out of it in comfort and security at least" (65). The frontier was still a part of the character and lives of these men who lived in a region of the South that was then a borderland, a place that would soon be firmly embedded in a slave system that would in large part be the basis of the crushing guilt that would lead Quentin to commit suicide in Cambridge, Massachusetts.

Although the impetus for Sutpen's drive to acquire money, land, slaves, children, and secondarily a wife is portrayed as the moment he is turned away at the front door by the African American slave at the Tidewater plantation, the narrative that comes to shape his life is the one that he is read by his teacher at the only school he ever attends. An effort by his teacher to settle restless students, the story is the get-rich-quick myth of opportunity and riches. This passage is one of the few in the entire book where Sutpen's actual words are quoted; in fact, not much of the section that we hear in Grandfather Compson's words is direct quote from Sutpen. Surely, the direct quotation was intentional on Faulkner's part. Sutpen says, "What I learned was that there was a place called the West Indies to which poor men went in ships and became rich" (195). He even points out that in listening to his teacher read, he didn't learn where the West Indies was located (although that would have been a handy detail for when he decided to make the journey) and by learning about the potential for such a journey, he "was equipping [him]self better for what [he] should later design to do than if [he] had learned all the addition and subtraction in the book" (195). The story itself is a powerful motivator that comes to dominate his life.

   Absalom, Absalom! is down to its core about borders and border crossers. By way of Haiti, Sutpen arrives in Yoknapatawpha County, where he carves out a plot of land measuring 100 square miles and tries to distance himself from the Other that he represents to the community and fashion himself as one of the local elite. Quentin is obsessed with this story of crossing and in drawing lines and borders that serve to valorize his own family's Southern past and to distinguish them from Sutpen and his progeny. As Quentin and Shreve retell the story of Sutpen's early life in western Virginia, for example, Quentin is intent on identifying the location as West Virginia, even though, as Shreve insists, Sutpen would have been born in Virginia. Quentin, of course, would have known this detail—western Virginia was admitted to the United States as West Virginia because of the antislavery and pro-Union sentiments of the region, but he is intent on fighting against any suggestion that Sutpen is connected with the South by birth. Quentin goes on to describe Sutpen's life in "West Virginia" as "where what few other people he knew lived in log cabins boiling with children like the one he was born in—men and grown boys who hunted or lay before the fire on the floor while the women and older girls stepped back and forth across them to reach the fire to cook" (179). Quentin insists on identifying Sutpen as "Other"—someone not born in a Southern state, someone who when he moved to Yoknapatawpha could not claim an ancestry like that of the Compson or the Coldfield families.

   In a similar fashion, as Rosa relates her version of Sutpen's story to Quentin, she identifies herself as from a family that knows where they came *from*. Perhaps in part because of the tragedy of the story of her father's suicide and because of her humiliation at Sutpen's proposal that he try to impregnate her before they marry, but likely, too, because of the aristocratic bearing she hopes to hold on to, Rosa identifies herself as from a family with a history solidly rooted in the South. Her father, of course, knew where he came from. The genealogy that she relates is as full of insistence as Quentin's response is to Shreve's labeling of Sutpen as Southern by birth. Rosa uses this, too, as a way to distance herself from Sutpen, and she seeks to "other" Sutpen as well. He is a barbarian—a satanic figure—who cannot claim even a past that might tie him to respectability. I have added boldface in the passage below to show the emphasis that Rosa places on "knowing," on being able to trace the trajectory of her family's line—both through the blood line and across physical, geographical borders—and having evidence to confirm her and her family's status in the community:

> our father **knew** who his father was in Tennessee and who his grandfather had been in Virginia and our neighbors and the people we lived among **knew** that we **knew** and we **knew** they **knew** we **knew** and we **knew** that they would have believed us about who and where we came from **even if we had lied**, just as anyone could have looked at him once and **known** that he would be **lying** about who and where and why he came from **by the very fact** that apparently he had to refuse to say at all. And **the very fact** that he had had to choose respectability to hide behind was **proof enough (if anyone needed further proof)** that what he fled from must have been some opposite of respectability too dark to talk about. . . . And he was no younger son sent out from some old quiet country like Virginia or Carolina with the surplus negroes to take up new land, because **anyone could look** at those negroes of his **and tell** that they may have come (and probably did) from a much older country than Virginia or Carolina but it wasn't a quiet one. (11)

Quentin, in his "All right all right" speech, pushes Sutpen literally into the borderlands, into a state that even now has trouble identifying itself as Northern or Southern. Rosa pushes him there as well, hiding behind what she claims is her own respectability because she supposedly knows where she came *from*. Rosa suggests that there was intent, reason, progression in her family—from "old quiet country like Virginia or Carolina," while to Sutpen she assigns a history of questionable moral values, deceit, and poverty.

Rosa is intent on controlling the narrative, intent on telling the story to Quentin to save not only her own reputation but also her family's. She frames her story of Sutpen by giving him the role of the displaced, wandering person, one who has no familial connections, no family status, and a worthless name. "He wasn't a gentleman. He wasn't even a gentleman," she tells Quentin. No one in Yoknapatawpha knew for certain if the name he used was actually his own, and the name was certainly one "nobody ever heard before." In search of "some place to hide himself," Sutpen, according to Rosa, "fled here and hid, concealed himself behind respectability." He "so far as anyone . . . knew either had no past at all or did not dare reveal it" (9–10). Rosa represents a supposedly virgin land and innocent citizens of Yoknapatawpha as existing in some sort of prelapsarian state as Sutpen enters their community: "out of quiet thunderclap he would abrupt (man-horse-demon)" (4), coming "*out of nowhere and without warning upon the land*" (5). He names his plantation Sutpen's Hundred, "as if it had been a King's grant in unbroken perpetuity from his great grandfather" (10). Rosa believes, too, that she understands the motivations and lures of young men who found their way to Mississippi in 1833, the year that Sutpen arrived. Claiming that 25-year-old men do not "voluntarily undertake the hardship and privation of clearing virgin land and establishing a plantation in a new country just for money"—and certainly not one "without any past that he apparently cared to discuss"—Rosa tells Quentin that young men were more likely to be interested in the overindulgence of alcohol and other temptations on nearby Mississippi riverboats. Anyone could have recognized that he was the type of person who would have "chosen the River" and ended up hanging from the end of a hemp rope, Rosa claims (11).

Similar stories are perpetuated by other community members, including Mr. Compson, Quentin's father. Details of Sutpen's entrance into the community emphasize the point that he arrived on a Sunday, on the Sabbath, stressing the supposed purity of the community he was intruding upon. Mr. Compson describes Sutpen and his horse—his "beast"—as "looking as though they had been created out of thin air and set down in the bright summer Sabbath sunshine in the middle of a tired foxtrot." Again and again the details are repeated that no one had seen his face before, heard the name Sutpen before, or knew from where he came (24). He was "underbred," according to Grandfather Compson. "It showed like this always . . . in all his formal contacts with people" (34). He brought in slaves—"wild blood"—"which he had brought into the country and tried to mix, blend, with the tame which was already there, with the same care and for the same purpose with which he blended that of the stallion and that of his own" (67). The African slaves he brought with him from Haiti speak no English, but people in the community cannot understand their "sort of French"—"not some dark and fatal tongue of their own" (27) that Sutpen uses to communicate with them. "A good part of the county" does not recognize the language they use as "civilised" (44), emphasizing the boundaries between the races and between Sutpen and his slaves and the community. Although the community was a new one, others in Yoknapatawpha are referred to as Sutpen's "adopted fellow citizens" (28). He never seems to have equal footing, but believes that money can be the great equalizer. By the time that Sutpen's story reaches Shreve, Sutpen has become "this Faustus, this demon, this Beelzebub." Again and again he is described as a man of façades—"a man who pretended to be civilised" (204), a demon who took advantage of "a poor ignorant Indian" (145) to gain the land where he built his plantation even though the supposedly more upstanding citizens of Yoknapatawpha were just as much to blame for pushing the Native Americans off their land. Sutpen is described as in flight, as hiding—as ultimately intent on evil-doings. Layer upon layer of reinterpretation make up Sutpen's story, effectively camouflaging the common guilt that the community shares but does not acknowledge.

Both Quentin and Rosa are intent on reframing Sutpen's story so that he is shown as a wanderer, but this sort of wanderer has more in common with a vagrant—not a wanderer in the Ulysses tradition or the struggles of the youthful American male making his way in the world. Quentin and Rosa seem not so much fearful of placelessness as fearful of not having a family line connected to that place and the place that they came from. Although *Absalom, Absalom!* revolves around Sutpen's intent in creating a "design," Rosa and Quentin are equally intent in casting Sutpen as a wanderer who did not have a design— someone not part of the same move west that brought Compson and Coldfield ancestors to Yoknapatawpha in the first place, someone more like the hoodlums and thrill-seekers on the Mississippi riverboats.

If we can take the word of Colonel Compson, he is the one with the most direct access to the story that Sutpen tells of his own past. Certainly Sutpen might have changed some details about his past—and he could have conceivably made up every single detail—but the story that he supposedly told to the young Compson and that was passed down through grandfather to son to grandson is a story that focuses on a transformation that takes place as Sutpen migrates from the mountains of western Virginia, into the Tidewater of Virginia with his family, on to the West Indies, and finally to Yoknapatawpha County. The version of Sutpen's story that comes from the grandfather begins with the words "His trouble was innocence." Earlier in the novel, Sutpen is described as "like a man who had been through some solitary furnace experience which was more than just fever, like an explorer say" (24). This story is at the heart of *Absalom, Absalom!* and in many ways seems to be the narrative that ultimately drives Quentin to commit suicide.

The Appalachia that Sutpen describes in this story seems incongruous. Despite the negative image he creates of the mountain community as steeped in poverty and the people as bogged down in a sense of purposelessness and depression, he represents it as a world of equality. "The land belonged to anybody and everybody," and people didn't fence off land and call it their own— that was "crazy." No one hoarded things: "nobody had any more of them than you did because everybody had just what he was strong enough or energetic enough to take and keep, and only that crazy man would go to the trouble to take or even want more than he could eat or swap for powder and whisky." As a child, Sutpen heard "vague and cloudy tales" of Tidewater wealth and luxuries, but he did not listen to them. Not able to comprehend what the stories meant, he still had nothing to compare them to. For Sutpen, the "fall" was associated with the knowledge of objects—the greed and materialism of a society specifically associated with slavery. The word "objects" is repeated again and again in his comparison of his Appalachian community and the Tidewater where he discovered "a land divided neatly up and actually owned by men who did nothing but ride over it on fine horses or sit in fine clothes on the galleries of big houses where other people worked for them." It was "a country all divided and fixed and neat" (179).

If Rosa tries to convince herself that her family knew where they came from and that there was a line of certainty and reason that brought her family to Yoknapatawpha, Sutpen, however, tells Grandfather Compson that he did not know why his family moved to the Tidewater, where his father had come from, whether their move to the Tidewater was because his father had come from there in the first place, or if someone traveling through their mountain region had told his father about an easier way of life he might find there. The only recollection he had was that one day his father told the girls to pack up some food, bundle the baby, and put out the fire, and then they all set off to walk down the mountain. Sutpen was 10 years old at the time. In a journey of a length that the child Sutpen seemed to confuse—whether it had been weeks, months, or a year, he couldn't remember—his father "began the practice of accomplishing that part of the translation devoted to motion," lying flat in the ox-driven cart that contained their belongings, "oblivious among the quilts and lanterns and well buckets and bundles of clothing and children, snoring with alcohol" (181). For the child Sutpen, there didn't seem to be a beginning or an end to the journey, but in referring to the "translation devoted to motion," Faulkner emphasizes the life-changing qualities of this journey, one that brought Sutpen out of innocence and into a world where he learned difference, where he learned about othering. He learned about not only lines drawn between races, but also lines drawn by society that defined different classes of people.

Sutpen's story tells of his feelings of displacement, isolation, and confusion. At first after making the move to the Tidewater, he held on to his "woodsman's instinct" that had been ingrained in him by the place that he came from in the mountains. That instinct was, quite obviously, what helped him to survive in the woods, and it "kept him oriented" (183). But the journey to the Tidewater left him unable even to figure out his own age; always from that time he could only give his age within a year or two. Likewise, he could not place himself geographically, he could not orient himself, for "he knew neither where he had come from nor where he was nor why" (184). Although his family lived in a cabin in the Tidewater that could almost have been a replica of the one where they lived in the mountains, and Sutpen began to see the class distinctions of the Tidewater, he still did not at the age of "eleven or twelve or thirteen" (for at that point he had lost all track of his age) covet what others had. Sutpen is described as having "fell into" that world (180); he is "innocent," according to Sutpen's version of the story, until the day he goes to the front door of the Tidewater plantation house and is told to go around to the back. From there on out, Sutpen lives his life intentionally and systematically attempting to control this threshold—who crosses it and who stands on both sides.

Sutpen hopes to be transformed by making the trip to Haiti. During the only time he had ever attended school in a brief three months in winter when his father had decided to send him off to school, Sutpen heard about the West Indies: "Enough [schooling] to have learned something about them, to realise that they would be most suitable to the expediency of my requirements" (194). Making the journey to the West Indies becomes for Sutpen an association with the riches he believed would be necessary to war against those who would make him go around to the back door. He believes he will be transformed and able to complete his "design" if he reaches the West Indies. Sutpen's descriptions of his journey there are, according to Quentin's account of his grandfather's story, not ones that relate a process. Quentin seems perplexed just as his grandfather before him that Sutpen never explained how he figured out where the West Indies was and how he was able to get there.

Yet in making the passage from western Virginia and then to the Tidewater, then from the Tidewater to Haiti, Sutpen claims that his journeys were ones he doesn't remember or that left him without a frame of reference. He is not sure how he got to Haiti or how he got into the house that is surrounded by slaves. When he reaches Haiti, he discovers that he must literally and figuratively learn a new language. In effect, he is stripped of many of the key elements that might identify him as an individual. Although not knowing one's age was not that unusual for someone living in poverty in nineteenth-century America, when this detail is added to the others, the lack of information seems to be part of a distinct pattern. He can't identify the date he entered the world and he can't explain how he made important journeys in his life from one place to the next. He finds himself in Haiti as a foreigner, looking at the planter and his daughter as "foreigners" (203), when, in fact, he is the one who is foreign, the one who must learn a new language in order to communicate with those around him and to pursue the design he plans to create. Grandfather Compson is firm in his assessment of Sutpen as still an innocent, believing—or at least trying to make his case to his son and then his grandson—that Sutpen "apparently did not know, comprehend what he must have been seeing every day because of that innocence" (203).

Sutpen's experiences in Haiti wash him in the blood of slavery, immerse him in the fires of the human tortures and injustices of the institution of slavery and in the literal fires of the slave revolt against the planters. Although Sutpen emphasizes his own innocence in the story that he tells, he also suggests—at least in the version that is passed on to General Compson—the savagery and

anguish of the Haitian slave system. He vividly describes the smell of burning
sugar during the slave revolt, and in the grandfather's words, Haiti is "a spot
of earth which might have been created and set aside by Heaven itself . . . as
a theatre for violence and injustice and bloodshed and all the satanic lusts of
human greed and cruelty for the last despairing fury of all the pariah-interdict
and all the doomed" (202). "A little island set in a smiling and fury-lurked and
incredible indigo sea," Haiti is the "halfway point," according to Compson,
"between what we call civilization, halfway between the dark inscrutable continent from which the black blood, the black bones and flesh and thinking
and remembering and hopes and desires, was ravished by violence" (202). The
book that supposedly set him on this journey to Haiti did not mention that to
become rich, Sutpen would need to assume the same corruption. Sutpen is a
transformed man when he reaches Yoknapatawpha. It is as if he has been to hell
and back. He has seen both the injustices of slavery and what all slaveholders
fear—slave insurrection. He has been immersed in fire and is now consumed
by more than the usual drive of someone going into new territory. As much
as Sutpen portrays himself as a victim of circumstance as a youth, as a young
man entering Yoknapatawpha, he becomes one solely motivated by power and
wealth. He is a remnant of a man—"gaunt now almost to emaciation." But the
lines of his face also suggest a malleability and a falseness: his beard looks like
a disguise and his skin has "the appearance of pottery" (24). It's surprising that
even though the Yoknapatawpha community questions Sutpen's appearance as
a façade, they are more than willing to accept the words of his story, perhaps
in large part because they are spoken by Colonel Sutpen.

The story of Sutpen's time spent in Haiti is also a manipulation. It's been well
established that Faulkner incorrectly places Sutpen in a pre-Revolution Haiti.
Sutpen arrives in the West Indies in 1827—years after the 1791 slave revolt that led
to the establishment of the republic of Haiti in 1804. Sutpen could not have put
down a slave revolt. Surely Faulkner knew this history. Only two years before he
published *Absalom* the United States ended its occupation of Haiti. A number of
scholars have discussed this problem in dating, with a wide variety of explana-
tions, ranging from Maritza Stanchich's reading that "Haiti becomes a dumping
ground for all Southern white anxiety" and John T. Matthews's reasoning that
"Caribbean places compromise the South's dream of uncontaminated origins, of
a benevolent pastoral paternalism unrelated to 200 years of colonial oppression"
(257) to George Handley's observations that this misdating reflects as well the US
effort "to create arbitrary borders among postslavery cultures in the Americas
and to deny kinship with them by means of its own imperialist pretensions, and
this for the sake of preserving an idea of its own racial purity." In effect, Sutpen's
story of putting down a slave revolt in Haiti destabilizes the Southern narrative of
plantation culture. Édouard Glissant argues that Yoknapatawpha "is linked with

its immediate surroundings, the Caribbean and Latin American, by the damna-tion and miscegenation born of the rape of slavery—that is, by what the county creates and represses at the same time. . . . In cultural terms, the southernmost parts of the United States are really rimlands of the Caribbean, and have been so ever since slaves were traded between the two areas, well before the Louisiana Purchase" (60–61). So if there was so much anxiety among slaveholders in the South over the revolt in Haiti, wouldn't Southerners, like Faulkner, have known that Haiti was a republic by the time that Sutpen arrived? Like Quentin's refusal to accept that Sutpen's birthplace was part of Virginia, here, too, there is refusal on the part of numerous narrators to recognize that Sutpen's story is just plain wrong, further embedding those narratives that reaffirm the narrative that they believe has "design."

As the people of Yoknapatawpha use the border region to attempt to control Sutpen and to try to distance themselves from the atrocities of slavery, so, too, does Sutpen use the border to control his own story. Sutpen recognizes that crossing borders can be a powerful act of subversion and that this border region can abet power. Sutpen revels in the image he creates for himself. He picks and chooses the details that he includes in his story and uses the border to control the narrative that Grandfather relates about him. We as readers tend to assume that the story that's passed down through Colonel Compson is the most accurate version of how Sutpen would tell his own story. And of course the timing of when he tells his story is important, too, but the fact remains that the original source of the story is Sutpen. This version of the story aims to portray Sutpen as a victim of sorts because of the way he was raised and because of the hardships of his youth. Sutpen also tries to rewrite the story and place someone else in the role as a way to obliterate the border region. Part of the power that Sutpen hopes to achieve will also be the result of his ability to control his story. Like Quentin who sits down with Shreve to tell why he doesn't hate the South, Sutpen sits down with Quentin's grandfather to explain himself. All along Sutpen has been desperately trying to control the narrative of his life, and he keeps forgetting the major parts of it, the major storyline that would explain why he is the way he is, and his motivations. He intentionally leaves out parts of the story as a way to gain control of it, to hold back the details that he believes his friend Compson might interpret in a particular way. If Sutpen is a man who wants control over everyone around him and the legacy that he will leave, certainly he is one who would want to control the story that is passed down about him. He wants power over the narrative that defines him. Although he might not recognize the similarities, Quentin, like Sutpen, is desperately trying to control the narrative of his life and keeps forgetting or leaves out details or perhaps even slants the truth as he sits down with Shreve to explain himself.

Controlling the narrative for Sutpen and for Quentin also means rewriting their stories—turning back time and distancing themselves from their own stories. Dirk Kuyk Jr. argues in his article "Sutpen's Design" that the ultimate goal that drives Sutpen is not his desire to create a dynasty, but instead his claim to a dynasty that he can "turn . . . against dynastic society itself." Sutpen is, in fact, creating a dynasty for himself so he can recreate the story of the moment of his life he identifies as pivotal and define himself by the moment when he passed from innocence into the experience that made him into a monster (204). Essentially, he wants to replace himself in the story of his own border crossing. The "boy symbol at the door" was not itself the design, but Sutpen desires land and slaves and money and children so that he will be prepared at the door when the knock comes—when a boy like the boy Sutpen arrives. This design, according to Kuyk, will "free the boy and his descendants forever from the backwoods brutehood in which Sutpen grew up," but in creating the design, Sutpen also "remains faithful to his innocent boyhood belief in what we might call an egalitarian noblesse oblige" (208). Although Kuyk in some ways suggests a more positive view of Sutpen than most can stomach, he also points to a way of looking at Sutpen that works neatly with Sutpen's desire to claim his own story and control it. Sutpen ultimately strives to replace himself in the narrative, to resituate himself as the planter who spares the child. He elevates his own role in the narrative by taking charge of it. I, however, have a more negative reading of Sutpen's motives. Sutpen wants to rewrite the story—place someone else in his role not as a way to react against the aristocracy, but to displace himself so that he can take on a new role and shed the old. In effect, he wants to take the role of position and power in the narrative. He wants to be the one in control of making the decision about the boy's future.

When Thomas Sutpen arrives in Yoknapatawpha, he follows a very detailed plan, he creates his "design" as a way to seek revenge and regain control of his life from a plantation system that he has both hated and yearned to be a part of. Creating that design means not only attaining fortune, slaves, and property, but also drawing lines around himself so that he sets himself off as superior to everyone else in the community. In the Appalachian Mountains where he was raised, lines and boundaries did not separate people, but in the Tidewater, he discovers "a country all divided . . . because of what color their skins happened to be" (179). Sutpen comes to equate this ability to draw lines and to partition off space as a sign of power and control over others. Sutpen's intentionality is in large part represented by his carving out of the wilderness a plantation that measures 100 square miles—like the "country all divided and fixed and neat" back in Virginia—and that he names Sutpen's Hundred. While societal borders had brought him shame and anger in the Tidewater, now in Yoknapatawpha he claims and names property in a god-like fashion, not unlike the way Faulkner measures out the boundaries of his Yoknapatawpha County. Plotting off space for his control, Sutpen also attempts to create his own design, create his own plan, map out his own life. Sutpen wants to control the borders that surround him. Sutpen tries to map out—leave out the parts of himself—that define him as Other.

But what seems a bit perplexing—especially in a novel that ends with a hand-drawn map created by the author of the fictional county represented in the book—is that Sutpen is never shown handling a map, looking over 100 square miles that he swindled from a Native American chief. Because Faulkner was so careful in delineating the boundaries and localities of his imaginary Yoknapatawpha County, it seems odd that Sutpen is not shown literally mapping out his Sutpen's Hundred as well. Laying claim as author of the map and "sole owner and proprietor," Faulkner carefully labeled over 30 event and place markers and meticulously enumerated the citizenry of his county, breaking down the numbers by race to the person. Much has been made in the scholarship on Faulkner's work as to how this map helps to create meaning. Robert Hamblin, for example, draws a parallel between Faulkner's map and Sutpen's claim to his hundred square miles of property, describing the map as "the artistic equivalent of the historical Sutpen's Hundred. Each is the result of its creator's great 'design' to impose order and meaning on chaos." But Sutpen never takes control of a rendering of his "hundred." He never makes that "hundred" actual with the lines on a page. Although Faulkner tells readers that Sutpen woke up the county recorder on a Saturday night "with the deed, patent, to the land and the gold Spanish coin" (26), Sutpen is never represented as mapping out the literal boundaries of his property—the space he lays claim to that is so vital a part of the design he hopes to create.

If, as cartographer Kate Harmon proposes, "I map, therefore I am" (11), Sutpen doesn't seem very successful. Map theory equates the visual representation of the map with the ability to contextualize, control, and lay claim. Amy Propen explains that "maps not only *reflect* renderings of the world, but they also *create* these renderings." In effect, "the map makes meaning," in large part because the mapmaker is able to make decisions about what should be included and what should be left out. Maps are a means "to possess and to claim, to legitimate and to name" (236–37). Sutpen partitions off his plantation "all divided and fixed and neat" as it could possibly be at 100 square miles. He names it with his own name. He marginalizes the other citizens of Yoknapatawpha by framing off his property and creating borders not unlike those he believes society drew to "other" him and his family in the Tidewater. Yet the only way that Sutpen believes he can achieve freedom from his past is by *remapping* his life, remapping himself. He believes he can "play God"—he can be the one to define the boundaries that contain him. He can create his own design—and it doesn't matter to him who or what he destroys in the process. Whether it be the lives of the people he holds in slavery or the children he fathers or the virgin land that he has torn from the wilderness, he believes he can force on his control. A large part of the tragedy of Faulkner's novel is that Sutpen believes he can realign the boundaries by forcing into the borderlands everything that his Sutpen's Hundred does not contain.

Yet why is Quentin so wrapped up in what we might describe in terms of border theory as a transgressive text? This story that is Sutpen's own attempt to wield power over others? Although characters such as Rosa, Mr. Compson, and Shreve are also readers of a border text—that is, the story of Sutpen's journey to Yoknapatawpha County—Quentin is the central figure and the one who is seemingly the most affected by Sutpen's narrative. In large part, Quentin's suicide can be traced to his inability to see beyond the Southern guilt and Southern code of honor that has shaped the society he has grown up in and that has warped his view of familial and romantic relationships. If reading a border text is "to cross over into another set of referential codes" (Hicks xxv), then Quentin is stymied. Although Quentin literally crosses the border into the North and he and Shreve spend hour upon hour talking about why Quentin "doesn't hate the South," Quentin never gains a perspective that can allow him to navigate the borderland. Perhaps Quentin is in part drawn to Sutpen's story because he and Sutpen have as young men both experienced a societal drive to cross boundaries. For Sutpen, that drive was the westward migration into new territories where land was supposedly freer for the taking and a past could be left behind. For Quentin, success for the young Southern man of means is associated with another border—the border between North and South—and the promise that an education at Harvard can bring for him and his family. Both crossed borders because of societal expectations of what they should be as men, but both crossings end in failure. Perhaps Quentin sees some part of himself in Sutpen. After all, they both are navigating the borderlands. Both attempt to navigate the psychological space between where they have come from and where they have landed.

Although Deacon acts as guide when Quentin arrives at Harvard in *The Sound and the Fury*, in many ways Deacon symbolizes the South that Quentin left behind. Quentin's time at Harvard becomes a downward spiral for him, and in the end, he ultimately finds himself wandering the streets of Boston and out into areas of the city where he has not been before. First, in his dorm room, breaking the crystal and twisting off the hands of his grandfather's watch that Quentin's father had passed on down to him, Quentin places the glass fragments and the hands in an ashtray. But the watch still keeps ticking. Given to him with the words from his father, "I give you the mausoleum of all hope and desire. . . . I give it to you not that you may remember time, but that you might forget it now and then for a moment and not spend all your breath trying to conquer it" (93), Quentin takes the watch to a clock repairman, entering the shop and asking the jeweler if any of the clocks in the shop have the correct time. Quentin, of course, is not interested in the jeweler telling him what the time is, but instead, he wants to know whether or not any of the clocks are "right" (103). Even though he is studying at Harvard, his guide is not the stereotypical professor. This first attempt to find "what time it really is" ends not with his seeking to repair his watch, but instead a response that he believes can prove his father's words wrong. He cannot as his father hopes "forget it now" and recognize that he cannot "conquer it."

Quentin did not want to make this journey to Harvard in the first place. He remembers his emotions about going, saying, "Let Jason have it. Give Jason a year at Harvard" (95). Benjy's pasture had to be sold off to raise the money to send Quentin, obviously adding a second layer of guilt and remorse. In the last pages of Quentin's section in *The Sound and the Fury*, memories intrude into his stream of consciousness narrative: "you will remember that for you to go to harvard has been your mothers dream since you were born and no compson has ever disappointed a lady and i temporary it will be better for me for all of us and he every man is the arbiter of his own virtues" (221). The lines connect the decision to sell the pasture, send Quentin to Harvard, and elevate ladies in Southern society, but the passage also suggests the temporary nature of Quentin's sojourn in the North. "It will be better for me for all of us" suggests perhaps a sense of relief for Quentin that he will be separated from the South, from Caddy, and from the incestuous feelings he has for her. But Quentin's departure from the South is not his own decision; it is instead one shaped by family expectations and pressures.

Even before he leaves Yoknapatawpha County for Boston, Quentin has become a divided self. At the opening of *Absalom, Absalom!* he is described as "two separate Quentins." He is both the Quentin Compson "preparing for Harvard in the South . . . and the Quentin Compson who was still too young to deserve yet to be a ghost." It is the "two separate Quentins now talking to one another in the long silence of notpeople in notlanguage, like this" (4–5). This divided self that creates the narrative in the first place has come about not because Quentin is remaining in the South, but because he is leaving it. This divided identity is the result of his impending border crossing—not because he is staying at home. He is haunted by the "deep South dead since 1865 and peopled with garrulous outraged baffled ghosts" (4), but the wandering that leads to his suicide comes about because he is unable to accept the parts of himself that come to the forefront with the introspection of Shreve's question, why does Quentin hate the South. Quentin seems forever unable to look from both sides.

If rivers across the continent flow in an elaborate web in Wolfe's *Of Time and the River*, so, too, does Faulkner note the "geologic umbilical" that connects the Southerner Quentin with the Canadian Shreve. Faulkner notes the relationship that ties Quentin to Shreve, although Quentin does not recognize the saving graces that that relationship might bring. Faulkner tells in *Absalom, Absalom!* of the two—"both young, both born within the same year"—who were

> born half a continent apart yet joined, connected after a fashion in a sort of geo-
> graphical transubstantiation by that Continental Trough, that River which runs
> not only through the physical land of which it is the geologic umbilical, not
> only runs through the spiritual lives of the beings within its scope, but is very
> Environment itself which laughs at degrees of latitude and temperature. (208)

Although Shreve has never seen the river, and Quentin and Shreve had "never laid eyes on one another" before they arrived at Harvard, now they share almost every moment together, sleeping in the same room, eating "side by side of the same food," reading the same books to complete the same assignments, and "facing one another across the lamplit table on which lay the fragile pandora's box of scrawled paper which had filled with violent and unratiotinative djinns and demons this snug monastic coign, this dreamy and heatless alcove of what we call the best of thought" (208).

Quentin carries literal and figurative weights with him. He carries the weight of the Southern past, never being able to forget time as his father hopes he will do. If his journey northward and his wandering in the Boston environ suggest life's journey and his potential growth into manhood, Quentin is unable to ditch the baggage of his youth and of his region's past. Thomas Wolfe writes, "The two things that haunt and hurt us: the eternal wandering, moving, questioning, loneliness, homesickness, and the desire of the soul for a home, peace, fixity, repose" (Qtd. in Bruccoli 36). Quentin physically carries the weights he will use to drown himself, sink himself to the bottom. The little immigrant girl follows him through the streets, another weight, another reminder of his regional and personal pasts.

This little hungry girl who follows Quentin accentuates the wandering and the border crossing that Quentin struggles with. Although she is typically read as a figure that Quentin believes he can protect—a symbol of the innocent girlhood that Caddy forsakes and that Quentin laments as lost—the girl also becomes a literal burden to him as she follows him through the streets and into the bakery. Thinking she must live near the railway station and assuming that she is from an immigrant family, Quentin defines her as border crosser and as "Other." She doesn't seem to know her own home, and she can't communicate with Quentin because she can't speak English. Quentin is desperate to unload her. She becomes baggage to him, and he finally dumps her and leaves her behind.

The entire Quentin section in *The Sound and the Fury* revolves around wandering and confusion. In many ways, Quentin recalls the modernist search for meaning, but Quentin also has the additional struggle with his Southern roots and the implications of those bonds. He, too, is like the little immigrant girl—a foreigner to the region who has crossed the boundary to a new place but who remains in the border region. Boys that he passes as he wanders, for example, discuss Quentin's accent, wondering if perhaps he is Canadian. Another comments that he speaks "like they do in minstrel shows" and "like a coloured man" (148). Ultimately, Quentin commits suicide because he is unable to throw over the baggage that he carries. He is not one of those survivor-narrators. Even though he puzzles over Sutpen's story of the borderlands, trying to explain to Shreve why he doesn't "hate the South," Quentin is overcome by cultural, familial, and personal pasts that haunt him. He cannot at once be Southern and look at himself from the perspective of someone looking at that person and region from a distance.

Quentin is part of the retelling (along with Rosa and Shreve and various other characters from his community) of a Southern border crossing narrative, and he tries to understand the implications of crossing borders in his own life and in the life of Thomas Sutpen. Sutpen may be selectively remembering, but he is forever trying to replace himself at the door—to halt the journey from the Western mountains to the Virginia Tidewater, from innocence to experience. Perhaps the tragedy is that Quentin as reader of a border text cannot recognize the implications of Sutpen's journeying, cannot understand the reflections of it in his own life, and cannot accept his own complicity in the same slave system upon which Sutpen created his design. The "telling and retelling" of Sutpen's story drags Quentin down into an abyss he can never escape. Quentin becomes obsessed with drawing lines around himself, forever seeing himself as marred by the past. He is unable to navigate the psychological borderlands, recognize and move beyond familial and personal guilt, and leave behind the crushing past of the South. Through Quentin, Faulkner makes clear the pressures and dangers of the divisions between black and white, between North and South, and the inability of Southerners like Quentin to successfully navigate the borderlands.

CHAPTER 7

"Anywhere South of the Canadian Border"

When my husband, son, and I head home from a trip down south to visit my parents, our drive to northern Illinois always has certain consistencies. It's just before sunrise. We always pack up early for our car ride home after a visit to the Weaks farm outside of Nashville. The moonlight still shimmers on the waters of the Cumberland River as we make our way north on the winding country road that runs alongside the riverbank. Years ago when I was a child, my grandmother packed homemade sausage and biscuits for us to eat on our way home, but my family's breakfast stop this time around will probably be McDonald's. Our drive is a long one and not particularly scenic. After we're about a third of the way up the state of Illinois, the landscape transitions from rolling hills to mostly cornfields—lots and lots of them, patterned here and there with large white farmhouses surrounded by groves of oak trees. One of my roommates from graduate school who was raised in central Illinois told me once about spending a year out east and feeling a sense of comfort and security as the train she was riding westward came out of the foothills of Ohio. Seeing from horizon to horizon with the full sky above meant she was in the open plains of the Midwest, and that line of demarcation was what meant she was home. For me, the opposite has always been true because the hills signify "home."

We have the car loaded as usual. I've smuggled along every copy of *Southern Living* that my mother had in the house. I didn't mean to take them all, but I did, squandering them away to ponder over on some cold winter night as I daydream about serving shrimp and grits and slow-cooked barbecue. The cover of the latest issue promises to fill me in on why Miss South Carolina says "No one understands the importance of pearls better than a Southern girl" and to show me how to cook "Southern Comfort Foods" that will remind me of the place I've left behind. I always look forward to the Idea Home plans—house plans that give readers a chance to build a home or at least dream about one that's been designed in a "Southern" style. I'm bringing back produce from my father's garden. This time around it's turnips, spinach, kale—winter crops down South that we can only hope to grow in hoop houses in northern Illinois. I'm still trying to figure out how to prepare the turnips and kale, and I've carefully written down my parents' suggestions. When I try to reproduce the recipe, I know I'll hear complaints from a husband and son not used to the strong Southern flavors, but I keep trying.

I'm surrounded by others who, like me, are navigating these Southern borderlands, who are stuck somewhere between South and NotSouth. The teaching pastor at our church in Rockford flies in from his home in Kentucky every weekend to give his sermon. I listen to my Performing Arts students from the South tell me about taking courses to rid them of their Southern accents.

I read Willie Morris, who writes in *North Toward Home* of "some easing of a great burden . . . some terrible weight off [his] shoulders . . . as if some grievance had suddenly fallen away" each time he left the South and "turned north toward home" (437–38). And about Minnie Bruce Pratt's character Beatrice, a white woman who returns to the South, who "has a dream sometimes she is walking the road / out of town, past the depot and the gin, on the road / to Selma, past burnt-up fields" (53). Yet while many still struggle with the implications of leaving, others have returned, reversed the out-migration. In *Call to Home* Carol Stack writes of a Great Return Migration of African Americans to the South and asks, "Why do they come back?" One reason, she speculates, may be that "some people come home with a mission, determined to draw on lessons learned up north to mobilize their community against old scourges" (6–7). Then there are Tracy Thompson, who returned south to research "the new mind of the South," and Barbara Kingsolver, who moved back south to Virginia with her family to live locally in *Animal, Vegetable, Miracle*. And even Harper Lee, who into her later years, lived in New York City, returning home for visits, but not living in Alabama permanently until she suffered a stroke. Return migration has become a phenomenon in itself in the last several decades as increasing numbers of Southerners have returned home because of greater economic opportunities in the South and the desire of many to be closer to family. It has also been well documented that increasing numbers of young people from Southern families that had moved north are moving south, not so much because of an attachment to place but instead because of the recognition that the South offers better job prospects than other regions of the country (Gregory 323).

So what does crossing the line from South to NotSouth mean now? Does crossing "the line" still hold meaning? Not just the Mason-Dixon Line, but also the border between Texas and Mexico, the ocean between Florida and the Caribbean? What does it mean now to pass through the liminal space? Can I—or anyone else—still linger there? In defining Southernness, moving beyond the South's borders has been as significant as the attachment to place. Leaving has in many ways been as important as the staying.

Southern border formation narratives *seemingly* don't hold the power they once did. After all, now the Mason-Dixon Line needs "saving" with global positioning devices, according to a 2002 *National Geographic* story. The physical remainder of the line is fading. The Mason-Dixon Preservation Partnership has been keen on restoring the line: stones are missing, while others that remain are weathered and in some cases vandalized (Trivedi). An expectant mother writes in a July 4 posting on the *Southern Living* website that she is 16 weeks pregnant and thinking about how to "instill strong Southern values within our child from the start." As she writes her post, she's sitting—appropriately—out on her front porch, musing over what she "think[s]" is "Southern": "manners, heart, integrity and tradition" ("What Does Southern Mean to You?"). She searches for a "script"—how to raise her child with a Southern group identity. Attempting to answer the question "What does it mean to be Southern?" and asking if we are headed toward a "No South," Allen Breed in a 2006 Internet wire story dispels many of those myths commonly held about Southernness:

1. Despite the fact that Southerners live in the Bible Belt, Midwesterners now outnumber Southerners in church attendance records.
2. Of the 10 states with the highest divorce rates in the nation, six are in the South.
3. Southerners tend to join the military more than Americans from any other region—but that might be because of economics.
4. Kentucky, Mississippi, and West Virginia have outlawed the marriage of first cousins, but such a marriage is still legal in Massachusetts, New York, and Rhode Island.

Breed goes on to point out that scholars have noted that the border between the South and the rest of the country is becoming blurred. The rest of the country is just as interested in traditionally Southern pastimes and marks of difference including country music and NASCAR. Traditionally "Southern 'institutions'" aren't just Southern anymore. The way Southerners lead their lives—make choices in their life narratives—isn't all that different now from the life choices and tastes of other Americans.

A large part of this blurring of the line between South and NotSouth is the result of the twentieth-century mass movement of Southerners from out of the South. A historical survey points to the magnitude of this movement and what was "exported" as Southerners left. According to James Gregory, the Southern diaspora "changed America":

> They transformed American religion, spreading Baptist and Pentecostal churches and reinvigorating evangelical Protestantism, both black and white versions . . . transformed American popular culture, especially music. The development of blues, jazz, gospel, R&B, and hillbilly and country music all depended on the southern migrants . . . transformed American racial hierarchies, as black migrants in the great cities of the North and West developed institutions and political practices that enabled the modern civil rights movement . . . helped reshape American conservatism, contributing to new forms of white working-class and suburban politics. Indeed, most of the great political realignments of the second half of the twentieth century had something to do with the population movements out of the South . . . transformed the nature of American regions, helping with the reconstructions that turned the South into an economic and political powerhouse and collapsing what had been huge cultural differences between that region and the rest of the United States. (xii)

Essentially, then, it was the movement of Southerners out of the South that reconstructed the region. Movement outward brought with it greater movement into the South by populations of "outsiders." As the South became more American, the rest of the United States in many ways became more "Southern."

In this movement outward across the South's border, group narrative identities framed by Southern "scripts" have been appropriated and revised—some more benign than others. Although country music, for example, was for a time a site of crossover, as country music secured a place as an industry in the 1960s, and particularly as the Country Music Association (CMA) claimed a stronger control of the industry, country music evolved into what Gregory describes as "a politicized entertainment medium with a target audience of lower-middle-income white Americans." With the competition for younger consumers by the rock-and-roll industry, the country music industry sought to survive by identifying with a narrative of "tough-guy masculinity and love-it-or-leave-it patriotism." As country music artists represented themselves as "'plain folks,' down-home and unpretentious," song lyrics spoke of "humble origins and dangerous and demanding work settings (especially trucks and coal mines) and occasional swipes at the silver spoon crowd." During the Vietnam era, country music songs like Johnny Wright's "Keep the Flag Flying," Loretta Lynn's "Dear Uncle Sam," and Ernest Tubb's "It's for God, Country and You Mom," "It's America," and "Love It or Leave It" responded to antiwar sentiments expressed in rock-and-roll music of the period. Expressing more conservative views of patriotism and traditionalism during those years of the late 1960s and early 1970s, country music identified with and played a role in shaping the values of an evolving blue-collar conservatism (Gregory 313). With lines like "we don't smoke marijuana" and "the kids still respect the college dean" in rural America, songs like Merle Haggard's 1969 "Okie from Muskogee" symbolized the threats to small-town America. The song became an "anthem of the angry white working class" and the press claimed it as "the ballad of the Silent Majority" (Gregory 315).

Although I certainly recognize that the decline and collapse of small-town America is a theme of communities across the United States, I think it is important to recognize here, too, the ways in which a specific form of Southern group narrative has been appropriated and claimed by a much broader and national audience. And I point here, not just to the influence of music and the popularity of country music, but to the ways narrative patterns have been claimed for political ends. Crossings made by Southerners have also had a significant influence on American politics and culture at large. Southern "scripts" have been rewritten and consumed by and for different groups of people beyond the South, as a means both to bind and to divide. In effect, the line between South and NotSouth has been blurred. Southern out-migrations and narratives about those crossings also give a window into the very real and very present conflicts that are now shaping our country and our world as that tension between crossing literal borders between nations, that urge to move freely between places and by association to go beyond one's self—the very human need to rely on and reach out to others—remains in conflict with the drive to frame off, to border, to identify as different from others, to retreat into isolationism.

Confederate symbols have, for instance, taken root in other societies around the world, emphasizing the powerful narratives attached to them that are clearly identified with hegemony and racism. Public Radio International reported recently on a trend in Germany to reenact American Civil War battles. Looking at the practice with a lighthearted tone, the reporter noted that overwhelmingly, the reenactors choose to fight on the Confederate side. One reason for the interest in the American Civil War is that 200,000 German immigrants to the United States fought in the war and thus many feel a "personal connection." She explains, too, that because in post–World War II Germany, "any talk of military glory became socially taboo here . . . for those at the reenactment, it is appealing that the U.S. Civil War took place in another country, in another time. It is safer, even romantic." In fact, though, the interest seems troubling. Professor of American Studies Wolfgang Hochbruck, who is a reenactor for the Union army, describes more sinister motives: "I think some of the Confederate reenactors in Germany are acting out Nazi fantasies of racial superiority. They are obsessed with your war because they cannot celebrate their own vanquished racists." The Confederate flag has also taken hold in Italy, not with a direct link to slavery, but on the athletic field and along the north-south division in the country. According to Alberto Testa, a criminology professor at the University of West London, "In Italy it is used generally in the south to symbolize the defeat and the frustration of the south against a north which has, in their eyes taken wealth and political powers and moved it to the north and the capital city of Rome. It symbolizes Italy's long running north and south divide." Testa points out that in France and Germany, however, the Confederate flag has been appropriated by the extreme right wing and is racialized and politicized because of ideological conflict over immigration into those two countries.

Back in the United States, during the 2016 election cycle, various media sources, including the *New York Times*, CNN, and the *Boston Globe*, reported that the flag, with "Trump 2016" emblazoned across the Confederate battle emblem, was flown briefly and taken down quickly at a Trump rally in Orlando (Figure 7.1). The 27-year-old man who owned the flag had purchased it just outside the arena (Corasaniti). Despite RNC chair Ken Mehlman's apology in a 2005 speech for the national convention of the NAACP for the use of the "Southern Strategy" by the Republican Party, and the acknowledgment by Michael Steele, the first African American RNC chair, that "For the last 40-plus years we had a Southern Strategy that alienated many minority voters by focusing on the white male vote in the South," the recent political climate has seen the reinvigoration of this political strategy in the United States (Jones). Despite an "autopsy report" orchestrated by RNC chair Reince Priebus following Mitt Romney's defeat in the 2012 presidential election that argued for the importance of engaging ethnic minorities in the Republican Party, Robert Jones, author of *The End of White Christian America*, in the months before the 2016 presidential election, described candidate Donald Trump's anti-immigration views and his "waffling denunciation" of white supremacy as "the antithesis of the big-tent recommendations of the Republican establishment." Jones identified the Trump campaign as making "a deliberate and conscious attempt to resurrect . . . discarded GOP tactics, recasting them for the current moment." A return to the Southern Strategy was even more deeply ingrained in the campaign when Trump chose Paul Manafort as the chair. Manafort, according to Jones, "brought decades of experiences as an overseer of the Southern Strategy," with business partnerships with Charles Black, who worked for the campaign to elect segregationist Jesse Helms to the US Senate and Lee Atwater, who, as head of George H. W. Bush's election campaign, oversaw the overtly racist Willie Horton ad campaign against Michael Dukakis. Summing up the preelection political landscape, Jones sees a clear connection between the "massive culture shifts" of the 1960s and 1970s with what is happening today in the United States:

To be sure, Trump has not simply exhumed and dusted off the old Southern Strategy. He has characterized illegal immigrants rather than black Americans as a threat to white women's safety. And he has redirected the Christian Right's focus away from its preoccupation with a "godless Communism." In its place, Trump has exploited the perception of Islam's growing power abroad against a backdrop of genuinely declining white Christian influence at home, where the U.S. finds itself for the first time a minority white Christian nation. And, significantly—in a demonstration of just how successful the old strategy was—he's discarded the dog whistle in favor of a bull horn. Trump's unlikely success with these old tactics is demonstrating William Faulkner's famous aphorism: "The past is never dead. It's not even past."

What Jones believed to be "Trump's unlikely success" is now a reality.

White supremacist narratives of seeking racial purity have never gone away and are once again gaining traction. During the trial of white supremacist Dylan Roof, who was ultimately convicted of the murder of nine parishioners of Emanuel AME Church in Charleston, South Carolina, the prosecutor reported that one of the victims, Tywanza Sanders, told Roof, "We mean you no harm." Roof responded, "Y'all are raping our white women. Y'all are taking over the world" (Sullivan). The "purity" of white womanhood is still a political tool to "preserve" the race, to "keep the white race pure." In summer 2016, Maine governor Paul LePage, commenting on efforts to reduce drug crime in his state, said that "the enemy right now . . . are people of colour or people of Hispanic origin," even though the local press pointed to recent statistics that show only 14.1% of those charged for manufacturing and selling drugs in Maine were African American and "almost all the rest were white." Despite the statistics, LePage attempted to rewrite the narrative. Identifying "the enemy" as "guys with the name D-Money, Smoothie, Shifty" from the states of Connecticut and New York, he explained that "they come up here, they sell their heroin, they go back home. Incidentally, half the time they impregnate a young white girl before they leave, which is a real sad thing because then we have another issue we have to deal with down the road" ("Maine Governor").

Are we at a crossroads? What will come of a push toward globalization? Will the borders be reconstructed again as nationalism becomes a driving force in the world? Or shall we drown like Quentin because we (or at least those in power) refuse to accept the natural movement outward across those lines? The movement of people across borders is at the forefront of our current political environment in the United States and abroad. In Europe, the flow of Syrian refugees fleeing their war-torn homeland has produced a flurry of wall building. "Leaders are succumbing to the keep-them-out syndrome," according to a recent report in the *Guardian*. "Hungary is building a fence

Figure 7.1. Confederate Flag at Trump Rally. Photo by Joey Roulette, photojournalist for *Orlando Weekly*.

(along its border with Serbia). Spain has done the same (in Ceuta and Melilla). Bulgaria followed suit (on the border with Turkey). More fencing is springing up in Calais. In Macedonia . . . they are deploying armoured vehicles against migrants" (Nougayrède). A 2015 report commissioned for the United Nations High Commission for Refugees found some important differences in the ways that media in five European countries—Spain, Italy, Germany, the United Kingdom, and Sweden—represent the migrant situation and speculate on the impact of these differences. While 91% of media in Germany and 75% in Sweden used the words "refugee" or "asylum seeker," in Spain, the word "immigrant" was used 67% of the time. In Italy (36%) and the UK (54%), the preference was "migrant" (Berry 7–8). The study found that media in Italy generally represented the issue as a humanitarian one, while in the UK, Italy, and Spain, "threat themes" including those to the country's welfare system or culture appeared more often. Only a small number of articles examined the "push factors" that motivated the migrants to leave their homes and the need to address these issues, despite the fact that war, abuse of human rights, and economic stratification were identified as causes (Berry 8). Likewise, the study found that reporting rarely told success stories or dealt with the positive impact of migrants in their host countries (Berry 12).

Competing narratives are lining up against each other: The iconic image of a three-year-old Syrian boy's body washed ashore in Turkey that came to represent the stories of tens of thousands of migrants seeking safety for their families. A viral photo of a dust and blood-covered five-year-old in the back of an ambulance after he had been pulled from a bombed-out building in Aleppo identified by Syrian president Bashar Al-Assad as a "fake." Political commentators in Europe warning of refugees who are responsible for what has been termed the "Migrant Rape Crisis." Because of this wall building and retreat into nationalism, long-standing alliances between countries are breaking down. The "take back control" political narrative that in part was an effort to reduce immigration promoted by those in the Brexit movement swayed UK voters to approve a June 2016 referendum to leave the European Union. In the United States, similar "take back control" narratives appeared in the 2016 presidential election. I present this context here because I believe that much of what is happening in the United States now and in other parts of the world is mirrored in the border building and isolationism of the American South. I am not, of course, equating the movements of repressed peoples in current-day Europe with Southerners who left the South in the twentieth century, but I see similar patterns in ways that narrative has been instrumental in the formation and deconstruction of borders. My hope is that by looking at this particular example, my study can give some insight not only into the Southern United States and its identity as a region, but also into bordering on both national and global scales. The South's long history of border formation stands as a record. We are reenacting many of those same narratives, unable to cross over, to live on the other side, unable to cross the divide.

As I write, I recognize that particular governments will come and go, but the issues here will not go away anytime soon. This struggle between bordering and bridging runs deep in humanity. The growth of nationalistic fervor clashes against globalization in a constant tension between two competing forces. Even for the South, a similar friction remains. Reconstruction of the South and the nation after the Civil War was the result of Southern migrations outward. The result was freer movement between South and NotSouth, the integration of Southern culture, politics, and social systems into American culture as a whole (for better or for worse), and the tremendous turn in the South to economic prosperity that has surpassed the economic and political power of industrialized cities where Southerners once fled. Yet neo-Confederate sentiments remain, not only trying to rebuild the South's borders but reconfiguring US borders as well, and "alternative" narratives lead the way in the building. The dangers are that people (like Quentin?) do not recognize or refuse to recognize where we have come from.

At the international Women's March the day after Donald Trump's inauguration, Ashley Judd in her remarks to an audience at the march in Washington, DC, stated, "I'm not as nasty as confederate flags being tattooed across my cities. Maybe the South is actually going to rise, maybe for some it never really fell" (Qtd. in Hopkins). Her words echoed those of Malcolm X: "As far as I am concerned, [the South] is anywhere south of the Canadian border" (479). Maybe that truth is even clearer now.

WORKS CITED

Introduction

Abbott, Shirley. *Womenfolks: Growing Up Down South*. New York: Houghton, 1998.

Agnew, John. "No Borders, No Nations: Making Greece in Macedonia." *Annals of the Association of American Geographers* 97.2 (2007): 398–422.

Altink, Henrice, and Chris Weedon. "Introduction." *Gendering Border Studies*. Ed. Jane Aaron, Henrice Altink, and Chris Weedon. Cardiff: U of Wales P, 2010. 1–15.

Anderson, Benedict. *Imagined Communities: Reflections on the Origin and Spread of Nationalism*. New York: Verso, 1983.

Anzaldúa, Gloria. *Borderlands: La Frontera: The New Mestiza*. San Francisco: Aunt Lute Books, 2007.

Appiah, K. Anthony. "Identity, Authenticity, Survival: Multicultural Societies and Social Reproduction." *Multiculturalism*. Ed. Amy Gutmann and Charles Taylor. Princeton: Princeton UP, 1994. 149–63.

Battat, Erin Royston. *Ain't Got No Home: America's Great Migrations and the Making of an Interracial Left*. Chapel Hill: U of North Carolina P, 2014.

Bhabha, Homi. *The Location of Culture*. London: Routledge, 1994.

Blotner, Joseph. *Robert Penn Warren: A Biography*. New York: Random House, 1997.

Bone, Martyn. "Introduction: Old/New/Post/Real/Global/No South: Paradigms and Scales." *Creating and Consuming the American South*. Ed. Martin Bone, Brian Ward, and William A. Link. Gainesville: U of Florida P, 2015. 1–23.

Border Poetics Research Group. "Border Aesthetics." *University of Tromsø*. 2010–13. Web. Accessed 17 Apr. 2017.

Brennan, Timothy. "The National Longing for Form." *Nation and Narration*. Ed. Homi Bhabha. New York: Routledge, 1990. 44–70.

Bromley, Roger. *Narratives for a New Belonging: Diasporic Cultural Fictions*. Edinburgh: Edinburgh UP, 2000.

Carcamo, Cindy. "With Only One Left, Iconic Yellow Road Sign Showing Running Immigrants Now Borders on the Extinct." *LA Times*. LA Times. 7 July 2017. Web.

Cash, W. J. *The Mind of the South*. New York: Vintage, 1941.

Cox, Karen. *Dreaming of Dixie: How the South Was Created in American Popular Culture.*
    Chapel Hill: U of North Carolina P, 2011.
Curry, Andrew. "Roman Frontiers." *National Geographic* 222.3 (Sept. 2012): 106–27.
Duck, Leigh Anne. *The Nation's Region: Southern Modernism, Segregation, and U.S. Nationalism.*
    Athens: U of Georgia P, 2006.
Friend, Craig Thompson, ed. *Southern Masculinity: Perspectives on Manhood in the South since
    Reconstruction.* Athens: U of Georgia P, 2009.
"Geno." *National Geographic Holiday 2012 Catalog* (2012): 65.
Gerrig, Richard J. *Experiencing Narrative Worlds: On the Psychological Activities of Reading.*
    New Haven: Yale UP, 1993.
Grafton, Earnie. "Caution." *San Diego Union-Tribune.* San Diego Union-Times, 10 Apr. 2005. Web.
Graham, Allison. *Framing the South: Hollywood, Television, and Race during the Civil Rights
    Struggle.* Baltimore: Johns Hopkins UP, 2001.
Greeson, Jennifer Rae. *Our South: Geographic Fantasy and the Rise of National Literature.*
    Cambridge: Harvard UP, 2010.
Gregory, James. *The Southern Diaspora: How the Great Migration of Black and White Southerners
    Transformed America.* Chapel Hill: U of North Carolina P, 2005.
Griffin, Farah Jasmine. *"Who Set You Flowin'?": The African-American Migration Narrative.*
    Oxford: Oxford UP, 1995.
Herrera, Juan Felipe. *187 Reasons Mexicanos Can't Cross the Border: Undocuments 1971–2007.*
    San Francisco: City Lights, 2007.
Jackson, Andrew. "Andrew Jackson's Annual Message." 1830. www.ourdocuments.gov. NHD,
    NARA, and USA Freedom Corps. Web. Accessed 11 Mar. 2014.
Kirby, Jack Temple. *Media-Made Dixie: The South in the American Imagination.* Athens: U
    of Georgia P, 1986.
Kristeva, Julia. *Nations without Nationalism.* Trans. Leon S. Roudiez. New York: Columbia
    UP, 1993.
Loftus, Mary. "Her Calling." *Emory Magazine* 88.3 (Autumn 2012): 20–25.
McPherson, Tara. *Reconstructing Dixie: Race, Gender, and Nostalgia in the Imagined South.*
    Durham: Duke UP, 2003.
Michaelsen, Scott, and David E. Johnson. Introduction. *Border Theory: The Limits of Cultural
    Politics.* Minneapolis: U of Minnesota P, 1997.
Morrison, Toni. *Jazz.* New York: Knopf, 1992.
Powell, Douglas Reichert. *Critical Regionalism: Connecting Politics and Culture in the American
    Landscape.* Chapel Hill: U of North Carolina P, 2007.
Reed, John Shelton. *The Enduring South: Subcultural Persistence in Mass Society.* Lexington,
    MA: Heath, 1972.
Rodgers, Lawrence R. *Canaan Bound: The African-American Great Migration Novel.*
    Champaign-Urbana: U of Illinois P, 1997.
Romine, Scott. *The Real South: Southern Narrative in the Age of Cultural Reproduction.* Baton
    Rouge: Louisiana State UP, 2008.
Ross, E. A. *Social Control: A Survey of the Foundations of Order.* New York: Macmillan, 1901.
Rubin, Rachel. "Sing Me Back Home: Nostalgia, Bakersfield, and Modern Country Music."
    American Popular Music: New Approaches to the Twentieth Century. Ed. Rachel Rubin and
    Jeffrey Melnick. Amherst: U of Massachusetts P, 2001. 93–109.
Trethewey, Natasha. "Southern Pastoral." *Native Guard: Poems.* Boston: Houghton, 2007. 35.
Turner, Frederick Jackson. *The Frontier in American History.* New York: Holt, 1921.
Turner, Victor. *Dramas, Fields, and Metaphors: Symbolic Action in Human Society.* Ithaca:
    Cornell UP, 1974.

————. *The Forest of Symbols: Aspects of Ndembu Ritual*. Ithaca: Cornell UP, 1967.

US Census Bureau. "Census Regions and Divisions of the United States." US Department of Commerce, Economics, and Statistics Administration. US Census Bureau. Web. Accessed 30 Oct. 2017.

Van Gennep, Arnold. *The Rites of Passage*. Trans. Monika B. Vizedom and Gabrielle L. Caffee. Chicago: U of Chicago P, 1960.

Wald, Priscilla. *Contagious: Cultures, Carriers, and the Outbreak Narrative*. Durham: Duke UP, 2008.

White, Paul. "Geography, Literature, and Migration." *Writing across Worlds: Literature and Migration*. Ed. Russell King, John Connell, and Paul White. London: Routledge, 1995. 1–19.

Williamson, J. W. *Hillbillyland: What the Movies Did to the Mountains and What the Mountains Did to the Movies*. Chapel Hill: U of North Carolina P, 1995.

Wilson, Charles Reagan. "History." *The Encyclopedia of Southern Culture*. Ed. Charles Reagan Wilson and William Ferris. Chapel Hill: U of North Carolina P, 1989. 583–94.

Wolfe, Stephen. "Border Aesthetics / Border Works." *Nordlit* 31 (2014): 1–5.

Wright, Richard. *12 Million Black Voices*. New York: Thunder's Mouth, 1941.

Chapter 1

"Alex Haley." *Kunta Kinte—Alex Haley Foundation, Inc*. Kunta Kinte—Alex Haley Foundation, 2018. Web. Accessed 18 Feb. 2018.

Ancholou, Catherine. "Catherine Ancholou on the Importance of Equiano's Narrative." *The Terrible Transformation*. Wisconsin Public Television. Web. Accessed 11 Mar. 2014.

Anzaldúa, Gloria. *Borderlands: La Frontera: The New Mestiza*. San Francisco: Aunt Lute Books, 2007.

Beam, Alex. "The Prize Fight Over Alex Haley's 'Tangled Roots.'" *Boston Globe* (30 Oct. 1998): D1. Web.

Bennett, Michael. *Democratic Discourses: The Radical Abolition Movement and Antebellum American Literature*. New Brunswick: Rutgers UP, 2005.

Burgert Brothers. "Lector in a Large Cigar Factory: Tampa, Florida, 1929. *Florida Memory*. Web. Accessed 21 Apr. 2016.

Cabeza de Vaca, Álvar Nuñez. *La Relación. Cabeza de Vaca's* La Relación *Online*. Southwestern Writers Collection. Texas State University-San Marcos. Web. Accessed 28 Feb. 2018.

Castronovo, Russ. "Compromised Narratives along the Border: The Mason-Dixon Line, Resistance, and Hegemony." In *Border Theory: The Limits of Cultural Politics*. Ed. Scott Michaelsen and David E. Johnson. Minneapolis: U of Minnesota P, 1997. 195–220.

Davenport, John C. *The Mason-Dixon Line*. Philadelphia: Chelsea, 2004.

Dodson, Howard, and Sylviane A. Diouf, comps. and eds. *In Motion: The African-American Migration Experience*. Washington, DC: National Geographic, 2004.

Douglass, Frederick. *Narrative of the Life of Frederick Douglass, An American Slave*. Ed. John R. McKivigan, Peter Hinks, and Heather Kaufman. New Haven: Yale UP, 2016.

Equiano, Olaudah. *The Interesting Narrative and Other Writings*. Ed. Vincent Carretta. New York: Penguin, 1995.

Feelings, Tom. *The Middle Passage: White Ships / Black Cargo*. New York: Dial, 1995.

Gilroy, Paul. *The Black Atlantic: Modernity and Double Consciousness*. Cambridge: Harvard UP, 1993.

Glissant, Edouard. *Faulkner, Mississippi*. Trans. Barbara Lewis and Thomas C. Spear. Chicago: U of Chicago P, 2000.

Hall, Roger Lee. *Lincoln and Liberty: Music from Abraham Lincoln's Era*. Stoughton, MA: PineTree, 2009.

Hentz, Caroline Lee. *The Planter's Northern Bride*. Philadelphia: Peterson, 1854.

Hernandez, Bernadine. "Rewriting Space in Ruiz de Burton's *Who Would Have Thought It?*" *CLC Web: Comparative Literature and Culture* 11.2 (2009). Article 10. Web.

Inman, Natalie. "'A Dark and Bloody Ground': American Indian Responses to Expansion during the American Revolution." *Tennessee Historical Quarterly* 70.4 (Winter 2011): 258–75.

Jacobs, Harriet A. *Incidents in the Life of a Slave Girl*. Cambridge: Harvard UP, 2000.

Kanellos, Nicolás. "Exiles, Immigrants, and Natives: Hispanic Print Culture in What Became the Mainland of the United States." *Print in Motion: The Expansion of Publishing and Reading in the United States, 1880–1940*. Ed. Carl F. Kaestle and Janice Radway. *The History of the Book in America* Series. Chapel Hill: U of North Carolina P, 2009. 312–38.

Loewen, James W. "Why Do People Believe Myths About the Confederacy? Because Our Textbooks and Monuments Are Wrong." *Washington Post* 1 July 2015. Web.

Lowe, John. "'Calypso Magnolia': The Caribbean Side of the South." *South Central Review* 22.1 (Spring 2005): 54–80.

McPherson, Tara. *Reconstructing Dixie: Race, Gender, and Nostalgia in the Imagined South*. Durham: Duke UP, 2003.

Nabokov, Peter, ed. *Native American Testimony: A Chronicle of Indian-White Relations from Prophecy to the Present, 1492–1992*. New York: Viking, 1991.

Office of the Historian. "Indian Treaties and the Removal Act of 1830." US Department of State. Web. Accessed 30 Oct. 2017.

Perdue, Theda. "The Legacy of Indian Removal." *Journal of Southern History* 78.1 (Feb. 2012): 3–36.

Price, David A. *Love and Hate in Jamestown: John Smith, Pocahontas, and the Start of a New Nation*. New York: Knopf, 2003.

Propen, Amy. "Visual Communication and the Map: How Maps as Visual Objects Convey Meaning in Specific Contexts." *Technical Communications Quarterly* 16.2 (2007): 233–54.

Ruiz de Burton, María Amparo. *Who Would Have Thought It?* Ed. and Intro. Rosaura Sánchez and Beatrice Pita. Houston: Arte Público P, 1995.

Sacks, Howard L., and Judith Rose Sacks. *Way Up North in Dixie: A Black Family's Claim to the Confederate Anthem*. Washington, DC: Smithsonian Institution, 1993.

Silva, Alan J. "Conquest, Conversion, and the Hybrid Self in Cabeza de Vaca's *Relación*." Ann Arbor: MPublishing, Winter 1999. Web. Accessed 17 Apr. 2017.

Smith, John. "John Smith's 1616 Letter to Queen Anne of Great Britain." *Digital History*. 2016. Web. Accessed 29 Oct. 2017.

Turner, J. M. W. "Slaves Throwing Overboard the Dead and Dying—Typhon Coming On." 1840. mfa.org. Web. Accessed 21 Mar. 2016.

Van de Passe, Simon. "Pocahontas." 1616. *Nova*. Wisconsin Public Television. Web. Accessed 11 Mar. 2014.

Vaughan, Alden T. *Transatlantic Encounters: American Indians in Britain, 1500–1776*. Cambridge: Cambridge UP, 2006.

Walker, Alice. "Everyday Use." *In Love and Trouble*. New York: Harcourt, 1973.

Weaver, Jace. *The Red Atlantic: American Indigenes and the Making of the Modern World, 1000–1927*. Chapel Hill: U of North Carolina P, 2014.

Wheatley, Phillis. "On Being Brought From Africa to America." *Poems of Phillis Wheatley: A Native African and Slave*. Bedford, MA: Applewood, 1969.

———. "To the University at Cambridge." *Poems of Phillis Wheatley: A Native African and Slave*. Bedford, MA: Applewood, 1969.

Chapter 2

Arnow, Harriette. *The Dollmaker*. New York: Macmillan, 1954.

Attaway, William. *Blood on the Forge*. New York: Doubleday, 1941.

Baldwin, James. "The Harlem Ghetto." *Notes of a Native Son*. Boston: Beacon, 1955.

Barlow, William. *"Looking Up at Down": The Emergence of Blues Culture*. Philadelphia: Temple UP, 1989.

Berry, Chad. *Southern Migrants, Northern Exiles*. Champaign-Urbana: U of Illinois P, 2000.

Bromley, Roger. *Narratives for a New Belonging: Diasporic Cultural Fictions*. Edinburgh: U of Edinburgh P, 2000.

Carlson, Oliver. *A Mirror for Californians*. New York: Bobbs-Merrill, 1941.

Darnton, Byron. "Arizona Cotton-Growing Scheme Abets Migration to California." *New York Times* 5 Mar. 1940: 20.

Douglass, Frederick. *Life and Times of Frederick Douglass, Written by Himself*. Boston: DeWolfe, Fiske, 1892.

Dunbar, Paul Laurence. "An Ante-Bellum Sermon." *Selected Poems*. New York: Penguin, 2004. 60–61.

———. *The Sport of the Gods*. New York: Dodd, 1902.

Feather, Carl. *Mountain People in a Flat Land: Popular History of Appalachian Migration to Northeast Ohio, 1940-1965*. Athens: Ohio UP, 1998.

Genovese, Eugene. *Roll, Jordan, Roll: The World the Slaves Made*. New York: Vintage, 1976.

Gregory, James N. *American Exodus: The Dust Bowl Migration and Okie Culture in California*. Oxford: Oxford UP, 1989.

Grossman, James R. *Land of Hope: Chicago, Black Southerners, and the Great Migration*. Chicago: U of Chicago P, 1989.

———. "Southern Distribution of the Chicago Defender, 1919." *Encyclopedia of Chicago*. Newberry Library. 2005. Web. Accessed 1 Mar. 2018.

Harper, Frances E. W. *A Brighter Coming Day: A Frances Ellen Watkins Harper Reader*. New York: Feminist P, 1990.

———. *Minnie's Sacrifice: Sowing and Reaping*. Boston: Beacon, 1994.

———. *Moses: A Story of the Nile*. Philadelphia: Merrihew, 1869.

Hartigan, John, Jr. *Racial Situations: Class Predicaments of Whiteness in Detroit*. Princeton: Princeton UP, 1999.

Hayden, Robert. "Runagate Runagate." *Poems and Poets*. Poetry Foundation. Web. Accessed 1 Mar. 2018.

Hemenway, Robert E. *Zora Neale Hurston: A Literary Biography*. Champaign-Urbana: U of Illinois P, 1980.

Henri, Florette. *Black Migration: Movement North, 1900–1920*. New York: Anchor, 1975.

Hopkins, Dwight N. "Slave Theology in the 'Invisible Institution.'" *Cut Loose Your Stammering Tongue: Black Theology in the Slave Narrative*. Ed. Dwight N. Hopkins and George C. L. Cummings. 2nd ed. Louisville: Westminster John Knox P, 2003. 1–32.

Hughes, Langston. "One Way Ticket." *The Collected Works of Langston Hughes: The Poems: 1941–1950*. Ed. Arnold Rampersad. Vol. 2. Columbia: U of Missouri P, 2001. 188–89.

Hurston, Zora Neale. *Moses: Man of the Mountain*. New York: Harper, 1990.

Johnson, James Weldon. *God's Trombones: Seven Negro Sermons in Verse*. New York: Viking, 1927.

Kerkhoff, Johnston D. "'He War Good to We Uns.' Says Bride, 11." *New York Post*. 4 Dec. 1941: 1, 3.

King, Martin Luther, Jr. "I've Been to the Mountaintop." AmericanRhetoric.com. Web. Accessed 1 Mar. 2018.

Kling, David. *The Bible in History: How the Texts Have Shaped the Times*. Oxford: Oxford UP, 2004.

Lange, Dorothea, and Paul Schuster Taylor. *American Exodus: A Record of Human Erosion in the Thirties*. New Haven: Yale UP, 1969.

Lawrence, Jacob. *The Great Migration: An American Story*. New York: HarperCollins, 1995.

Levine, Lawrence. *Black Culture and Black Consciousness: Afro-American Folk Thought from Slavery to Freedom*. Oxford: Oxford UP, 1977.

Mankiller, Wilma, and Michael Wallis. *Mankiller: A Chief and Her People*. New York: St. Martin's, 1993.

Morgan, Stacy. "Migration, Material Culture, and Identity in William Attaway's *Blood on the Forge* and Harriette Arnow's *The Dollmaker*." *College English* 63.6 (July 2001): 712–40.

Morrison, Toni. *Jazz*. New York: Knopf, 1992.

Neal, Mark Anthony. *What the Music Said: Black Popular Music and Black Public Culture*. New York: Routledge, 1999.

Obermiller, Phillip, E. Bruce Tucker, and Thomas E. Wagner, ed. *Appalachian Odyssey: Historical Perspectives on the Great Migration*. West Port, CT: Praeger, 2000.

Rodgers, Lawrence R. *Canaan Bound: The African-American Great Migration Novel*. Champaign-Urbana: U of Illinois P, 1997.

Sernett, Milton. *Bound for the Promised Land: African American Religion and the Great Migration*. Durham: Duke UP, 1997.

Sisson, Matt. "Cleveland Electric Illuminating Co." *The Encyclopedia of Cleveland History*. Cleveland Historical. Web. Accessed 23 Feb. 2018.

Taylor, Paul S. "Again the Covered Wagon." *Survey Graphic* 24.7 (July 1935): 348–51, 368.

Todd, Charles. "The 'Okies' Search for a Lost Frontier." *New York Times Magazine* (1939): 10–11.

Turner, Victor. *The Forest of Symbols: Aspects of Ndembu Ritual*. Ithaca: Cornell UP, 1967.

Woodson, Carter. *A Century of Negro Migration*. Washington, DC: Association for the Study of Negro Life and History, 1918.

Chapter 3

Alger, Horatio. *Luck and Pluck*. Boston: Loring, 1869.

——. *Ragged Dick; or, Street Life in New York with the Boot Blacks*. Boston: Loring, 1868.

Baker, Houston A., Jr. "Battling the Ghouls of a Southern Boyhood." *Chronicle of Higher Education* (June 15, 2001). Web. Accessed 11 Mar. 2014.

Bruccoli, Matthew, and Park Bucker, eds. *To Loot My Life Clean: The Thomas Wolfe-Maxwell Perkins Correspondence*. Columbia: U of South Carolina P, 2000.

Capote, Truman. *Breakfast at Tiffany's*. New York: Vintage, 1993.

Donald, David Herbert. *Look Homeward: A Life of Thomas Wolfe*. New York: Little, 1987.

Ellison, Ralph. *Invisible Man*. New York: Vintage, 1995.

Friend, Craig Thompson, ed. *Southern Masculinity: Perspectives on Manhood in the South since Reconstruction*. Athens: U of Georgia P, 2009.

Griffin, Farah Jasmine. *"Who Set You Flowin'?": The African-American Migration Narrative*. Oxford: Oxford UP, 1995.

Holliday, Shawn. *Thomas Wolfe and the Politics of Modernism*. New York: Lang, 2001.

Jarenski, Shelly. "Invisibility Embraced: The Abject as a Site of Agency in Ellison's *Invisible Man*." *MELUS* 35.4 (Winter 2010): 85–109.

Kerouac, Jack. *Vanity of Duluoz*. London: Penguin, 1994.

Kimmel, Michael. *Manhood in America: A Cultural History*. New York: Oxford UP, 2006.

McGraw, Eliza. *Two Covenants: Representations of Southern Jewishness*. Baton Rouge: Louisiana State UP, 2005.

Mencken, H. L. *H. L. Mencken on Religion*. Ed. S. T. Joshi. New York: Prometheus, 2002.

———. *Prejudices, Second Series*. New York: Knopf, 1920.

Millichap, Joseph. *Dixie Limited: Railroads, Culture, and the Southern Renaissance*. Lexington: UP of Kentucky, 2002.

Nowell, Elizabeth, ed. *The Letters of Thomas Wolfe*. New York: Scribner's, 1956.

Rubenstein, Richard. "The South Encounters the Holocaust: William Styron's *Sophie's Choice*." *Michigan Quarterly Review* 20.4 (Fall 1981): 425–442.

Rubin, Louis D. *A Gallery of Southerners*. Baton Rouge: Louisiana State UP, 1982.

Snyder, William. *Thomas Wolfe: Ulysses and Narcissus*. Athens: Ohio UP, 1972.

Styron, William. *Sophie's Choice*. New York: Random House, 1979.

Turner, Victor. *The Forest of Symbols*. Ithaca: Cornell UP, 1967.

Warren, Robert Penn. *A Place to Come To*. New York: Random House, 1977.

———. *Segregation: The Inner Conflict in the South*. Athens: U of Georgia P, 1994.

———. "The South: Distance and Change. A Conversation with Robert Penn Warren, William Styron, and Louis D. Rubin, Jr." *The American South: Portrait of a Culture*. Ed. Louis D. Rubin Jr. Baton Rouge: Louisiana State UP, 1980. 318.

Whites, Lee Ann. *The Civil War as a Crisis in Gender: Augusta, Georgia, 1860–1890*. Athens: U of Georgia P, 2000.

Wolfe, Thomas. *Of Time and the River: A Legend of Man's Hunger in His Youth*. Garden City: Sun Dial, 1944.

———. *You Can't Go Home Again*. New York: Harper, 1998.

Wright, Richard. *Black Boy*. New York: Harper, 1945.

Chapter 4

Abbott, Shirley. *Womenfolks: Growing Up Down South*. New York: Houghton, 1998.

Abrams, Lynn, and Karen Hunt. "Borders and Frontiers in Women's History." *Women's History Review* 9.2 (2000): 191–200.

Allen, Henry. "Katherine Anne Porter: The Vanity of Excellence." *Katherine Anne Porter: Conversations*. Ed. Joan Givner. Jackson: UP of Mississippi, 1987.

Arnow, Harriette. *The Dollmaker*. New York: Macmillan, 1976.

Berry, J. Bill. *Located Lives: Place and Idea in Southern Autobiography*. Athens: U of Georgia P, 1990.

Billingslea-Brown, Alma Jean. *Crossing Borders through Folklore: African American Women's Fiction and Art*. Columbia: U of Missouri P, 1999.

Bonifacio, Glenda Tibe, ed. *Feminism and Migration: Cross-Cultural Engagements*. New York: Springer, 2012.

Brantley, Will. *Feminine Sense in Southern Memoir: Smith, Glasglow, Welty, Hellman, Porter, and Hurston*. Jackson: UP of Mississippi, 1993.

Chung, Haeja K. "Fictional Characters Come to Life: An Interview." *Harriette Simpson Arnow: Critical Essays on Her Work*. Ed. Haeja K. Chung. East Lansing: Michigan State UP, 1995. 263–80.

———. "Harriette Simpson Arnow's Authorial Testimony: Toward a Reading of *The Dollmaker*." *Critique: Studies in Contemporary Fiction* 36.3 (Spring 1995): 211–23.

Cook, Martha. "*Background in Tennessee*: Recovering a Southern Identity." *Evelyn Scott: Recovering a Lost Modernist*. Ed. Dorothy Scura and Paul Jones. Knoxville: U of Tennessee P, 2001. 53-66.

Glasgow, Ellen. *Life and Gabriella*. Garden City: Doubleday, 1916.

Goodman, Charlotte. "The Multi-Ethnic Community of Women in Harriette Arnow's *The Dollmaker*." *MELUS* 10.4 (1983): 49–54.

Hansen, Liane. "Zora Neale Hurston, Through Family Eyes." *Weekend Edition Sunday*. National Public Radio. 11 Mar. 2018. Web.

Harrison, Elizabeth. *Female Pastoral: Women Writers Re-Visioning the American South*. Knoxville: U of Tennessee P, 1991.

Hurston, Zora Neale. *Dust Tracks on a Road*. New York: HarperCollins, 1996.

———. *Their Eyes Were Watching God*. New York: Harper, 2006.

Johnston, Mary. *Hagar*. Boston: Houghton, 1913.

Lerner, Gerda. *The Grimké Sisters from South Carolina: Pioneers for Women's Rights and Abolition*. Chapel Hill: U of North Carolina P, 2004.

Mitchell, Margaret. *Gone with the Wind*. New York: Simon and Schuster, 2008.

Reely, Mary Katherine. "Excellent Novels of Married Life Problems." *Ellen Glasgow: The Contemporary Reviews*. Ed. Dorothy Scura. Cambridge UP, 1992. 175–76.

Roberson, Susan L., ed. *Women, America, and Movement: Narratives of Relocation*. Columbia: U of Missouri P, 1998.

Rubin, Rachel Lee. "'My Country Is Kentucky': Leaving Appalachia in Harriette Arnow's *The Dollmaker*." *Women, America, and Movement: Narratives of Relocation*. Ed. Susan L. Roberson. Columbia: U of Missouri P, 1998. 176–89.

Scott, Evelyn. *Background in Tennessee*. Knoxville: U of Tennessee P, 1980.

———. *Escapade*. Charlottesville: U of Virginia P, 1995.

———. *Migrations*. New York: A & C Boni, 1927.

Stout, Janis P. "South from the South: The Imperial Eyes of Evelyn Scott and Katherine Anne Porter." *Evelyn Scott: Recovering a Lost Modernist*. Ed. Dorothy Scura and Paul Jones. Knoxville: U of Tennessee P, 2001. 15–36.

Thomas, James G. "Evelyn Scott." *The New Encyclopedia of Southern Culture: Literature*. Ed. Thomas Inge. Chapel Hill: U of North Carolina P, 2008. 410–12.

Welty, Eudora. *One Writer's Beginnings*. Cambridge: Harvard UP, 1983.

Chapter 5

"American Roots Music." *PBS Wisconsin*. PBS. 2001. Web. Accessed 29 Oct. 2017.

Barlow, William. *Looking Up at Down: The Emergence of Blues Culture*. Philadelphia: Temple UP, 1990.

Berry, Chad. *The Hayloft Gang: The Story of the National Barn Dance*. Champaign-Urbana: U of Illinois P, 2008.

Braziel, Jana Evans. "'Bye, Bye Baby': Race, Bisexuality, and the Blues in the Music of Bessie Smith and Janis Joplin." *Popular Music and Society* 27.1 (2004): 3–26.

Carlson, Marvin. *Performance: A Critical Introduction*. New York: Routledge, 2003.

Davis, Angela. *Blues Legacies and Black Feminism: Gertrude "Ma" Rainey, Bessie Smith, and Billie Holiday*. New York: Vintage, 1999.

Filene, Benjamin. *Romancing the Folk: Public Memory and American Roots Music*. Chapel Hill: U of North Carolina P, 2000.

Frith, Simon. "Music and Identity." *Questions of Cultural Identity*. Ed. Stuart Hall and Paul DuGay. London: Sage, 1996. 108–27.

Garman, Bryan K. *A Race of Singers: Whitman's Working-Class Hero from Guthrie to Springsteen*. Chapel Hill: U of North Carolina P, 2000.

Gregory, James. *The Southern Diaspora: How the Great Migrations of Black and White Southerners Transformed America*. Chapel Hill: U of North Carolina P, 2005.

Griffin, Farah Jasmine. "Who Set You Flowin'?": *The African-American Migration Narrative*. Oxford: Oxford UP, 1995.

Huber, Patrick. "Black Hillbillies: African American Musicians on Old-Time Records, 1924–1932." *Hidden in the Mix: The African American Presence in Country Music*. Ed. Diane Pecknold. Durham: Duke UP, 2013.

Hughes, Langston. "Music at Year's End." *Chicago Defender* 9 Jan. 1943: 14.

Jackson, Mark Allan. *Prophet Singer: The Voice and Vision of Woody Guthrie*. Jackson: UP of Mississippi, 2007.

Jones, LeRoi. *Blues People: Negro Music in White America*. New York: Morrow, 1963.

Keil, Charles. *Urban Blues*. Chicago: U of Chicago P, 1991.

Logsdon, Guy. "Liner Notes." *Hard Travelin'*. Created and performed by Woody Guthrie. Smithsonian Folkways Recordings, 1998.

Malone, Bill. *Country Music, U.S.A*. Austin: U of Texas P, 1985.

———. *Don't Get Above Your Raisin': Country Music and the Southern Working Class*. Champaign-Urbana: U of Illinois P, 2002.

Mason, Bobbie Ann. *Elvis Presley*. New York: Penguin, 2003.

"Muddy Waters Bio." *Rolling Stone*. Rolling Stone. 2017. Web. Accessed 31 Oct. 2017.

Oliver, Paul. *The Story of the Blues*. Philadelphia: Chilton, 1969.

Palmer, Robert. "Muddy Waters: 1915–1983." *Rolling Stone*. 23 June 1983. Web. Accessed 31 Oct. 2017.

Rubin, Rachel. "Sing Me Back Home: Nostalgia, Bakersfield, and Modern Country Music." *American Popular Music: New Approaches to the Twentieth Century*. Amherst: U of Massachusetts P, 2001. 93–109.

Smith, Suzanne. *Dancing in the Street: Motown and the Cultural Politics of Detroit*. Cambridge: Harvard UP, 1999.

"Willie Dixon Biography." *Rock and Roll Hall of Fame*. Rock and Roll Hall of Fame and Museum, Inc. 2016. Web. Accessed 24 May 2016.

Chapter 6

Bruccoli, Matthew, and Park Bucker, eds. *The Thomas Wolfe-Maxwell Perkins Correspondence*. Columbia: U of South Carolina P, 2000.

Faulkner, William. *Absalom, Absalom!* New York: Vintage, 1990.

———. "A Courtship." *The Collected Stories of William Faulkner*. New York: Random House, 1950. 361–80.

———. *The Sound and the Fury*. New York: Vintage, 1954.

Glissant, Édouard. *Faulkner, Mississippi*. Trans. Barbara Lewis and Thomas C. Spear. New York: Farrar, 1999.

Hamblin, Robert. "Faulkner's Map of Yoknapatawpha: The End of *Absalom, Absalom!*" *Center for Faulkner Studies: Teaching Faulkner*. 2016. Web. Accessed 25 Apr. 2016.

Handley, George B. "Oedipal and Prodigal Returns in Alejo Carpentier and William Faulkner." *Mississippi Quarterly* 52.3 (Summer 1999). Web.

Harmon, Kate. *You Are Here: Personal Geographies and Maps of the Imagination*. New York: Princeton Academic P, 2004.

Hicks, D. Emily. *Border Writing: The Multidimensional Text*. Minneapolis: U of Minnesota P, 1991.

Kuyk, Dirk, Jr. "Sutpen's Design." *William Faulkner's* Absalom, Absalom! *A Casebook*. Ed. Fred Hobson. Oxford: Oxford UP, 2003. 189–217.

Ladd, Barbara. *Nationalism and the Color Line in George Washington Cable, Mark Twain, and William Faulkner*. Baton Rouge: Louisiana State UP, 1997.

Lester, Cheryl. "Racial Awareness and Arrested Development: *The Sound and the Fury* and the Great Migration (1915–1928)." *The Cambridge Companion to William Faulkner*. Ed. Philip M. Weinstein. Cambridge: Cambridge UP, 1995. 123–45.

Libby, David J. *Slavery and Frontier Mississippi, 1720–1835*. Jackson: UP of Mississippi, 2004.

Matthews, John T. "Recalling the West Indies: From Yoknapatawpha to Haiti and Back." *American Literary History* 16.2 (Summer 2004): 238–62.

Propen, Amy. "Visual Communication and the Map: How Maps as Visual Objects Convey Meaning in Specific Contexts." *Technical Communications Quarterly* 16.2 (2007): 233–54.

Stanchich, Martiza. "The Hidden Caribbean 'Other' in William Faulkner's *Absalom, Absalom!*: An Ideological Ancestry of U.S. Imperialism." *Mississippi Quarterly* 49.3 (Summer 1996). Web.

Chapter 7

Anzaldúa, Gloria. *Borderlands: La Frontera*. San Francisco: Aunt Lute Books, 1999.

Berry, Mike, Inakio Garcia-Blanco, and Kerry Moore. *Press Coverage of the Refugee and Migrant Crisis in the EU: A Content Analysis of Five European Countries*. Report prepared for the United Nations Higher Commission for Refugees. Dec. 2015. Web.

Breed, Allen G. "What Does It Mean to Be Southern—Special Series." *Rome News-Tribune* 2006. Tribune.com. Web.

Corasaniti, Nic. "At a Donald Trump Rally, a Confederate Flag Goes Up, and Quickly Comes Down." *New York Times* 11 Aug. 2016. Web.

Gregory, James. *The Southern Diaspora: How the Great Migrations of Black and White Southerners Transformed America*. Chapel Hill: U of North Carolina P, 2005.

Hopkins, Anna, and Anneta Konstantinides. "Secret Service WILL Investigate Madonna." *Daily Mail*. Dailymail.com. Web. 17 Apr. 2017.

Jones, Robert. *The End of White Christian America*. New York: Simon, 2016.

Kingsolver, Barbara. *Animal, Vegetable, Miracle*. New York: HarperCollins, 2007.

"Maine Governor Paul LePage Criticised for 'Racist' Remarks." *BBC News* 27 Aug. 2016. Web.

Morris, Willie. *North toward Home*. Boston: Houghton, 1967.

Nougayrède, Natalie. "Angela Merkel Is Right: The Migration Crisis Will Define This Decade." *Guardian* 21 Aug. 2015. Web.

Pratt, Minnie Bruce. *Walking Back Up Depot Street*. Pittsburgh: U of Pittsburgh P, 1999.

Reeg, Caitlin. "Why Germans Like to Reenact U.S. Civil War Battles." *PRI's The World*. Public Radio International. 30 May 2011. Web.

Stack, Carol. *Call to Home: African Americans Reclaim the Rural South*. New York: HarperCollins, 1996.

Sullivan, Kevin. "'Evil, Evil, Evil as Can Be': Emotional Testimony as Dylan Roof Trial Begins." *Washington Post* 7 Dec. 2016. Web.

Thompson, Tracy. *The New Mind of the South*. New York: Simon, 2013.
Trivedi, Bijal P. "Saving the Mason-Dixon Line." *National Geographic News*. 10 Apr. 2002. NationalGeographic.com. Web.
"What Does Southern Mean to You?" *Southern Living* July 4, 2008. community.southernliving.com.
X, Malcolm, and Alex Haley. *The Autobiography of Malcolm X*. New York: Random House, 1964.

SONG LIST

This list includes name of artist, title of song, recording company, and date of release. If information is not included, then it was unavailable or not applicable. For Guthrie I have included the date for recording by the Library of Congress (LOC) as well as for the first commercial recording.

Allman Brothers. "Ramblin' Man." Capricorn, 1973.
Anonymous. "What Am I Doing Up Here?"
Bare, Bobby. "When Am I Ever Gonna Settle Down." RCA, 1968.
Berlin, Irving. "God Bless America." RCA, 1939.
Campbell, Glenn. "Country Boy." Capitol, 1975.
Carter Family. "Can't Feel at Home" ("I Don't Feel at Home in This World Anymore"). 1931.
Cole, Kid. "I'm Going to Cincinnati." MCA Coral, 1936.
Davenport, Cow Cow. "Cow Cow Blues." Vocalion and Brunswick, 1927.
———. "Jim Crow Blues." Paramount, 1927.
Flatt and Scruggs. "I'm Gonna Settle Down." Mercury, 1959.
Gaither, Little Bill. "Creole Queen." Okeh, 1941.
Gillum, Jazz. "Down South Blues." Bluebird, 1942.
Guthrie, Woody. "Do-Re-Me." LOC, 1940. RCA, 1940.
———. "Dust Bowl Refugee." LOC, 1940. RCA, 1940.
———. "God Blessed America for Me." Released as "This Land Is Your Land." Folkways, 1951.
———. "Goin' Down the Road Feelin' Bad" ("Blowing Down That Old Dusty Road"). LOC, 1940. Asch, 1944.
———. "Hard Travelin'." Asch, 1944.
———. "I Ain't Got No Home in This World Anymore." LOC, 1940. RCA, 1940.
———. "Jolly Banker" (also known as "The Banker's Lament"). LOC, 1940.
———. "Pastures of Plenty." Columbia River, 1941.
———. "Pretty Boy Floyd." LOC, 1940. RCA, 1940.
———. "So Long, It's Been Good to Know Yuh" (originally titled "Dusty Old Dust"). LOC, 1940. RCA, 1940.
———. "Talkin' Dust Bowl Blues." LOC, 1940. RCA, 1940.
———. "Tom Joad." LOC, 1940. RCA, 1940.
———. "Vigilante Man." LOC, 1940. RCA, 1940.
Haggard, Merle. "Ramblin' Fever." MCA, 1977.
Hooker, John Lee. "Boogie Chillum." Modern, 1948.
Jenkins, Bobo. "Bad Luck and Trouble." Chess, 1954.
———. "24 Years on the Wrong Road." Big Star.
Jennings, Waylon. "I'm a Ramblin' Man." Capital, 1967.
Jones, Maggie. "North Bound Blues." Columbia Records, 1925.

Ledbetter, Huddie (Lead Belly). "Bourgeoisie Blues." 1938.

———. "Cotton Fields." 1962.

Maddox Brothers and Rose. "Dust Bowl Blues" ("Do-Re-Mi").

———. "In the Land Where We'll Never Grow Old." 4-Star, 1953.

———. "The South." 4-Star, 1951.

Merriweather, Big Maceo. "Texas Blues." 1941.

Nelson, Woody. "On the Road Again." Columbia, 1980.

Parton, Dolly. "Smoky Mountain Memories." Columbia, 1994.

Rodgers, Jimmie. "Train Whistle Blues." RCA, 1958.

Smith, Bessie. "Young Woman's Blues." Frank Music, 1927.

Snowden, Ben, and Lew. "Dixie." (pre-recording era)

Waters, Muddy. "Feel Like Going Home." Aristocrat, 1948.

———. "My Home Is in the Delta." Chess, 1964.

———. "Southbound Train." Chess, 1959.

Whitter, Henry. "Lonesome Blues." 1924. Also recorded by Big Bill Broonzy. Okeh, 1940.

Williams, Hank. "Ramblin' Man." MGM, 1953.

Wonder, Stevie. "Living for the City." Tamla, 1973.

INDEX

CPSIA information can be obtained
at www.ICGtesting.com
Printed in the USA
BVHW070008101118
532730BV00003B/9/P